Critical Thinking
Reading and Writing
Across the Curriculum

Anne Bradstreet Grinols

Wadsworth Publishing Company
Belmont, California
A Division of Wadsworth, Inc.

Acknowledgments

I am pleased to thank, first of all, the forty-three contributors who made this work possible through their articles, which form the basis of this text. I would also like to thank Charlotte Kiefer for her helpful comments, perseverance, and enthusiasm for our collaboration; Arelene Bradstreet, Sue Achtemeier, Cindy Garver, and Judy Reichard for their crucial assistance when it was most needed; John Strohmeier, Kevin Howat, and Serina Beauparlant from Wadsworth for their support; and my family for their patience and encouragement.

This text is dedicated to Daniel, my youngest student.

A.B.G.

English Editor: John Strohmeier
Editorial Assistant: Sharon Wallach
Production Editor: Lisa Danchi
Managing Designer: Andrew H. Ogus
Interior and Cover Design: Design Office/Peter Martin
Cover Photographer: Nick Pavloff
Print Buyer: Barbara Britton
Copy Editor: Betty Duncan-Todd
Compositor: Omegatype Typography, Inc.
Signing Representative: Serina Beauparlant

Printed in the United States of America 34

1 2 3 4 5 6 7 8 9 10—92 91 90 89 88

Library of Congress Cataloging-in-Publication Data
Critical thinking: reading and writing across the curriculum/[edited] by Anne Bradstreet Grinols.
    p.   cm.
  ISBN 0-534-08838-4
  1. College readers.   2. English language—Rhetoric.
3. Interdisciplinary approach in education.   I. Grinols, Anne Bradstreet.
PE1417.C73 1988
808'.0427—dc19   87-20287
                                                                                          CIP

CONTENTS

Contents

Contents

PART IV. HUMANITIES

Contents

PART V. MORE QUESTIONS, A RHETORICAL GUIDE,
AND A LIST

A Note to the Instructor:

Bridging the Gap

In recent years, college faculty and teaching staff have noted a widening gap between the reading, writing, and thinking skills they require of their students and those the students are able to demonstrate. Many students must make a major adjustment from previously acceptable levels of endeavor; yet little, if any, time or teaching emphasis is devoted to encouraging this transition. Instead, instructors and textbook writers all too often assume that students are already in command of the processes necessary for critical thinking, evaluative reading, and creative writing. The growing number of learning skills centers and the proliferation of books on reading and study skills are responses to this problem. Yet materials and resources are by no means complete.

Although this text is not intended to replace all the "how-to" books currently available on the instruction of reading, writing, and study skills, it will fill a definite need. First, it is based on the now-recognized fact that learning content is not the same thing as—nor does it necessarily lead to—acquiring the learning processes that are necessary to learn that content. A student assigned to read an essay will (it is hoped) read that essay. He can then tell you the content of the essay, but he won't be able to tell you how he read it. Another student might tell you some thoughts she had about the essay without necessarily being able to tell you the intellectual validity of those thoughts, or even how she arrived at them. And rare indeed is the student who can put down on paper, in reasonably coherent form, an analysis of that essay. This book, then, addresses the learning process and the critical thinking, objective reading, and clear writing skills that are necessary components of the learning process.

Second, although the content is of lesser importance in this approach to learning, it is nonetheless critical. The ability to read is useless unless it is applied to some form of content. The articles in this book were selected because they were considered to be the most appropriate to which students could apply their new learning skills. In fact, they are unique in a book of this kind in that they were written, for the most part, by college-level faculty and teaching staff on a broad variety of topics in many academic disciplines. They are therefore relevant to students who are concerned about their expertise in academic areas. This attribute of *Critical Thinking* makes the text extremely valuable to a college student or to anyone who wishes to improve his ability to read academic material with maximum effectiveness.

When considering content, the importance of vocabulary cannot be overlooked. Often a student has no difficulty understanding the author's message once she can break through the unfamiliar vocabulary. From similes and metaphors to literary allusion and technical jargon, the language the author chooses is often the key to understanding and appreciating the points being made. Thus the article-by-article treatment of the book found in the instructor's manual lists for each article the words and phrases that may be unfamiliar or troublesome to your students. This section of the manual also contains additional analysis questions and some suggestions for comparative treatment of the articles.

Elsewhere in the instructor's manual are a discussion of the instructional section of the text, sample syllabi, an answer key to the comprehension questions that accompany each article, and some information about the computer-assisted instruction (CAI) materials that accompany the text.

The CAI materials for *Critical Thinking* have been developed for the IBM-PC and compatibles. The package consists of two disks, each with two articles from the text. For each article, the student completes skimming, reading, and questions sections as well as a set of schema evaluation and main idea exercises. In addition, each article has a set of exercises concerning important critical thinking skills especially developed for use on the computer. These are separate programs that are executed after the main program has finished. Included are exercises in writing style, exercises in identifying main concepts and concept mapping, and work with schema, freewriting, and thesis statements. Students can start the program or return to different parts of the program with a menu. This CAI package is available to all departments using *Critical Thinking*. For more information, contact your Wadsworth representative or write to: English Editor, Wadsworth Publishing Company, Ten Davis Drive, Belmont, CA 94002.

In sum, *Critical Thinking: Reading and Writing Across the Curriculum* exposes students to many subject areas, topics, and ideas they are likely to confront as they pursue their college education. Most articles are purposefully brief. Even a subject that is totally unfamiliar to a student will not be daunting when the student sees that the article covering it is only four pages long. The approach of breadth rather than depth also allows students to become acquainted with many academic disciplines that they may not otherwise encounter. Consider an engineering student who finds integrated circuits a safe topic, but Greek tragedy, well, "Greek to her"! Even such a brief exposure to an article in this book can contribute to the goal of a well-rounded education. And who knows? Perhaps interest may be aroused in a previously ignored area. Yet no matter what content is retained, the learning processes and critical thinking skills that are demonstrated and then exercised throughout this book should be reinforced to accomplish long-term retention and to enable skill transfer to your students' areas of learning across the curriculum.

A Note to the Student:

Fighting the College Frights

Sarah had been valedictorian of her high school class. She had found most of her subjects in the small New England college she had attended for the next two years fairly easy and was proud that she had never really had to study much to succeed. Now she wondered if being a transfer student to a large university would present more of a challenge.

Juan, too, had done well in his high school class, although the school was small and its standards perhaps not the highest. He had moved to the United States from Puerto Rico during his junior year, and his English was still a bit uncertain, requiring him to study harder than his class-mates. After graduation, he had deferred his college acceptance for a year to earn money for his tuition.

Michael, on the other hand, had attended a large high school in Minneapolis, where he had excelled in both academics and sports. Easy-going and popular, Mike had been Student Council president, National Honor Society president, and the person voted most likely to succeed by his class.

And what about you? What would a thumbnail sketch of you, an incoming freshman or transfer student, portray? After all, it is not only freshmen who have these adjustments to make. Students transferring from other colleges may be surprised at the stress they encounter as they try to adjust to a new environment, routines, and challenges all over again. And what if your record—high school or college—was not as strong as Sarah's or Michael's? What about that student next to you in class who seems to know all the answers? Indeed, what if you are returning to formal education after it was interrupted by marriage, career, or time in the armed forces, and you are afraid your academic skills are rusty or forgotten?

Well, take heart. Obviously, you have some strong points, including a fair share of basic intelligence, or you wouldn't have arrived here. Yet what about your weak points? (There even may be some you haven't discovered yet!)

Matriculating at any college or university is going to produce some surprises and necessitate some adjustments. The large lecture classes or the sprawling campus may seem forbidding. The volume and complexity of study material often come as a shock. The sudden isolation from old friends, family, and familiar routine makes most new students feel very much on their own. And this can be unsettling to anyone, no matter how successful academically or socially he had been in the past. Even those students attending a community college or a large urban university while living at home will find that the demands of their new schedules leave little time or energy for old pastimes. Whether or not the home environment changes, virtually everything else does.

Any major change or upheaval in an individual's life-style induces stress. Thus, it should come as no surprise that the many changes experienced in college can be stressful. Yet this fact is often overlooked in the excitement of beginning the new venture. Indeed, most college-bound students have found high school and home schedules confining and have longed for the freedom and opportunities they anticipate college will offer them. Likewise, older or returning students often are dissatisfied with present job opportunities or life-style and hope that their new college experience will open new doors.

What happens when real experience clashes with eager expectations? A second look at our three students is enlightening.

Sarah was rueful, finding her lack of study skills to be more properly a cause for alarm than a source of pride. She realized that she would have to obtain some help in this area before she would lose too much ground in her coursework. Juan, after consulting with his adviser, enrolled in a linguistics course for bilingual students and planned to allow more time for reading assignments than the usual two hours for every one in class. Even Michael was somewhat chagrined to find many of his new peers possessing academic, social, and athletic skills to rival his; he soon realized that he would have to apply himself to the many challenges of his new situation to have even a chance at the success he had anticipated.

Like many of their peers, Sarah, Juan, and Michael had to seek out and adopt new approaches to their academic endeavors, their personal development, and the balance between the two. Learning skills, writing fluency, study habits, time management, goal setting, priority assigning, and problem solving are necessary components of success. Assistance in these areas is available, and students are encouraged to seek out and tap the many resources their college or university offers.

This assistance takes the form of special courses, academic survival workshops, academic and personal counseling, tutorials and seminars, student organizations, and university offices and programs concerned with specific themes, situations, and problems. Large universities abound in these programs. Even small colleges and two-year programs are making these services available in increasing numbers, and most programs and resources are available not only to freshmen but to all students.

Yet even before such external resources can be fully utilized, you must examine and put to use your own personal resources. It is often surprising how much information is gleaned from an hour or two of self-examination based on appropriate questions and honest, thoughtful answers. As you reconsider your expectations as contrasted with reality, begin by asking yourself, "Why am I here?" Next, make a list of your goals, both short-term and long-term. Set your priorities to ensure that immediate goals, as well as the most important long-range ones, are not neglected for others of lesser significance or value.

Finally, develop a good time-budgeting system—by the week, month, and semester. Once such a schedule is established and maintained, time and energy are not needlessly wasted in the constant remaking of decisions about what to do and when to do it. A good time-management schedule eliminates this kind of repetition and the anxiety that accompanies it, while allowing enough flexibility so that unexpected tasks, illnesses, and opportunities can be accommodated with only minor adjustment rather than elaborate revision.

In the establishment of a daily schedule, certain guidelines are invaluable. First, assign priorities. Determine which activities are absolutely necessary, which would be beneficial, and which are easily accomplished without sacrificing more important ones. For example, lectures scheduled from 10:00 am to 1:00 pm *must* be attended; writing a lab report that is due next week would be beneficial; and returning a library book on the way to the lab would be both helpful and cost-free in time, because the library is on the way to the lab.

Second, set aside time for personal tasks, meals, sleep, recreation, and exercise. Skimping in these areas will only extract a price later: Your ability to study, learn, and prepare for exams will be impaired unless you are mentally and physically in the best possible condition.

Finally, reserve a small segment of time for the unexpected problem or opportunity that is bound to arise. If you expect the unexpected, you will be able to attend that special seminar, fly that kite, or even catch a nap without disrupting the entire schedule. This allowance for spontaneity acts as a safety valve, providing enough flexibility and freedom so that you will be both able and willing to carry out the schedule you created.

In the long run, motivation is more powerful than will power. If your daily to-do list (which should, of course, include several hours of reviewing notes, previewing texts, and downright, no-bones-about-it *studying*) is based on priorities, which are in turn based on personal goals you have established for yourself, then you will be motivated to complete that list. After all, you made the list for your own good, didn't you? Sheer will power, or just "gutting it out," is less effective and quickly exhausting, producing more anxiety and frustration than learning.

With goals determined, priorities established, and a realistic time schedule in effect, refer again to your personal assessment; now is the time to take care of any weaknesses or shortcomings that will hinder your efforts toward academic success.

For instance, most students discover that the reading efficiency and writing and study skills that served them well in the past are no longer adequate. Some students find that a little personal assistance in a specific area or two is all they need; others find they need more detailed instruction, which is available in workshops or even a full-semester course. Additional help may be offered through the dean of students' office; through academic departments' teaching assistants, tutors, and advisers; and through a network of programs and offices on campus. Various texts, workbooks, reading-efficiency devices, tapes, handouts, and other audiovisual aids are usually available through these programs and offices. Without a doubt, one or more of these resources will enable you to raise your academic survival skills to a level of proficiency that will allow you to achieve academic success. The vital ingredient is *you*. Unless you take advantage of these resources, they cannot help you.

Academic achievement is attainable. Although many students arrive on campus less than ready to compete effectively, a well-reasoned approach to resolve problems and eliminate inadequacies should go a long way toward eliminating anxiety about academic survival. Your mental outlook and physical condition are two of your best resources: Safeguard them wisely. At the same time, use the resources of your university: They are there for *you*. Finally, do not hesitate to seek assistance for any problem or situation for which you cannot find an already-established answer. The "college frights" need refer only to the subject of this essay, not to a malady from which you suffer.

And when you have successfully survived your first semester or quarter, what then? Periodically going over the following points can help you avoid sophomore slump, junior jitters, and senior shock as well. Let us be realistic: Proper consideration of these points is vital for *all* stages of education to ensure success.

Things to Think About

Time Management

1. Establish a schedule for the current semester, current week, and today or tomorrow. Include papers, exams, and projects. Are tasks of the short-term schedules specific in nature? Will successfully completing them lead to completion of the semester schedule?

2. Have you allowed sufficient time for sleep? Meals? Exercise? (Note: Not all recreation is exercise!)

3. Have you allowed some spontaneity time each day? This flexibility allows your schedule to function.

4. Have you allowed time to review your lecture notes as soon as possible after class? Immediately after taking in new information, you begin to forget it. Reviewing your notes helps you remember. Even a twenty-minute review after each lecture will increase considerably the amount of material you will retain.

5. You will surely have more and longer writing assignments than ever before. In your long-term time schedule, have you allotted time to draft, edit, and retype each paper?

6. Time is like money: You can spend it only once. Budget it wisely to reflect your priorities, and you will never run out of it before the "big-ticket" items are taken care of.

Priorities

1. Why are you in college? What goals do you expect to achieve here?

2. Does completion of your short-term goals lead to completion of your long-term goals?

3. Guard against neglecting your *important* priorities as you handle your *immediate* needs. Keep your perspective. For example, don't let a short-term, dead-end job interfere with your *main* job, which is to be a student. Your success as a student is your primary concern.

4. Reexamine your established priorities regularly. Do they still reflect your goals? Have your goals changed? If so, other changes are most likely in order. For instance, if your career goals have changed, perhaps your major should be reexamined.

5. Goals, like time-management schedules, are best made by you rather than established by others. Your strongest commitment will be to priorities *you* make.

6. Remember: "Nothing succeeds like success." This well-known saying loses its triteness when the success is yours, as it certainly can be. Your success will be your best motivation. So, go for it!

Overview

Part I is a brief synthesis of teaching instruction in the areas of critical thinking, reading, and writing. Assimilation of this material is the key to your being able to successfully understand and complete the rest of the text. More than that, though, it will reveal to you the knowledge of and attitude toward the learning process, which will enable you to think rationally and creatively throughout your college years (and beyond!).

Parts II, III, and IV of this book consist of articles written by faculty and teaching staff representing many of the academic fields and disciplines found at colleges and universities. No claim is made that these articles are necessarily the best examples of writing in their respective fields. Rather, they are representative of the kinds of writing you, the student, will confront in your academic career.

Each article is followed by ten multiple-choice comprehension and evaluation questions plus general questions to serve as springboards for further analysis (both written and verbal) and discussion. Additional skill development and reinforcement of learning are offered through exercises in such areas as writing, schema, concept mapping, and multiple-stimulus reinforcement.★

The articles themselves are grouped according to field, and the fields are brought together under the general headings of physical sciences, social sciences, and humanities. This format lends itself to analysis of two or more articles to compare differences in style and perspective. Comparative analysis questions are given at the end of each major section to get you started.

Part V consists of some additional study aids and information. The first section is a sampling of open-ended discussion questions that require comparative analysis of ideas, approaches, and attitudes in the various

---

★These terms are explained in the instructional section that follows.

articles and that are not limited to field groupings. Thus, in another example of the across-the-curriculum approach of this text, you are encouraged to consider such topics as the purpose of education, methods of persuasion, cultural patterns, and sexism in language. You are challenged to examine your own schema—knowledge and opinions—on the subjects in the context of those offered by various authors in this collection. Reading for understanding and comparative analysis leads to critical thinking both as a goal of tangible results and as an ongoing process: At the completion of the text you will have new thoughts *and* a new way of thinking.

The second section in Part V is a rhetorical guide. Should you wish to examine the articles from the point of view of thesis/main idea, bias, tone, structure, or theme—rather than by field (as the contents are organized)—this guide should provide a good frame of reference.

The final section in Part V is an alphabetical listing of the forty-three contributors to this text. A bit of biographical information is included as well.

———————

PART I

Instruction

Learning in College:
Critical Thinking, Reading, and Writing

College students are called upon to use analytic reading and thinking processes that presume highly developed learning abilities, but where are these abilities supposed to have been acquired? How many students finish high school with any knowledge of how the mind takes in and evaluates information? Yet college reading assignments and exam questions all too often presuppose cognitive abilities that are virtually impossible to develop without such knowledge.

As a college student, what is *your* ability to read effectively for understanding? What is your perception of the concepts of style or structure? Can you separate the wheat from the chaff—identify the author's main idea, the supportive points, the details, and the filler? These are the evaluative processes that college students are called upon to use every day in their coursework. Improving your skills in these vital areas is what this book is about.

In her essay "The Goal of Undergraduate Education: Can Colleges Serve Adult Students?" (which appears later in this book), Helen Brown Burris points to a long-running controversy in the field of education:

What is the purpose of a college education? Traditionalists have claimed that the only valid purpose is to train the mind, to develop aesthetic sensitivity, and to encourage intellectual excellence. Today's modernists point to changing demographics, exploding technological development, and a vastly altered employment environment as they insist that career preparation be one (if not *the*) primary function of a college education.

Yet on one point there is total agreement. The ability to think clearly and precisely is necessary for both intellectual pursuit and career preparation. Furthermore, the abilities to read critically and write coherently are vital components of the learning process, whether in formal education, on the job, or simply as an effective member of society.

For example, although you may suspect that your current approach to academic reading is not ideal, you already have a lifetime commitment to your present pattern of reading. To train yourself to think and read more critically, you must be persuaded to break this commitment and change your current pattern. It may not be enough to be told *what* to do. But knowing the *whys* and *hows* will have a vital impact on your motivation to change. To increase your reading effectiveness when the material is unfamiliar in content or complex in structure, you need to understand something about the reading process itself. Then you can learn how to apply this understanding to your academic reading. The same points are valid for accurate writing and critical thinking.

There are six areas to consider: cognition, schema, technique, thesis, format, and writing. Each is examined in turn.

Cognition: The Reader's Goal

Research into the learning process indicates that people learn with least effort when the new information comes from more than one source of stimulus. This is why children are taught to trace a *P* in peanut butter as they say the letter aloud and watch the letter being formed. They take in the desired information with concurrent reinforcement through all five senses: seeing, hearing, feeling, smelling, and (no doubt) tasting. In addition, they have the advantage of kinetic involvement—learning by doing. Similarly, students listening to a lecture find their comprehension enhanced if the lecture is accompanied by diagrams, or similar visual reinforcement, on the blackboard. And hands-on involvement such as that gained in a laboratory experiment or a field trip is added kinetic reinforcement that makes it all come clear.

What about reading? Obviously, the only sensory mode being used is the visual. Furthermore, even if the text is well-reinforced by charts and illustrations, the presentation of academic material is likely to be abstract rather than concrete in nature, adding to the difficulty in comprehension. How then do you replace the reinforcement that comes from multisensory learning?

The answer lies in the final step of the learning process: using the information. Reading about or even memorizing a concept in isolation is not true mastery. True mastery comes when you can, in the terms of Benjamin Bloom, translate, apply, analyze, synthesize, and evaluate the concept.[1] You, the reader, supply your own additional reinforcement by testing yourself. You might apply any or all of the steps in Bloom's list as follows:

Translate	Put the concept in your own words.
Apply	Relate the concept to other information.
Analyze	Break down the concept into its simplest components.
Synthesize	Fit the concept into previously learned concepts.
Evaluate	Consider the broad significance of the concept.

Summary

True cognition comes not just from simple assimilation of information, but also from assessment of its accuracy, its relevance, and how it fits in with other information you already have. Therefore, question and evaluate *as you read*.

---

[1]B. S. Bloom, M. D. Englehart, E. J. Furst, W. H. Hill, and D. R. Krathwohl, eds., *Taxonomy of Educational Objectives: Handbook I: Cognitive Domain* (New York: McKay, 1956).

Schema: The Learning Process

Imagine that you are going to construct a building. One method is to start at the bottom and put one brick down, then some mortar, another brick, some more mortar, then another brick, and so on. The building slowly takes shape as you add the bricks, one at a time. Another method of building is to construct the frame and then hang the sides from the frame. The frame provides the model, and almost from the very beginning, you have a rough picture of the finished result.

Many of us try to assimilate new information as if our minds process data one bit at a time, as in the first method outlined above. We take in a pile of facts and concepts, one at a time, until we can't hold any more. There is no organization or method. The first facts are covered up or dropped and lost as new facts are added.

The truth is that the mind learns in a manner much more like the second method described. A model is established, and new information is then added to the model or rejected because it does not seem to fit properly. If the model is adjusted, the new information may ultimately find acceptance, but only after an evaluation process has taken place.

A model is established in one of two ways. In the first, previously held information, ideas, and opinions relating to a topic constitute a schema (or model) by which you evaluate all new data related to the topic. The more information you have, the more developed is your schema, and the stronger your commitment to it. Without thoughtful consideration, you will be much more likely to reject any new information that does not fit into your schema than to change your schema. Because schemas are made up of opinions and conclusions that may be inaccurate or outdated, it is vital for you to consider new information as objectively as possible before deciding to accept or reject it.

If you have absolutely no schema (no knowledge or views) about the new information, then a model must be created. The model will take form as you first confront, and then take in, the new information. It will take form with or without your awareness or active cooperation! Therefore, it is very important that your first approach to this new information be conducted as effectively as possible. The recommended procedure is discussed in the following section.

Summary

We learn best by assimilating information into a model created from already established data and views and by altering that model as needed. If we have no schema, and thus no model, we create it as we read.

Skim, Read, Reinforce: The Reader's Technique

The many approaches to studying and reading are indicated by the acronyms that abound: PREP, OARWET, OK5R, SCORE, and the old stand-by SQ3R, recently modified to SQ4R and then to SQ5R. In case this is beginning to sound like alphabet soup, the fundamental message in all these approaches is the same. It is SRR: skim, read, reinforce.

Skim

The purpose of skimming is to get an overview of the material—an idea of the author's purpose in writing and the main idea of what she wishes to convey to you, the reader. Skimming also serves to establish a model of the material covered. When the next step, the actual reading of the text (or chapter or article), is begun, the reader already has in mind a perspective on the topic gleaned from the skimming step. This is why reading without skimming, particularly when there is no well-developed schema on the topic, is difficult at best and fruitless or confusing at worst.

Skimming methods vary. Most involve reading the first paragraph or two, followed by reading the key sentences (usually the first ones in each paragraph), then the phrases (unfamiliar terms, names, numbers that catch your eye), and then the final paragraph or two (usually the summary). The goal is to grasp the main idea of the text as quickly as possible. Although all the material is "covered," less than half of the material is actually read.

Read

During the reading step, the text is read from the beginning. Since the first paragraph was already read in the skimming step, this important introductory material is now familiar and thus is read more easily and with better comprehension. As the rest of the text is read, the facts and ideas are sorted out and put into the model or outline formed during the skimming process. Questions that developed naturally during the skimming process are answered. Indeed, because you are now looking for the answers to the questions *you* formulated, the answers are more likely to leap off the page instead of remaining buried in the text. Reading should not be the passive process it often becomes, but an active one. The key is to read for ideas and answers rather than word-for-word absorption. Be aggressive!

Reinforce

Following skimming and reading comes the final step—reinforcement. Reinforcement may take the form of asking questions, summarizing, making notes, recitation, or any other appropriate method of review. Remember: The purpose of reinforcement is to carry out the final step in the learning process and so encourage mastery. Because multisensory reinforcement is reinforcement at its best, it is beneficial to seek approaches or techniques that employ a variety of visual, aural, and other modes of reinforcement.

Concept mapping, for example, is a form of visual reinforcement whereby the main subject is identified, written down in the center of the paper, and boxed or circled. Subordinate points from the text are likewise written down and circled. Connecting lines are drawn from each point to the main idea and to each other when appropriate. Lesser points, examples, and descriptions are added with appropriate connecting lines. Other main ideas are added, along with their salient points, until a graphic representation of the text is apparent. Thus illustrated, the proper relationships and relative significance of the points are clear.

Concept maps are particularly useful for quick assessment of the detailed definition of an important term, as well as for analysis of obscure, complex ideas. As an example, consider the following explanation of the term *experimental research,* identified as a definitive type of research methodology. The text is accompanied by a concept map of the same information (Figure 1).

When educational research is properly described as "experimental" the researcher has specified a finite set of researchable hypotheses and has

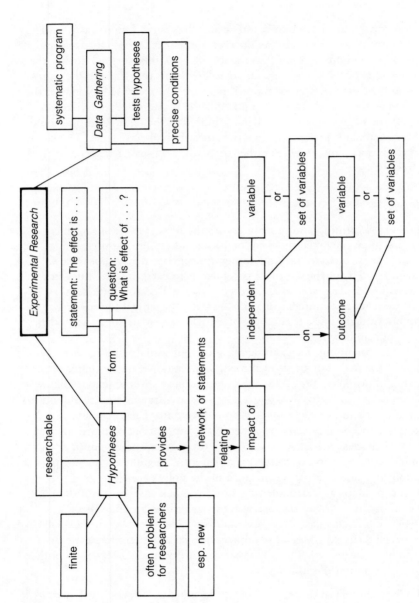

Figure 1.
Concept map on experimental research.

established a systematic program of data gathering, under precisely defined conditions, in an effort to test those hypotheses. The hypotheses provide a network of statements relating the impact of an independent variable or set of independent variables on some outcome variable or set of variables. A hypothesis may be presented as a direct statement describing the impact of one variable upon another such as, "Students who are trained in word analysis skills are less likely than those who have not received such training to make spelling errors during composition writing." Or it may be stated in the form of a question, "What is the effect of training students in word analysis skills on their spelling error production during composition writing?" . . . The fundamental weakness of many new researchers is their failure to make a satisfactory statement of the research question. Although this failure is especially common among new researchers, experienced researchers often have the same difficulties.[2]

The basic information in the passage condenses in the concept map to a definition of experimental research, with descriptions of its main components. Moreover, the relative significance of the data is clear.

Now let us examine another concept map (Figure 2), drawn from material in the same encyclopedia concerning the definition and explanation of the phrase *optimal (or best) experiment.*

Even without consulting the text, the three main points about an optimal experiment are readily recognizable from the map:

1. External validity and internal validity yield optimal experiments.

2. An optimal experiment requires precise analysis of data, conditions for sampling, application of treatments, and assessment of outcomes.

3. An optimal experiment does not necessarily require complexity.

Now compare the information derived from the map with the text from which it was constructed:

---

[2]*Encyclopedia of Educational Research,* 5th ed. (New York, 1982), vol. 2, p. 625.

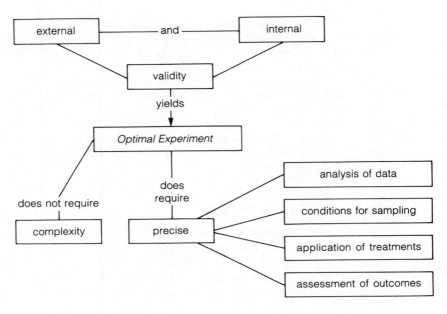

Figure 2.
Concept map on optimal experiment.

> The optimal experiment is one that is valid both internally and externally.
> The more precisely the researcher is able to define the conditions for
> sampling, application of treatments, assessment of outcomes, and analysis of
> data, the more likely the study is to meet those requirements. . . . There is a
> common misconception that for an experimental design to be seen as
> competent it must be complex. In reality, complexity and competence are
> only partially related.[3]

For a difficult passage the mapping technique can be carried an
additional step to highlight further the relative importance of the concepts. In this step, the individual concepts are laid out in a hierarchical
pattern: More general, important concepts are placed at the top of the
page, subordinate ones are placed underneath, and any specific details

---

[3]Ibid., p. 630.

and examples are at the bottom. Relationships and directional flows among the concepts are identified and labeled. When using this technique, you will find that the hierarchical ordering of concepts is often different from the order in which the concepts appear in the text.

How much better, when reviewing, to note the main points in a glance at your map, than to seek them out as you reread a complicated passage of several hundred words.

Creating a concept map also involves kinetic reinforcement because you are producing it yourself, both mentally and physically. Drawing pie charts or bar graphs are other forms of reinforcement that are both visual and kinetic. Such charts are particularly helpful in analyzing chronological or quantitative material such as characterizes economics, history, sociology, government, and demography. Obviously, your choice among these and other modes of visual reinforcement will depend on the nature of your material. Not all materials lend themselves to visual reinforcement. The next best choice is usually auditory, or aural, reinforcement.

Auditory reinforcement can be attained through recitation, lecture attendance, and group discussion. Most subject areas, with the exception of science laboratory work, do not allow reinforcement through the other sensory modes. However, visual and auditory modes are sufficient if accompanied by reflection. After all, the reflection process is the vital component in any learning situation. This is particularly true in the reinforcement step in critical reading.

Does this sound like a lot of time-consuming effort? If so, please note that, with a little practice, it will take you less time to accomplish these steps than it presently takes you just to read the text, because you will be coordinating your efforts with the way your mind most effectively processes information.

Summary

Skim for the main idea. Read for understanding. And finally, create an appropriate method of reinforcement: Use it or lose it!

Thesis: The Author's Message

The first information acquired in the skimming and reading process is the author's topic, or subject area. This is often confused with the thesis, or main idea, of the text. It is important to clarify these two concepts in order properly to identify and evaluate the author's points.

Topic, or subject	What the author is writing about (can be written in a word or phrase). *Example:* college registration
Thesis, or main idea	The point, or message, the author is making (must be a complete sentence). *Example:* College registration is a boring hassle, but necessary.

The importance of the main idea is that it is exactly what the phrase says it is—the author's *main idea*—the focal point, or fundamental position, he is trying to convey. All other information is intended to illustrate, defend, elucidate, or otherwise enhance the thesis. Comprehension is more fluent as related ideas and data in the text fit into the framework provided by the main idea. This organization of ideas can be effected only if you know what they are supposed to be organized around; it is the thesis that gives meaning, relevance, and perspective to all other information. This is why your task is to grasp the main idea *first,* as outlined in the SRR step.

Summary

The author had a purpose in writing. Reading for the main idea reveals that purpose and establishes the basis for understanding the entire passage or text.

Format: The Author's Packaging

Although the main idea constitutes the framework, or skeleton, it is only part of the author's whole message. Often the whole message, or body of what she is trying to convey to the reader, can be understood only after considerable reflection and consideration, which should, of course, be part of the reinforcement process.

Analysis of the author's packaging of ideas often provides an excellent guide to the complete message contained therein; for in addition to what they have to say, authors are concerned with *how* they say it. To get the most out of your texts, you must share that concern. The author's ideas come packaged in terms of bias, style, tone, and structure. Your perception of these attributes will assist you in understanding the text, as well as add immeasurably to your ability to evaluate the material critically.

Bias, for example, relates to schema concerning the knowledge and viewpoints each person has on a subject. However, even if you, the reader, have no prior knowledge about a given topic, you still have a bias that will affect how you accept or reject the material as it becomes known to you (as you read). Your bias is made up of all you have experienced—your heritage, your culture, your education, your family, your peers—the list is nearly endless. Both author and reader have biases. Your goal is to be aware of your own bias and the author's, so that you can consider these biases as part of your evaluative process. Then you consider your own ideas and the author's ideas and retain what is true. Open-mindedness is critical to learning, just as reflection is. Indeed, unless you are open to new ideas, reflection is useless.

Style, according to the *Random House College Dictionary,* refers to the "mode or form of expression, as distinguished from the content." It describes the way an author writes, rather than what he is writing about. Style may be formal, informal (or semiformal), colloquial, or slang. It also may be technical—that is, filled with words or phrases that may be obscure to the layman but would be understood by someone with knowledge or expertise on the topic being discussed. Formal, or scholarly, writing involves strict conformance to traditional writing conventions and tends to consist of complicated sentence structure, as well as traditionally acceptable vocabulary. Informal writing is more straightforward and features up-to-date vocabulary. Colloquial, or conversational, writing resembles the way people speak, using correct but informal sentence patterns. Contractions and other familiar terms are common. Slang includes fad idioms, street-talk, jargon, and other features that do not meet language conventions and would be inappropriate for business or other conventional use.

Tone is similar to style but more accurately represents the author's attitude or feelings toward the topic. For example, the author may be optimistic, pessimistic, cynical, angry, romantic, or enthusiastic about the topic.

The author's *structure* is simply the way in which she organizes ideas. Perceiving the author's structure is like having a map and road signs as you progress through the material. The easiest way to do this is to be familiar with the typical organizational patterns of the type of reading you are doing. These include, but are not limited to, the following:

Analytic	A method of breaking into parts for examination and evaluation
Expository	A method to expound, set forth, or explain objectively
Descriptive	A statement of a situation, idea, or problem with amplification (explanation, examples, and so forth)
Question and answer	A question (or series of questions) followed by an answer (or answers)
Thesis–proof	A statement (or series of statements) followed by a proof (or series of proofs)
Narrative	The telling, or relating, of a story or incident
Cumulative narrative	The telling of a series of stories or incidents
Enumeration	A listing of facts or events
Descriptive enumeration	A listing of facts or events, each briefly described
Spatial	Organization according to location of subjects discussed
Chronological	Organization according to order of events
Problem–solution	Description of a situation followed by proposal of a solution
Instructional, or how-to	A method of teaching, or instruction, usually including steps to follow

Summary

The earlier in the reading process you identify the forms of packaging used by the author (bias, style, tone, structure), the more quickly this knowledge guides you to meaningful reading and analysis. Like a road map, an author's organizational patterns can guide your "journey" through the text.

Writing: A Learning Tool

One learns by writing. Writing is an integral part of the learning process because it enhances and supports what one reads and thinks about. One way to help remember something is to write it down: The act of writing reinforces what is spoken aloud or pictured in the mind. Concept maps (see Figures 1 and 2) add graphic form to the content being written down. And almost any writing exercise takes the writer further into what he is reading or thinking about, shedding new light on the topic while reinforcing its impact on long-term memory.

Writing encourages the learning process in other ways, too. When asked to write a summary, analyze information, or report on research done by others, you must have a clear grasp of the subject you are addressing. If not, your writing on that subject will not be clear. "Fuzzy" writing is often due to a lack of understanding of the subject being written about.

In her essay in this text, "How Johnny Can Write: Thinking About a Composition Theory," Miriam Brody makes the following statement: "Before there is a writing process, there is a cognitive process. The work of a writer's process of cognition is to understand the world so it may be written out." Whether the subject to be written about is a concept, a short story, an experience, or a scientific discovery, it must be understood clearly in the mind of the writer before it can be written about with any clarity. Most students have less difficulty writing from their own experience ("My First Date," "The Day I Almost Drowned") than writing about an unfamiliar subject ("Integrated Circuits," "Irony in Greek Tragedy"). Have you ever attempted to write an essay exam on a subject covered in a chapter you did not read or in a class discussion you missed? It was almost surely an unsuccessful (as well as unpleasant) experience, and what you wrote lacked clarity (among other desirable qualities).

Yet just as some real understanding of the subject is necessary before writing begins, the writing process itself can help clarify your understanding of the subject further. Capturing an idea or opinion into words and writing them with some coherence on paper forces you to become precise in your understanding of what you are saying. If this procedure proves difficult, one technique that can be helpful to get you started is *freewriting*. First, write down your topic. Then, as quickly as possible, write down all words and phrases about the topic that come to mind. Do not worry about punctuation, capitalization, or coherence. Simply get the words down on paper. (This step is also called *brainstorming*.) When you cannot think of another word or idea to write, go over the paper. Using circles or arrows, connect and complete your ideas as much as possible. For an example, see Figure 3.

Consider the results. Now, try to write a coherent statement about your subject, using the results of this exercise. Note that it is not necessary to use all the ideas you jotted down.

The following statement is the result of this exercise:

> Autumn is a time of contrast. The slow pace of summer quickens with the cool crisp air, as if hurrying to prepare for the winter ahead. Children in fresh new clothes step smartly off to school, greeting their old friends along the way. At roadside stands and in every farmers' market, the fruits and vegetables are lined up in a vibrant display of contrasting color, texture and taste.

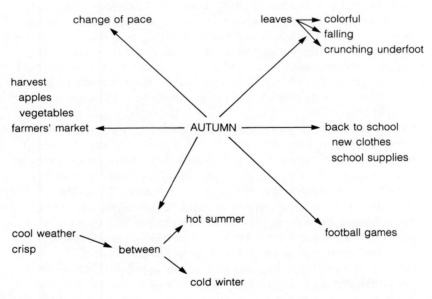

Figure 3.
An exercise in freewriting.

As shown, freewriting is helpful in writing an essay, in choosing or narrowing a topic, and in simply getting started. It also can help you determine your thesis. In the example, the topic supplied was "autumn." Because this is too broad a subject to write about, the writer had to find something to say about autumn. After the freewriting process was done, the writer had her thesis: Autumn is a time of contrast.

With a definite thesis in mind, the first step in the actual process of writing is to put your mental impressions into words on paper. Words are formulated into sentences, which are arranged into paragraphs, which take their proper places in essays, essay exams, research papers, articles—or letters to Mom!

Let us now examine those forms that most college writing takes: the essay, the essay test, and the report.

The Essay

An essay consists of an introductory paragraph, a concluding paragraph, and one or more paragraphs between them. Each paragraph contains a thesis, or main idea—the point you are making. The sentence that makes this point is called the topic sentence. Other sentences in the paragraph support the topic sentence.

Usually, although not always, the topic sentence in expositional writing is the first sentence in the paragraph. Why? Put yourself in the role of the reader: It is easier to follow writing if the writer establishes the point and then discusses it, rather than launching into a discussion of an as yet unidentified topic. Unless the writing is a personal journal, intended for the writer's eyes only, it must be shaped by the needs of the would-be reader to understand it.

One exception to the rule about placement of topic sentences is often made in the introductory or first paragraph for the whole essay. Usually the purpose of the first sentence(s) here is to introduce the topic for the essay—to lay claim to the reader's attention. Just as a public speaker often begins a speech with an anecdote to command the attention of the audience, so a writer may use the opening sentences of an essay with an "attention grabber." Thus, the topic sentence is often the last sentence of the paragraph. Indeed, this topic sentence usually expresses the thesis for the whole essay.

Another exception may be the last paragraph of the essay. Because the purpose of this paragraph is to conclude the essay, a restatement of the original thesis statement, although not in the same words, is likely to be made in the last sentence.

The remaining paragraphs form the body of the essay. Because most college essays are between 200 and 800 words, the number of paragraphs will vary according to the length of your specific assignment. The purpose of all of them is the same: to support or explore the thesis that was set forth in the introductory paragraph. This support may be in many forms (or combination of forms), such as explanation, illustration, question and answer, cause and effect, comparison and/or contrast, and persuasion.

The Essay Test

In an essay test, you can rarely choose the topic but must respond to the question given. This may seem obvious, but the most common mistake students make is to write everything they know about the topic. Unless the question states "Write everything you know about. . . . ," do *not* do it! Instead, answer the question. To paraphrase the legal directive: Answer the question, the whole question, and nothing but the question. This is the main point to remember about an essay test.

Next, organize your answer. Usually it is best to state your main points at the outset and then support them. Paragraph development is similar to that of a regular essay, although the "attention grabber" type of introduction is omitted in favor of starting off with your main point, or thesis.

Finally, allow time to go over your answer to correct any errors in spelling, punctuation, grammar, and so forth. Although your instructor is concerned primarily with content, the form he finds it in will undoubtedly affect its impact on him and, consequently, *your* grade.

The Report

In a summary, a writer gives a condensed version of the main points of an article, in her own words. A research report is like a summary except that the writer is summarizing, or synthesizing, material from more than one source.

The chosen topic should have ample, available resources yet be sufficiently limited to allow the writer to cover it with depth and thoroughness. See how an appropriate topic was produced in the following process:

Gardening

Vegetables and fruits	Too broad
Farm produce	Still too broad
Tomatoes	Better
Growing tomatoes in home gardens	Best

After the topic is chosen, the source materials should be read closely. Take notes on index cards (in your own words when possible), noting the references on the cards. Arrange the cards to yield a coherent order, and your outline is practically done.

Now write and let it rest. Revise and let it rest, repeating as necessary. Each time you return to your work after a few days of letting it rest, your perspective should be fresh, resulting in better editing in less actual working time.

Finally, compare your report to the original sources. Check for accuracy. Be certain you did not add to your sources, attributing to them your own opinions. Accuracy is the most important feature of a good research report. Your creativity and originality can show through in your choice of topic or your approach to it, but let the facts remain the facts.

An Important Note

It is impossible to discuss writing without mentioning vocabulary, grammar, and speech. Competence in grammar and a large, precise, working vocabulary are necessary prerequisites to good writing—indeed, to any form of communication. Any weaknesses in these areas should be dealt with continually until they are resolved. Vocabulary, in particular, should continue to grow over one's lifetime.

Speech is a means for sending communication, which is received through listening just as writing is a form of communication, which is received through reading. Writing differs from speaking in that it can be edited or even erased, or it can be chiseled into concrete to last indefinitely. On the other hand, once spoken, words cannot be changed or erased, only added to; and a speech usually does not last very long in the minds of the audience—unless, of course, it is written down in words and preserved!

Summary

Writing supports the learning process as a mode of reinforcement and as a method of communication. Whether in a personal essay or in a research report, clear writing is more likely to result when the subject is clearly understood. Choose your topic carefully. Follow the informal guidelines, or rules, governing the development of the appropriate forms of college writing. Techniques such as concept mapping and freewriting are often helpful at various stages of the writing process. And improvement in grammar, vocabulary, and speaking ability will contribute immeasurably to proficiency in writing. Remember: when carried out properly, writing can be a most versatile learning tool.

In conclusion, successful college students are those who can read, write, and think effectively in the academic areas they will explore. To do this, students must have a certain degree of awareness of what they know, along with some anticipation of what will be expected of them by their professors and textbook writers. Consideration of the principles outlined above, when applied to the critical academic readings and accompanying questions that make up this book, can enhance your expertise as you work for the success that *can be yours*.

Application

Now that you have read the instructional section, apply what you have learned to the articles. As directed, first skim, then read, an essay. Next, look at the questions that follow. These questions are not intended to be exhaustive, but they do serve several purposes. First, the multiple-choice questions provide a check of your basic understanding of the article. The first few questions (under the heading "Assimilation") test your recognition of some of the basic facts in the essay. Because they are multiple-choice, the correct answer is one of the choices listed. You are not required to remember the correct answer, only to *recognize* it. The process of recognition will also, of course, serve as reinforcement of these facts. Even where the correct choice seems fairly obvious, just going through the question and the answer serves to emphasize and reinforce that particular piece of information.

The next few multiple-choice questions (under the heading "Interpretation") test your ability to make inferences and draw conclusions. The correct answer may not be spelled out in the reading, but enough information is available to enable you to choose the most appropriate inference or conclusion from the choices given. Some of these more thoughtful questions require you to examine your perception of several critical characteristics of the writing itself. These characteristics include tone, style, and the organization of ideas (structure), as well as the bias of the author as revealed in the essay.

The final multiple-choice question (under the heading "Main Idea") always concerns the main idea, or thesis, of the article. This provides you with the opportunity to discover your success in extracting the underlying message of the essay from all the supporting information, illustrations, and lesser details. Moreover, because the correct response to this question was, in most cases, supplied by the author, you can compare your evaluation with the point the author set out to make. Simply formulate your own one-sentence statement of the main idea before looking at the choices given.

The analysis questions are intended to lead you deeper into the reflection process, which is vital to critical thinking, clear writing, and true learning. Some of these questions are meant to serve as springboards for discussions in your class or with your friends. Some you may wish to mull over by yourself. Some may give you ideas for creative writing or topics for research papers. A few may not be appropriate for your level of knowledge about the topic—this is why there are several choices. In any case, "thought" questions to stimulate your analysis and reflection should not be limited to the choices given. Create your own. Go beyond What? Where? and When? Consider How? and Why? Muse over What if? and Where do we go from here?

Whether these questions are your own or come from the book, the point to remember is this: It is the *process* of critical thinking rather than its result, the specific thought, which is best served by the questions.

The last section of each article offers still more opportunity for reinforcement and reflection through one or more exercises. Although most of these are writing exercises, variety is provided through concept mapping, exploration of bias, construction of graphs and tables, poll-taking, and so forth.

Summary

In most college texts, emphasis is on the content rather than the procedure for assimilating the content: the "what" rather than the "how." In this book, the reverse is true. The emphasis is on the procedures: careful reading, clear writing, and the critical thinking processes on which they both depend.

The articles themselves provide practice for applying the procedures to the content: the "how" to the "what." This practice will yield deeper understanding and reinforcement of these procedures while demonstrating how diversely they may be applied. Your final goal, of course, will be to apply these procedures to the content you will encounter in *all* your college courses.

PART II

Physical Sciences

Can We Know the Universe? Reflections on a Grain of Salt

Nothing is rich but the inexhaustible wealth
of nature. She shows us only surfaces, but
she is a million fathoms deep.

Ralph Waldo Emerson

Science is a way of thinking much more than it is a body of knowledge. Its goal is to find out how the world works, to seek what regularities there may be, to penetrate to the connections of things—from subnuclear particles, which may be the constituents of all matter, to living organisms, the human social community, and thence to the cosmos as a whole. Our intuition is by no means an infallible guide. Our perceptions may be distorted by training and prejudice or merely because of the limitations of our sense organs, which, of course, perceive directly but a small fraction of the phenomena of the world. Even so straightforward a question as whether in the absence of friction a pound of lead falls faster than a gram of fluff was answered incorrectly by Aristotle and almost everyone else before the time of Galileo.

Science is based on experiment, on a willingness to challenge old dogma, on an openness to see the universe as it really is. Accordingly, science sometimes requires courage—at the very least the courage to question the conventional wisdom.

Beyond this the main trick of science is to *really* think of something: the shape of clouds and their occasional sharp bottom edges at the same altitude everywhere in the sky; the formation of a dewdrop on a leaf; the origin of a name or a word—Shakespeare, say, or "philanthropic"; the reason for human social customs—the incest taboo, for example; how it is that a lens in sunlight can make paper burn; how a "walking stick" got to look so much like a twig; why the Moon seems to follow us as we walk; what prevents us from digging a hole down to the center of the Earth; what the definition is of "down" on a spherical Earth; how it is possible for the body to convert yesterday's lunch into today's muscle and sinew; or how far is up—does the universe go on forever, or if it does not, is there any meaning to the question of what lies on the other side? Some of these questions are pretty easy. Others, especially the last, are mysteries to which no one even today knows the answer. They are natural questions to ask. Every culture has posed such questions in one way or another. Almost always the proposed answers are in the nature of "Just So Stories," attempted explanations divorced from experiment, or even from careful comparative observations.

But the scientific cast of mind examines the world critically as if many alternative worlds might exist, as if other things might be here which are not. Then we are forced to ask why what we see is present and not something else. Why are the Sun and the Moon and the planets spheres? Why not pyramids, or cubes, or dodecahedra? Why not irregular, jumbly shapes? Why so symmetrical, worlds? If you spend any time spinning hypotheses, checking to see whether they make sense, whether they conform to what else we know, thinking of tests you can pose to substantiate or deflate your hypotheses, you will find yourself doing science. And as you come to practice this habit of thought more and more you will get better and better at it. To penetrate into the heart of the thing—even a little thing, a blade of grass, as Walt Whitman said—is to experience a kind of exhilaration that, it may be, only human beings of all the beings on this planet can feel. We are an intelligent species and the use of our intelligence quite properly gives us pleasure. In this respect the brain is like a muscle. When we think well, we feel good. Understanding is a kind of ecstasy.

But to what extent can we *really* know the universe around us? Sometimes this question is posed by people who hope the answer will be in the negative, who are fearful of a universe in which everything might one day be known. And sometimes we hear pronouncements from scientists who confidently state that everything worth knowing will soon be known—or even is already known—and who paint pictures of a Dionysian or Polynesian age in which the zest for intellectual discovery has withered, to be replaced by a kind of subdued languor, the lotus eaters drinking fermented coconut milk or some other mild hallucinogen. In addition to maligning both the Polynesians, who were intrepid explorers (and whose brief respite in paradise is now sadly ending), as well as the inducements to intellectual discovery provided by some hallucinogens, this contention turns out to be trivially mistaken.

Let us approach a much more modest question: not whether we can know the universe or the Milky Way Galaxy or a star or a world. Can we know, ultimately and in detail, a grain of salt? Consider one microgram of table salt, a speck just barely large enough for someone with keen eyesight to make out without a microscope. In that grain of salt there are about 10^{16} sodium and chlorine atoms. This is a 1 followed by 16 zeros, 10 million billion atoms. If we wish to know a grain of salt, we must know at least the three-dimensional positions of each of these atoms. (In fact, there is much more to be known—for example, the nature of the forces between the atoms—but we are making only a modest calculation.) Now, is this number more or less than the number of things which the brain can know?

How much *can* the brain know? There are perhaps 10^{11} neurons in the brain, the circuit elements and switches that are responsible in their electrical and chemical activity for the functioning of our minds. A typical brain neuron has perhaps a thousand little wires, called dendrites, which connect it with its fellows. If, as seems likely, every bit of information in the brain corresponds to one of these connections, the total number of things knowable by the brain is no more than 10^{14}, one hundred trillion. But this number is only one percent of the number of atoms in our speck of salt.

So in this sense the universe is intractable, astonishingly immune to any human attempt at full knowledge. We cannot on this level understand a grain of salt, much less the universe.

But let us look a little more deeply at our microgram of salt. Salt happens to be a crystal in which, except for defects in the structure of the crystal lattice, the position of every sodium and chlorine atom is predetermined. If we could shrink ourselves into this crystalline world, we would see rank upon rank of atoms in an ordered array, a regularly alternating structure—sodium, chlorine, sodium, chlorine, specifying the sheet of atoms we are standing on and all the sheets above us and below us. An absolutely pure crystal of salt could have the position of every atom specified by something like 10 bits of information.[1] This would not strain the information-carrying capacity of the brain.

If the universe had natural laws that governed its behavior to the same degree of regularity that determines a crystal of salt, then, of course, the universe would be knowable. Even if there were many such laws, each of considerable complexity, human beings might have the capability to understand them all. Even if such knowledge exceeded the information-carrying capacity of the brain, we might store the additional information outside our bodies—in books, for example, or in computer memories—and still, in some sense, know the universe.

Human beings are, understandably, highly motivated to find regularities, natural laws. The search for rules, the only possible way to understand such a vast and complex universe, is called science. The universe forces those who live in it to understand it. Those creatures who find everyday experience a muddled jumble of events with no predictability, no regularity, are in grave peril. The universe belongs to those who, at least to some degree, have figured it out.

It is an astonishing fact that there *are* laws of nature, rules that summarize conveniently—not just qualitatively but quantitatively—how the world works. We might imagine a universe in which there are no such laws, in which the 10^{80} elementary particles that make up a universe like our own

---

[1] Chlorine is a deadly poison gas employed on European battlefields in World War I. Sodium is a corrosive metal which burns upon contact with water. Together they make a placid and unpoisonous material, table salt. Why each of these substances has the properties it does is a subject called chemistry, which requires more than 10 bits of information to understand.

behave with utter and uncompromising abandon. To understand such a universe we would need a brain at least as massive as the universe. It seems unlikely that such a universe could have life and intelligence, because beings and brains require some degree of internal stability and order. But even if in a much more random universe there were such beings with an intelligence much greater than our own, there could not be much knowledge, passion or joy.

Fortunately for us, we live in a universe that has at least important parts that are knowable. Our common-sense experience and our evolutionary history have prepared us to understand something of the workaday world. When we go into other realms, however, common sense and ordinary intuition turn out to be highly unreliable guides. It is stunning that as we go close to the speed of light our mass increases indefinitely, we shrink toward zero thickness in the direction of motion, and time for us comes as near to stopping as we would like. Many people think that this is silly, and every week or two I get a letter from someone who complains to me about it. But it is a virtually certain consequence not just of experiment but also of Albert Einstein's brilliant analysis of space and time called the Special Theory of Relativity. It does not matter that these effects seem unreasonable to us. We are not in the habit of traveling close to the speed of light. The testimony of our common sense is suspect at high velocities.

Or consider an isolated molecule composed of two atoms shaped something like a dumbbell—a molecule of salt, it might be. Such a molecule rotates about an axis through the line connecting the two atoms. But in the world of quantum mechanics, the realm of the very small, not all orientations of our dumbbell molecule are possible. It might be that the molecule could be oriented in a horizontal position, say, or in a vertical position, but not at many angles in between. Some rotational positions are forbidden. Forbidden by what? By the laws of nature. The universe is built in such a way as to limit, or quantize, rotation. We do not experience this directly in everyday life; we would find it startling as well as awkward in sitting-up exercises, to find arms outstretched from the sides or pointed up to the skies permitted but many intermediate positions forbidden. We do not live in the world of the small, on the scale of 10^{-13} centimeters, in the realm where there are twelve zeros between the decimal place and the one. Our common-sense intuitions do not count. What does count is experiment—in this case observations from the far infrared spectra of molecules. They show molecular rotation to be quantized.

The idea that the world places restrictions on what humans might do is frustrating. Why *shouldn't* we be able to have intermediate rotational positions? Why *can't* we travel faster than the speed of light? But so far as we can tell, this is the way the universe is constructed. Such prohibitions not only press us toward a little humility; they also make the world more knowable. Every restriction corresponds to a law of nature, a regularization of the universe. The more restrictions there are on what matter and energy can do, the more knowledge human beings can attain. Whether in some sense the universe is ultimately knowable depends not only on how many natural laws there are that encompass widely divergent phenomena, but also on whether we have the openness and the intellectual capacity to understand such laws. Our formulations of the regularities of nature are surely dependent on how the brain is built, but also, and to a significant degree, on how the universe is built.

For myself, I like a universe that includes much that is unknown and, at the same time, much that is knowable. A universe in which everything is known would be static and dull, as boring as the heaven of some weak-minded theologians. A universe that is unknowable is no fit place for a thinking being. The ideal universe for us is one very much like the universe we inhabit. And I would guess that this is not really much of a coincidence.

Comprehension Questions

Assimilation

1. In this article science is depicted as:
   a. stranger than fiction
   b. an enormous body of knowledge
   c. a system of natural laws
   d. a search for rules

2. According to Sagan, "When we think well, we . . .":
   a. share ideas
   b. feel good
   c. grow tired
   d. are creative

3. Sagan describes our universe as:
   a. bewildering and fearful
   b. ideal

c. static
d. shrinking

4. Sagan states that questions about our world have arisen from every culture, along with answers:
   a. based on careful observation
   b. based on scientific experiments
   c. based on the religion of ancestors
   d. based on stories

5. In the field of scientific exploration, man must rely on:
   a. his experiment results
   b. his intuition
   c. the opinion of his peers
   d. his own common sense

Interpretation

6. Sagan's attitude toward science, as expressed in this article, is:
   a. didactic
   b. clinical
   c. querulous
   d. romantic

7. The title of the article refers to:
   a. an experiment that failed
   b. an accident in the lab that had surprising results
   c. a reference to a poem by Walt Whitman
   d. an example used to illustrate a point

8. The author's writing style is enhanced with:
   a. allusions to literature
   b. lengthy quotes from the classics
   c. biblical references
   d. inverted matrices

9. The amount of information needed to know a grain of salt:
   a. is equal to the number of its 10^{16} atoms
   b. is found in the description of the pattern in which its atoms are arranged
   c. is equal to the amount of information needed to know the universe itself
   d. varies with each grain of salt

Main Idea

10. The main idea of this article is:
     a. The universe cannot be understood by man's finite mind despite all the efforts he makes to do so.
     b. Man is forced to depend more on intuition and less on facts as he tries to learn about his world.
     c. The study of science can be defined as man's quest for the natural laws that govern the universe.
     d. Man's knowledge of the universe comes through the patterns of its natural laws and his understanding of them.

Analysis Questions

1. Although this essay concerns a scientific topic, the author introduces it with a quotation from a poet. How effective is this technique? How does this establish the tone for the essay?

2. Does respect for the natural world necessarily lead to respect for science?

3. The author's writing technique includes the posing of unusual, thought-provoking questions. How does this technique help get us interested in the topic?

4. Is this essay meant for scientists? Nonscientists? How would the topic be approached differently if meant for a different audience? Give examples.

Exercise

Sagan tells us that "when we think well, we feel good." Do you agree? Can you think of an occasion when this proved to be true for you? (How about the last exam you "aced"? That difficult equation you solved?) In a few paragraphs, describe the situation, what brought it about, and how you felt about it.

The Scientific Method in Biology

*A*lmost everyone knows that biology is one of the natural sciences, like physics and chemistry. As such, the science of biology ultimately depends on careful observation of the natural processes going on in the world around us. However, some people think that "doing biology" involves hours of complicated research in sterile, white-walled, windowless laboratories. Well, sometimes it does; but for many biologists, the doing of biology involves much, much more. To get a better understanding of what biologists really do, we will begin where the best of such studies begin—with the unexpected discovery of the beauty and complexity of living systems, as exemplified by the story of Karl von Frisch and the honeybee.

One of the most common observations anyone can make about honeybees is that they are extraordinarily good at finding honey. Furthermore, not long after one bee finds a source of honey, the whole hive seems to show up to carry it off. A young biologist named Karl von Frisch noted this fact

Reprinted from Allen D. MacNeill and Nina Macginn, *Concepts of Biology,* a forthcoming Prentice-Hall publication. Reprinted by permission of Prentice-Hall, Inc., Englewood Cliffs, New Jersey.

and then asked what seemed to be a very simple question: How does the whole hive find out about a source of honey so quickly? To answer this question completely took him the rest of his life and changed the science of biology in ways still not fully appreciated. Without complicated equipment and with very little laboratory work, von Frisch and his co-workers discovered a whole universe of previously unsuspected senses and behaviors in honeybees. For more than five decades they painstakingly explored the perceptual world of the honeybee, and in recognition of his discoveries and his contribution to the founding of the modern science of animal behavior, Karl von Frisch was awarded the Nobel Prize in physiology and medicine in 1973. It all began with an observation, a question, and application of the scientific method.

During research into the color vision and sense of smell in bees, von Frisch noted that a sheet of cardboard with some honey on it set on a table in the open would usually attract one bee in a few hours. Very soon there would be dozens or even hundreds of bees at the cardboard. He thus inferred that the first bee to find the honey was somehow communicating the existence of this food source to its hive mates. To investigate this possibility, early in the spring of 1919 he set up an observation hive with glass sides in a darkened room of the old Klosterhof of the Zoological Institute in Munich. He also erected a feeding station nearby and marked any foraging bee finding this food source with a tiny dot of red paint on the back of her thorax. Sitting in the fragrant darkness of the observation booth, he noticed that such returning foragers exhibited curious behavior immediately upon their return to the interior of the observation hive. Instead of milling about fairly aimlessly the way the nonforaging bees seem to, a bee who had just returned from the feeding station ran in a series of tight circles about two or three bee-lengths in diameter on the vertical surface of the hive. Von Frisch called such circles *round dances* and observed that other bees were quickly attracted to such a dancing bee, touching it with their antennae and forelegs and often following it during its gyrations. When marked inside the hive with their own drop of paint, such "followers" were observed to leave the hive quickly and fly away, often showing up at the feeding station fairly soon afterward.

Von Frisch made several important observations about the round dances: (1) such dances were very stereotyped; in nearly all cases, a dancing bee ran in tight circles several times, then reversed direction and ran in several more, very similar, circles in the opposite direction; (2) as a returning forager danced her round dance, her hivemates touched her repeatedly with their antennae (and occasionally their forelegs), closely following the dancer as she circled; (3) the dancing bee almost always danced in the most crowded area of the hive and periodically stopped to feed her followers with nectar from her honey stomach; (4) once her dancing was finished, the forager left the hive and flew back to the original food source; and (5) several new foragers appeared at the food source fairly soon thereafter.

These observations certainly suggested that foragers were communicating at least the availability of food to their hivemates. However, we can imagine other possibilities. For instance, the observed relationship between dancing and food finding might be entirely accidental: there might be no direct causal relationship of any kind between round dancing and the discovery of the new food source by other foraging bees. Alternatively, an indirect relationship might exist, but the actual availability of the food source might *not* be communicated to hivemates: instead, the returning forager might dance simply because she was "excited." That excitement would be communicated to her hivemates, some of whom might fly out of the hive and discover the new food source essentially by accident. Finally, the round dance might not communicate the availability or location of the new food source, but simply attract the attention of the dancer's hivemates, some of whom might find the new food source by following her when she left again to return to the food source, or by following the scent of the food source, or by using some other purely external cue to food location.

To distinguish which of these possible explanations was most likely to be correct, von Frisch formulated an ingenious experimental test based on the assumption that the dancing forager was communicating the availability of the food source using the round dance. He reasoned that if the round dance actually communicated the availability of a food source near the hive, then *preventing* foragers from returning to the hive to dance should prevent the usual rapid discovery of the food source by the hivemates of the detained forager. Von Frisch's experiment was an elegant example of the scientific method in biology. To appreciate this more fully, let us look at the scientific method in more detail, using as an example von Frisch's research into the functions of the round dance of honeybees.

The very first step in all scientific investigations is the simple observation of natural phenomena. As the observer watches (or listens or smells or whatever), patterns begin to emerge from the repetition of particular phenomena, and the observer wonders, Are these patterns real or figments of my imagination? A sense of curiosity, then, seems to be one of the most important characteristics of a good scientist. Another valuable characteristic is an understanding of the basic concepts of natural science in order to formulate valid, interesting questions.

Karl von Frisch first observed that once one bee discovers a food source, other bees quickly discover it also. He also observed that as each bee discovers the food source, she returns to her hive and round dances. This happened so often that it appeared to be a regular pattern in the foraging behavior of honeybees. Whenever one's original observations seem to exhibit such a regular pattern, that pattern can be used to formulate a *research hypothesis*. A research hypothesis is a tentative general explanation of the observed pattern of regularity. Von Frisch's research hypothesis was that the function of the round dance in honeybees is to communicate the availability of a food source to the dancer's hivemates.

Most research hypotheses share several general characteristics. First, they are usually too generally applicable to be tested directly. Instead, they are used to guide the formulation of specific predictions about the future behavior of an observed system—predictions that *can* be easily and directly tested. Second, research hypotheses are almost always stated in such a way that they can be tested using observation (as opposed to "just thinking more" about the "reasonableness" of the hypothesis). As we have stated before, if predicted processes cannot be observed in any way, they are absolutely useless as scientific generalizations.

Finally, most scientists agree that to be useful, research hypotheses should be stated in such a way that they can be *falsified;* that is, it should be possible to obtain information that would contradict a given research hypothesis. Why this should be the case can easily be seen by looking at von Frisch's research hypothesis. Let us assume that, for some reason, it is absolutely impossible to obtain any information that would indicate that honeybees do *not* communicate the availability of food sources to each other via round dancing. In that case, further research into the question would be downright silly, since the question is not really even a question anymore, but rather a statement of so-called fact. If you cannot think of any way that you could disprove a hypothesis, then that hypothesis is basically useless *as science.*

Because research hypotheses are not usually directly testable, they are usually supported (or *validated*) via a process called *logical inference.* By this method, research hypotheses are used to formulate specific predictions that *can* be directly tested through careful observation. If the results of such further observations support the specific predictions that were based on the research hypothesis, then the research hypothesis itself has also been indirectly supported. We call them research hypotheses, therefore, because they are used to direct the research done to validate them. If they are stated in very general terms, research hypotheses can often result in many individual investigations involving many investigators over very long periods of time. This was certainly the case in Karl von Frisch's work on honeybees.

To test his prediction about the round dance, von Frisch performed an *experimental test of hypothesis*. Such a test is called experimental because an important variable in the system being investigated is actively manipulated by the investigator. Experimental tests of hypotheses are often tests in which two experimental situations are set up which differ with respect to only *one* variable. Such an experimental design has been the dominant tradition in the physical sciences, but has been somewhat less common in the biological sciences until quite recently, for two reasons. First, it is often difficult to reduce an experimental setup to the point where it tests the effects of the manipulation of only one variable, biological systems being so much more complex and interactive than the relatively simple systems investigated by physical scientists. Second, valuable information about biological processes can often be obtained through simple observation, not requiring experimental intervention into the system under study; indeed, the science of biology grew out of this system of simple observation of nature, which is called *natural history*.

In his experimental test of his hypothesis on the function of round dancing, von Frisch set up two observation hives, with two corresponding feeding stations. One hive served as the *experimental test* (often simply called the experimental). As specified in the test hypothesis, foraging bees discovering this feeder were prevented from returning to the hive and round dancing. Furthermore, the number of new foraging bees finding the experimental feeder was counted and recorded. The other observation hive and feeding station served as the *control test* (often simply called the control). As with all controls, this setup differed from the experimental only in the fact that foraging bees finding the feeding station were marked but *not* detained; allowed to return to their hive, these same marked bees were then observed to see if they performed the round dance in the hive. Again, the number of new foraging bees finding the control feeder was counted and recorded, and then these results were compared with the experimental results.

As you may have guessed, von Frisch found that many new bees found the control feeder (several hundred in at least one case), while there was no significant increase in the number of foraging bees arriving at the experimental feeder in almost all cases. This evidence therefore supported von Frisch's test hypothesis and research hypothesis that honeybees use the round dance to communicate the availability of a food source to their hivemates.

This was just the beginning of Karl von Frisch's study of honeybees. Yet already we can identify two major concepts relating to science and scientific research. The first is that the science of biology is not simply the contents of textbooks. The *real* science of biology can be found in the day-to-day results that pour out of the laboratories and field stations where biologists work.

The second important concept is related to the first: Science cannot absolutely "prove" anything, at least in the everyday sense of the word *prove*. As we have seen, hypotheses and conclusions are ultimately validated through induction. Inductive reasoning cannot be and never is absolute; it provides only the relative probability of future events, not their absolute certainty. Scientific "truth," if we may call it that, is therefore *never* absolute, because it ultimately depends on the statistical verification of its principles. To be biologists, therefore, we must be ready to modify or abandon even our most cherished beliefs and to observe the workings of nature without prejudice.

The world of living things is a powerful and subtle teacher. Her power rests in her ability to reveal to us her innermost secrets which we receive via the simple act of observation. Her subtlety resides in her ability to bend our minds and our senses gently but firmly to her ways. As we become more familiar with the science of life we gain a deep and lasting insight into, and appreciation of, the beauty and complexity of life on earth.

Comprehension Questions

Assimilation

1. Von Frisch discovered that the round dance:
    a. had nothing to do with communication in honeybees
    b. communicated only the type of food available

    c.   communicated the availability of food near the honeybee hive

    d.   communicated the availability and distance of a food source

2.   To test his hypothesis about the function of the round dance, von Frisch:
    a.   simply observed returning foraging bees to see if they performed a round dance
    b.   prevented foragers from returning to see if new foragers would find the food source anyway
    c.   allowed marked foraging bees to round dance in the hive to see if other bees would find the food source
    d.   allowed only marked bees to return to the hive

3.   A research hypothesis:
    a.   has no place in the scientific method
    b.   is a tentative general explanation of the observed pattern of regularity
    c.   indicates that there is no significant difference between manipulated and unmanipulated test situations
    d.   is always better than an alternative hypothesis

4.   Which of the following statements is true?
    a.   Von Frisch never used experimental tests on his honeybees.
    b.   Only hypotheses that can be tested via controlled experiments are useful in science.
    c.   Scientific method depends on inductive reasoning alone.
    d.   Experimental predictions are formulated from research hypotheses.

5.   Which of the following best describes a scientific theory?
    a.   An educated guess about the cause of some phenomenon, based on uncontrolled observations
    b.   A controlled investigation of a particular phenomenon involving the manipulation of test conditions
    c.   A hypothesis that has been rigorously tested, either by experiment or by further observation, and found to be valid under most conditions
    d.   An untested hypothesis that is used to guide further research

Interpretation

6.   Which of the following is the best example of *inductive* reasoning?
    a.   The last three green apples I ate were sour, therefore all green apples are sour.
    b.   All students are overworked; you are a student, therefore you are overworked.

    c. The professor I just met was arrogant, therefore all professors must be arrogant.

    d. Green apples are sometimes sour, so the green apple I am about to eat will be sour too.

7. Which of the following is the best example of *deductive* reasoning?

    a. The last three green apples I ate were sour, therefore all green apples are sour.

    b. All students are overworked; you are a student, therefore you are overworked.

    c. The professor I just met was arrogant, therefore all professors must be arrogant.

    d. Green apples are sometimes sour, so the green apple I am about to eat will be sour too.

8. Which of the following statements is true?

    a. The science of biology is a never-ending process.

    b. The science of biology is essentially a collection of facts about living organisms.

    c. Once a hypothesis has been confirmed, it is never contradicted again.

    d. "Doing biology" usually involves a lot of complicated scientific apparatus.

9. In a later experiment, von Frisch predicted that foraging bees would be more numerous at a feeder that was only 50 meters from the hive, as opposed to one that was 100 meters from the hive. However, many more bees found the distant hive. Therefore:

    a. von Frisch should modify his original hypothesis to include these new findings

    b. von Frisch should disregard this result

    c. the original hypothesis about the function of dancing in bees must be wrong and therefore should be rejected

    d. the unusual results were probably wrong and therefore useless to science

Main Idea

10. The main idea of the article is:

    a. Scientific theories, since they are based on the scientic method, are always true.

    b. The scientific method in biology is ultimately based on deductive reasoning.

  c. The science of biology is based on a combination of inductive and deductive reasoning and always involves observations of some kind.
  d. Karl von Frisch's work with honeybees proved once and for all that honeybees can communicate with each other.

Analysis Questions

1. What do you think are the most important characteristics of a good scientist? Why?

2. From what you know of other scientific disciplines (such as chemistry, physics, and so on), how is biology the same? How is it different?

3. Does science, including biological science, understand the world in essentially the same way as, or in different ways from, other systems of thought? How and why?

4. What implications does your understanding of the scientific method have for your understanding of other systems of thought, such as art, music, or religion?

5. Public controversy sometimes arises over the role of science in formulating values, both personal and social. Does science (including biology) have any place in the formulation of such values? Why or why not?

6. How much science should students in secondary schools be required to take? Which areas are most important (biology, chemistry, geology, physics, anthropology, and so on), or are they all equally important? How much coursework should college students be required to take in these areas?

7. How vital are the lab components of college science courses? Could they be eliminated? Discuss.

Exercise

Consider some scientific discovery (for example, gravity, photosynthesis, lunar effect on the tides, the solar system, the freezing or boiling points, germ-caused disease). Imagine that you are a scientist involved in that discovery. Describe a possible hypothesis, observations you could make, and your subsequent actions, as you follow the scientific method. In addition, you may wish to follow one or more of the steps below.

  a. Maintain a log or journal of the above actions, in which you record entries of your observations and actions.

b. Compare your imaginary scenario with history; check what really happened concerning the scientific discovery you chose.

c. Write a brief letter to an imaginary colleague describing your experimentation and observation. Now write a letter to your 12-year-old niece or nephew describing the same things. Compare the two letters. How are they different? Why?

d. Was it difficult to go through the exercise in the main question above? Why or why not?

e. How has going through the exercise in the main question above influenced your understanding of the scientific method? Explain.

f. Rank the following kinds of exercises according to your preference: objective, essay, and imaginary enactment (such as that in the main question above). Explain your preferences.

How Are Scientific Discoveries Made?

*T*he view of science that is usually passed on to nonscientists in their high school courses is one that accounts for scientific advances in strictly logical terms. An observation of nature is made that, for one reason or another, puzzles the observer. The observer then devises a hypothesis to account for the observed fact and checks this hypothesis by doing experiments. If the experiment verifies the hypothesis, a new theory is born; if the experiment fails to give the desired results, further hypotheses are devised until success is obtained. This view of science places primary emphasis on the observed fact and upon experiment as an instrument of verification. The actual course of scientific advance in history is quite different. I should like to illustrate the true path of science by examining four cases in the history of science.

Kepler's First Law, as it is now known, was enunciated by the German astronomer Johannes Kepler (1571–1630) in 1609. It states what appears to be a simple astronomical fact: the orbits of the planets are ellipses with the sun at one of the foci. This law was based on the excellent observations of the path of the planet Mars made by the greatest observational astronomer of the sixteenth century, Tycho Brahe. One could argue that the astronomical facts spoke for themselves and that Kepler was merely the calculating instrument that produced the ellipse from the observations. Any calculator would have done the same. Here is that wonderful objectivity of which science boasts! But when the historical situation is examined, the story turns out to be quite different. The facts spoke, if at all, in a very obscure tongue, and it took the mystical vision of Kepler to translate the "facts" into an astronomical law.

When Kepler first worked up the data he inherited from Brahe, he discovered an orbit for Mars that fit the data nicely. Almost any other astronomer of the time would have stopped there and proudly announced his solution. But this orbit was ovoid—egg-shaped—and this deeply offended Kepler's mathematical mind. Kepler was convinced that God was a mathematician who had ordered the cosmos by mathematical laws. The Deity was not a hen, to lay egglike orbits, but, rather, the supreme origin of all mathematical and physical truth. Hence, the first orbit *must* be a mistake. Kepler, therefore, recalculated and recalculated his data until he found the ellipse. An ellipse fit his preconceptions perfectly. It is the curve formed by a plane cutting a right cone obliquely to the axis. The limiting case of an ellipse is a circle, the orbit astronomers had assigned to planets since antiquity, but one that did not provide the basis for accurate calculations. How wise of God to have devised the ellipse! Circles are simple and would have lulled men into complacency before the mysteries of creation, whereas ellipses provide just the necessary intellectual spice to stimulate further research and lead men on to Truth.

Kepler's First Law was fundamental to Sir Isaac Newton's (1642–1727) "discovery" of universal gravitation. Here is a case that does fit the common view. Newton, sitting in his orchard in Lincolnshire, observed an apple fall. What, he asked himself, if the same force that caused that apple to fall extended to the moon? The centrifugal force of the moon in its orbit must, then, balance the force of gravity, if gravity varied inversely as the square of the distance between earth and moon. When he calculated the effect, he ran into difficulty, for he could not decide how the distance between earth and moon should be measured. Should it be from the surface of the earth to the surface of the moon, or from center to center? Experiment was of no use. Instead, Newton had to invent a mental instrument to answer the question. That instrument was the calculus, by which he could prove that all the mass of both earth and moon could be considered concentrated at the center of gravity of each and, therefore, that the distance was the distance between these two centers.

The success of Newton's calculations, which appeared in the greatest book in the history of science, *Philosophiae naturalis principia mathematica* (*Mathematical Principle of Natural Philosophy,* 1687), led him, in turn, to enunciate three fundamental laws of motion. The first of these is the law of inertia, which states that a body at rest stays at rest and a body in motion remains in motion in a straight line unless acted upon by external, unbalanced forces. This law, we now know, is totally incapable of experimental verification. After the revolution accomplished by Einstein, we can no longer even define such terms as rest and motion in a straight line. Classical physics was founded upon a metaphysical proposition completely removed from experience!

New scientific ideas need not come from simple observations of fact influenced by preconceptions, as was the case with both Kepler and Newton. They sometimes spring from deeper sources. The classic case is that of Friedrich August Kekulé (1829–1896). Kekulé, a chemist, suggested that the central element involved in organic chemistry, carbon, had four bonds by which it united itself to other elements. The tetravalent carbon atom revolutionized the study of carbon compounds, for it allowed chemists, for the first time, to understand how molecules with fairly large molecular weights can be composed of a small number of elements. Indeed, the hydrocarbons consist only of carbon and hydrogen, and what Kekulé saw clearly was that this is accomplished by linking the carbon atoms together in long chains to which the hydrogen atoms are then attached. He further realized that the links between carbon atoms can involve two or even three of the four bonds with which the carbon atom is endowed. A bright and powerful new light shone on the analysis of organic compounds, for with these new concepts, all became clear in hydrocarbon structure. Not quite all. One common substance defied Kekulé's analysis. This was benzene. It had been analyzed over and over again since its isolation by Michael Faraday in the 1820s. It was undoubtedly C_6H_6. But such a formula necessarily implied double and even triple bonds, and Kekulé knew perfectly well that such bonds were associated with very energetic molecules. Benzene, however, is strangely inert. How to reconcile the known composition with the known inertness? Kekulé has told us how the answer came to him. He was, he said, musing before a fire one chilly night and drifted off to sleep. He dreamed of snakes dancing until, suddenly, one snake grabbed its own tail in its mouth, forming a circle. Kekulé sprang awake and shouted, "That's benzene!" Benzene had a ring, not a chain, structure.

It might be argued that this idea was simply the result of a rational process occurring in Kekulé's mind while he slept. But what is of interest is that it appears to have sprung from the deepest levels of his subconscious mind. Depth psychology, a twentieth-century invention, has shown that snakes are phallic symbols and have important sexual significance. And the image of a snake biting its own tale is as old as recorded history. It was a basic symbol of the ancient alchemists, representing the cosmic circularity of both space and time. In short, Kekulé's dream had little or nothing to do with benzene. Indeed, had he dreamed it in 1925, instead of 1863, he probably would have felt obliged to visit a psychiatrist to discover what was wrong with him! But in 1863, depth psychology was still unknown, and so Kekulé turned the dream to account and used it to make a fundamental advance in organic chemistry. The moral here is that scientific ideas of fundamental importance can come from anywhere, not just from observations.

My final example is chosen because it deals with a mental obsession rather than with any observations of the real world. At the age of sixteen, the young Albert Einstein asked himself a question. What would the world look like if he, Albert Einstein, were perched on the crest of a light wave and traveling with it through space at the speed of light? This was a problem in philosophy, of epistemology to be exact, with which physics apparently had little to do. Yet it was a question of such fundamental importance that it ultimately drove Einstein to revolutionize physics. His adolescent question could be answered only by denying the reality of Newtonian metaphysics. There could be no rest or absolute motion through absolute space in absolute time, as Newton had insisted. Instead, all motions must be relative, and the revolutionary conclusion to be drawn from that simple statement is that the speed of light must be the same wherever it is measured, regardless of the speed of the light source or the place of measurement relative to the light source. This is such a contradiction of common sense that most physicists of the time thought Einstein demented and, certainly, wrong. But he was neither, and the Special and General Theories of Relativity are now the common coin of physics. To be sure, they agree with observations; otherwise no one would have considered them for a moment. But they were not *born* from observations or experiments. They were, rather, the creation of an original mind contemplating the universe. In that sense, they resemble great paintings or symphonies as much as they do physics.

What are we to make of these examples? I would argue that they are not exceptions, but the rule, in the history of scientific progress. This progress is not a logical, step-by-step affair determined by the efforts of busy researchers making measurements in laboratories. It is, rather, the result of the creative human intelligence leaping to wild conclusions on the basis of almost totally insufficient evidence. Creative scientists, like other creative people, have visions of reality that they represent as scientific theories. What distinguishes the history of science from the history of art or of literature is that these visions must pass the test of critical comparison with nature. Experiment is not an instrument of discovery, but a critical tool by which theories, when attacked, can be shown to be insufficient or to stand up. Theories lead to facts; only rarely do facts lead to theories. That is what makes the history of science so fascinating.

Comprehension Questions

Assimilation

1. According to the author, the strictly logical view of scientific discovery calls for:
    a. hypothesis, then observation, then experiment
    b. experiment, then observation, then hypothesis
    c. hypothesis, then experiment, then observation
    d. observation, then hypothesis, then experiment

2. The first orbit Kepler found for Mars was rejected because it was:
    a. an ellipse
    b. round
    c. considered inappropriate and unmathematical
    d. not in accordance with Brahe's data

3. The second orbit Kepler found for Mars was:
    a. ovoid
    b. circular
    c. elliptical
    d. egg-shaped

4. Kekulé's solution to the benzene question:
    a. was finally reached in the early 1900s after much work
    b. was proved wrong by Einstein's work

c. was discovered originally by Michael Faraday
d. came to him in a dream

5. Einstein's Special and General Theories of Relativity were born of:
    a. a philosophical question
    b. an old but unproved hypothesis
    c. an observation
    d. an experiment

6. According to the author, the greatest book in the history of science is by:
    a. Kepler
    b. Newton
    c. Kekulé
    d. Einstein

Interpretation

7. The author's organizational structure is:
    a. cumulative narrative
    b. spatial
    c. thesis–proof
    d. descriptive enumeration

8. The question posed in the title "How Are Scientific Discoveries Made?" is appropriate because:
    a. it is a rhetorical question
    b. it is never really answered, thus keeps the reader thinking on his own
    c. it is answered in the text of the article
    d. it is demonstrated to be an unanswerable question

9. The author's mode of development combines all the following types *except:*
    a. spatial
    b. expositional
    c. humorous
    d. narrative

Main Idea

10. The main idea of this article is best expressed as:
     a. Man's observations of the world around him give rise to scientific theories or discoveries, which are then tested by laboratory experimentation to ascertain the truth.

b. Johannes Kepler, Isaac Newton, Friedrich August Kekulé, and Albert Einstein were successful scientists because they had original minds and were able to prove their original theories through experimentation.

c. Scientific discoveries and theories do not, as is usually thought, come simply from the observation of nature, but arise from the creative human mind and are then tested against nature by experiment.

d. Down through the ages, major discoveries in scientific areas have had tremendous impact on man's world and—even more—on how man views his world.

Analysis Questions

1. How does Williams's view of scientific discovery compare with the traditional view? Which one do you think is correct?

2. Williams compares Einstein's Special and General Theories of Relativity to great paintings and symphonies. Comment.

3. Have you ever awakened with a fresh insight or solution to a problem that had not previously occurred to you? Do you believe that people can think creatively in their dreams? Discuss. (Include appropriate examples, if any.)

4. Is this article more appropriately categorized as a history topic or as a science topic? Why? (Support your opinion.)

5. Does Williams support his point through the four cases he describes? Does he *prove* his point? Is proof possible?

6. What other case of scientific discovery can you find that would support Williams's point? Can you find any that refute it?

Exercise

Create a schema graph as follows: On the vertical side list the names of the four scientists whose modes of discoveries were discussed in the article. Label the horizontal side as follows: no previous knowledge of the scientist, knew of the scientist, knew of the discovery of the scientist, knew the information about how the discovery was made (as Williams described it), and agree with Williams about it. Then put an *x* in appropriate locations on the graph to indicate your knowledge in these areas. Finally, consider how your knowledge and opinions influenced your grasp and acceptance of Williams's information and ideas.

Year-to-Year Climate Fluctuations: The El Niño/Southern Oscillation Phenomenon

*I*n 1982–1983 a strong climatic disturbance occurred over a large part of the earth. In the central Pacific, the Marquesas Islands were drenched with a record five times their normal rainfall, and the Tuamotu archipelago recorded its worst hurricane since 1906. Rainfall records in Ecuador and northwestern Peru were shattered month after month and led to Ecuador's worst floods in a century. By contrast, the Indonesian–Australian region, southern Africa, and southern India suffered severe drought, bushfires, and famine. Western Pacific equatorial winds changed direction, eastern tropical Pacific Ocean surface temperatures rose by as much as 9° F, and a major ocean current—the Pacific equatorial undercurrent—stopped flowing. In the United States, California and the South experienced torrential rains and floods, and the

Rocky Mountains had record snowpacks. These events are all related to the El Niño/Southern Oscillation phenomenon, the single most prominent signal in year-to-year climate variability.

The meteorological aspects of this phenomenon were first recognized by meteorologist Sir Gilbert Walker more than one-half century ago. He claimed that there was a year-to-year climate variation on a vast scale occurring between the Pacific and Indian Oceans. Atmospheric pressure in the eastern Pacific increased when pressure over the western Pacific and Indian Oceans decreased, then a reversal took place, and so on. Pressure thus swayed back and forth like a gigantic seesaw every several years; Walker named this climate fluctuation the *Southern Oscillation*. However, scientists of Walker's day were skeptical. To them it seemed highly unlikely that pressure and associated climate disturbances in widely separated regions of the globe would be linked. It is only in the last decade that the Southern Oscillation has been intensively studied and its importance widely recognized.

The Southern Oscillation is strongly coupled to the ocean, and the oceanography component is known as *El Niño*. When an El Niño occurs, the surface waters in the eastern Pacific near the equator are abnormally warm; a gigantic pool of warm surface water extends one-quarter of the way around the earth from the South American coast to the central Pacific. This warm-water pool appears irregularly every several years. In the last 15 years, major El Niños occurred in 1972, 1976, and 1982–1983.

El Niños have a major effect on the biology of the eastern and central equatorial Pacific and along the western coasts of North and South America. For example, consider the Peruvian coastal upwelling region, a narrow strip of coastal water 30 miles wide and 800 miles long. Although this strip of coastal water is only 0.02 percent of the world's ocean surface, in 1967 it produced approximately 20 percent of the world's fish catch. In this region, upwelling (the vertical upward movement of water) causes chemical nutrients, principally phosphates and nitrates, to be brought to the surface. Phytoplankton (minute marine plants) synthesize them using sunlight, and abundant plankton growth enables extremely dense fish populations to develop. When an El Niño occurs, upwelling is suppressed, phytoplankton blooms cease, and fish starve, as do the birds that live on them. The result is an ecological disaster. The El Niño of 1972, together with overfishing, virtually destroyed what was once the world's largest fishing industry. Clearly, the potential economic and social benefits from understanding the El Niño phenomenon would be great.

Probably the biggest El Niño of this century was the most recent one in 1982–1983. The suppression of upwelling along the equator and the South American coast caused small fish and squid to disappear. As a result, millions of sea birds that nest on Christmas Island (central equatorial Pacific) abandoned their young, and all fur seal pups born in the Galápagos Islands (eastern equatorial Pacific) in 1982 had died by March 1983.

Swings in the Southern Oscillation and accompanying El Niños are clearly of major importance. What causes a climate fluctuation of this type? To understand something of the mechanism we first must understand the normal Pacific atmosphere and ocean circulation near the equator. Because ocean temperature decreases with depth, the normal pattern of eastern equatorial Pacific upwelling causes cool water to be brought to the surface in the east. The warmer surface water in the west heats the overlying air and causes it to rise; clouds and heavy rain result. The rising air is replaced by air in the lower atmosphere moving westward from the eastern Pacific. This westward wind causes upwelling and cold surface water in the east, so the resultant atmospheric and oceanic circulation is self-perpetuating.

When an El Niño occurs, a gigantic pool of warm water in the central and eastern Pacific near the equator causes the heating region, rising air, clouds, and precipitation to shift eastward. Consequently, desert Pacific Islands in the central Pacific are drenched with rain while Indonesia, New Guinea, and adjacent areas experience drought. Hurricanes, which need warm sea-surface water to maintain their strength, are seen much farther to the east. Due to the change in heating pattern, the atmospheric pressure at the earth's surface is higher than normal in the western Pacific and lower than normal in the central and eastern Pacific. This pressure change causes the western Pacific surface winds to weaken or even flow in the opposite direction.

The changed heating near the equator also affects regions far from the equator. High- and low-pressure cells form in the North Pacific and over North America, causing normal wind patterns over North America to be altered. Abnormal weather, like the 1982–1983 record Rocky Mountain snowpacks and the torrential rains in the South and California, results.

All the above noted changes in atmospheric circulation are due to the appearance of the huge warm-water pool near the equator in the central and eastern Pacific. Why does it form? It seems to be caused by a slackening of the winds months earlier in the western equatorial Pacific. Why do the winds relax? We are not sure. The tropical Pacific Ocean and atmosphere are strongly coupled together, and only within the last year have coupled ocean–atmosphere models been developed. Probably an understanding of the overall mechanism is just around the corner.

Year-to-year climatic fluctuations in the tropical Pacific and Indian Ocean regions, as well as in parts of North America, seem to be largely due to the El Niño/Southern Oscillation phenomenon. If we can better understand this major climatic fluctuation, we may significantly improve our forecasts of average weather conditions several months into the future. The potential benefits of such long-range forecasting would be tremendous.

Comprehension Questions

Assimilation

1. The El Niño/Southern Oscillation phenomenon refers to:
    a. a year-to-year climate variation occurring between the Pacific and Indian Oceans
    b. a condition of severe drought in the Marquesas Islands and Tuamotu archipelago
    c. a major increase in the Pacific equatorial undercurrent
    d. a hypothetical chain reaction of climate disturbances between the northern and southern hemispheres

2. Sir Gilbert Walker first recognized the meteorological aspects of the El Niño/Southern Oscillation phenomenon:
    a. over a century ago
    b. more than 50 years ago
    c. less than 30 years ago
    d. during the major disturbance of 1972

3. The term *upwelling* refers to:
    a. minute marine plants
    b. the fishing area along the Peruvian coast
    c. vertical upward movement of water
    d. the huge pool of warm water near the equator in the central and eastern Pacific

4. All the changes in atmospheric circulation described by the author are, according to him:
    a. due to the weakening of El Niño

b. due to the appearance of the huge warm-water pool near the equator in the central and eastern Pacific

c. due to the upwelling recently discovered in the Arctic and Antarctic Oceans

d. due to an unknown cause

5. The slackening of the winds in the western equatorial Pacific are, according to the author:
   a. caused by El Niño as it forms
   b. caused by El Niño as it dies out
   c. caused by random weather and climate variations
   d. due to an unknown cause

Interpretation

6. We can infer that the author believes that an understanding of what he calls the "overall mechanism" of the interaction between the Pacific Ocean and the atmosphere:
   a. will be discovered in the distant future
   b. will be discovered very soon
   c. will never be discovered
   d. is no longer of vital significance in weather forecasting

7. Concerning the effect of better long-range weather forecasting on social and economic conditions, the author:
   a. seems unaware of the connection
   b. is pessimistic about any possible impact
   c. refers to such effects, but does not discuss them
   d. discusses several areas where the impact will be especially noticeable

8. The author uses several modes of development of his ideas. These include all the following *except:*
   a. spatial organization
   b. question and answer
   c. cause and effect
   d. descriptive enumeration

9. From reading this article, we can infer that the writer is most likely:
   a. a fisherman
   b. a weather forecaster for network television
   c. an oceanographer
   d. a geologist

Main Idea

10. The main idea of this article is:
    a. Scientists have identified and are beginning to understand the El Niño/ Southern Oscillation phenomenon, the single most prominent signal in year–to–year climate variability.
    b. The economic impact of the El Niño/Southern Oscillation phenomenon is especially obvious along the Peruvian coastal upwelling region where less than 1 percent of the world's ocean surface produces approximately 20 percent of the world's fish catch.
    c. Although Sir Gilbert Walker's discovery of the meteorologic aspects of the El Niño/Southern Oscillation phenomenon was met with skepticism by his colleagues, it has been proven to be accurate.
    d. Scientists and meteorologists who study conditions in the climate on land, in the air, and in the oceans are making discoveries that will lead to more accurate weather forecasting.

Analysis Questions

1. What economic benefits can you think of that would result from improved, long-range weather forecasting? What social benefits?

2. Why are scientific discoveries, such as the one made by Sir Gilbert Walker, so often met with skepticism?

3. Have there been unusual weather patterns in the area in which you live? If so, what are they? What might be the causes?

4. Describe the effect of upwelling.

5. What actions has man taken to influence the weather? What is your opinion of these actions?

6. Why do you think weather is such a common conversational topic? What makes the topic of this article interesting?

Exercise

One of the writing techniques that Clarke uses in his article is a mode of development called *spatial organization*. Explain this term; then, graphically demonstrate the information given in the text by drawing a rough map of the world and locating the occurrences he discusses in their proper locations on the map. If you had to learn this information, which representation would be easier to study from, the map or the text? Why?

Geomorphology of the Finger Lakes Region

When the first great glacier swept down from Labrador 1 million years ago, the Finger Lakes region of New York State had already undergone 200 million years of erosion of its seabed form. For over 300 million years the huge inland sea had covered much of what is now the northeastern portion of the United States. During that time layer upon layer of salt, lime, mud, and sand were laid down on the sea floor as a result of evaporation, precipitation, and sedimentation. In time, by the combined weights of newer upper layers and the salt water the lower layers were compressed to an eventual thickness of 2,400 meters. These compressed, hardened strata are the dominant rockbed forms of the region: sandstones and shales in the south; limestones in the north. Three formations of preglacial rock in particular helped shape the area's eventual look: Onondaga limestone in the north, Tully limestone throughout the middle of the region, and the Portage escarpment of sandstones and shales in the south. The glaciers would gouge and shape these into rough form; subsequent weathering would give them today's finish.

The sea retreated north and east some 200 million years ago when the land was uplifted. A relatively flat, but not featureless, plain resulted from the uplift, tilted toward the south. Composed of soft and hard sea-bottom rock forms, which weathered and eroded at differing speeds, this plain was gradually reduced from its 3,000-foot height back almost to sea level, forming a peneplain.

The eroded sediments flowed with the existing drainage south into what are now the Delaware and Susquehanna river systems. Cutting through every type of rock it encountered, the water also carved new drainage channels to the north. The divide between these two drainage systems was a line running southwest from the Adirondacks. When, 100 million years ago, the land experienced another uplift, these two systems produced different topographical structures: a deepening of the existing system to the south, but a radical re-formation of the new system to the north. The subsequent headwater erosion created a broad, gently rolling basin in the north and, down into the region where the Finger Lakes lie today, a deeply channeled area in a belt running east and west, fifty to sixty miles high and two times as wide. These features would have major consequences when the glacier moved south.

Exactly what caused the Ice Age is still a matter of conjecture. Whether it arose from a partial blockage of the sun's radiation caused by volcanic activity or a change in the atmospheric concentration of carbon dioxide, or from a change in the tilt of earth in relation to the sun, or simply from a much greater than normal amount of snow leading to greater radiational cooling, several things are clear: temperatures across the world dropped fifteen to twenty degrees long enough to arrest summer snow melt, radiational cooling led to further accumulations of snow and ice, and, starting roughly 1 million years ago, at least four advances and declines of ice occurred over much of the northern hemisphere. Two glaciers swept down on the Finger Lakes region, separated by a long interglacial period.

As the first great glacier crept southward at a speed of two or three feet per day, it carried before it, much as a chisel does wood, great amounts of debris picked up from the north. The weight of the ice and debris, pressing inexorably on the weathered peneplain, gouged, chiseled, and scored the rockbed. Because more ice could be accommodated in the wide north basin than in the narrower southern channels, the ice was forced to higher, heavier levels; the greater thicknesses speeded the glacier's advance and caused the ice to push even harder. Carried within and atop the ice was the debris: rock flour, huge boulders erratics, gravel, sand, and clay. Some of this debris was deposited directly when the glacier retreated, left lying where the ice melted. The rest, borne by the huge floods of water released by the melting, was carried along the now deeper and wider drainage channels to spots where the second glacier would find it and sweep it away.

In the interglacial period—the time between the first and second stages of the ice's advance, estimated to be as long as 200,000 years—the climate in the Finger Lakes region was even warmer than it is today. The types of plants and animals that could live successfully in the area are indications of this milder climate. During this period, all the debris deposited by the first glacier was weathered and eroded, and much of it was washed away. When the second glacier arrived, it found the way prepared.

From above, a glacier appears to be solid, hard, immovable ice. But the interior of the ice sheet is in constant motion, the very weight of overlying ice compressing that below and heating it enough to create a watery medium in which individual ice particles can swirl, eddy, rise, and fall. This interior movement is what allows the sheet to move forward, as the front is supplied with fresh material from behind and inside. During its maximum stage, the first glacier to cover the Finger Lakes region was 2,500 feet thick, with a 200-foot hard crust riding atop the slowly churning, creeping mass. As the glacier moved south, slender tongues of ice first filled the prepared valleys, deepened them, grew in height and length and weight, pushing forward. As the glacier melted, these valley extensions were the last to melt. The interior movement also allowed the ice to transport huge quantities of materials great distances. The hundreds of tons of ice pushing chisellike boulders before it scoured the area as it moved, clearing the land of plant life, forcing animals south, and picking up any loose material. It also plucked or quarried huge boulders out of the landscape, especially crystalline rock from the Adirondacks and the belts of Tully and Onondaga limestone. Today we find these erratics embedded in the ground and lying in streambeds scores and even hundreds of miles from their origins.

After the 200,000-year interglacial period, the second glacier started south. It picked up and moved what debris was left from the first ice cover, and following the channels routed by the first, it deepened, gouged, and chiseled the land even further. Although this action was similar to the earlier glacier's, the debris carried by the second ice advance most changed the countryside. Since the melting of the second glacier, only weathering has affected the piles of moraine it deposited. No third ice cover has yet come along to sweep away the remnants, and so these piles of debris still exist.

As the last glacier retreated, its melting released tremendous floods that carried the gravel, clay, sand, rock flour, and other types of moraine. Depending on the configuration of the ground at the point of melt, and the speed with which the ice gave up its load, these piles were left in distinctive shapes. Where the retreat stalled for long periods, from 200 to 500 years, evident just south of the lakes of today, terminal moraines exist. These are the largest land forms left by the ice, hundreds of feet high and winding for miles. Other, smaller forms include the "swarm" of 10,000 drumlins just north of the Onondaga escarpment, distinctive half-egg-shaped hills called hoddy-doddies, which range in height from 50 to several hundred feet and in length from a few hundred feet to over a mile; the winding sandy ridges called eskers, also common in the area; cone-shaped kames; and kettles, created when huge ice chunks were deposited below the level of the moraine, which then collapsed when the ice melted.

The floods of water were at much higher levels than the lakes are today. There is evidence of eleven separate and distinct levels of Cayuga Lake, each one a stage in the ice's retreat and the subsequent erosion of the blocking moraine. The numerous small streams and tributaries to the main trunk rivers flowing north–south thus acted on the land high above today's levels. When the second glacier scooped out the loose material and then melted away, the water level fell, leaving these small valleys hanging far above the main north–south valleys the lakes themselves fill.

The glacier's actions also left eleven nearly parallel lakes which today look like fingers of hands spread out on the land. As the lake levels fell, still blocked to the north by the ice, the runoff was to the south, into the Susquehanna and Delaware river systems. But the two glaciers did their work: today, the Finger Lakes drain to the north, into the Mohawk and Saint Lawrence systems and out to the Atlantic. The ice so altered the height of the northern basins, and the amounts of terminal moraine in the south were so high, the water had easier work reversing its flow and punching an exit in the other direction.

In the 10,000 years since the ice melted, the land around the Finger Lakes has reforested, the animals have returned, and the commonly wet winters and rainy springs have continued their work on the land. The postglacial changes in the countryside seem unremarkable compared with those wrought by the huge forces at work before, but they have created some of the distinctive land forms for which the area is famous. Most spectacular are the numerous gorges, with impressive high-walled chasms of slate and shale cut by rushing water. The Taughannock River, running from Schuyler County to Tompkins County, has created a gorge more than 400 feet high and over a mile long, depositing the material in a fan-shaped delta out into Cayuga Lake. The Genesee River in Livingston and Wyoming counties has created Letchworth Gorge, a spectacular "Grand Canyon of the East" over ten miles long. Enfield Glen, Watkins Glen, Buttermilk Falls Glen, and Fillmore Glen are other nearby examples of the effect of water on moraine over relatively short periods of time. Had the rivers been running solely over bedrock, these spectacular postglacial formations would not have occurred.

Comprehension Questions

Assimilation

1. A glacier is most accurately defined as:
   a. solid ice
   b. Portage escarpment
   c. watery medium
   d. all of the above

2. The "Grand Canyon of the East" refers to:
   a. Niagara Falls
   b. Letchworth Gorge
   c. Fillmore Glen
   d. Watkins Glen

3. The climate of the Finger Lakes region:
   a. was once warmer than it is today
   b. was always cooler than it is today
   c. is in a continuing warmer trend
   d. cannot be specified since the area was underwater until after the glacial age

4. Which of these conditions is not a probable cause of the Ice Age, according to the article?
   a. partial blockage of the sun's radiation
   b. greater amount of snow than usual
   c. slowing down of the earth's spin
   d. change in tilt of the earth in relation to the sun

5. In the last million years, the Finger Lakes region has undergone:
   a. one ice cover
   b. two ice covers

    c.   four ice covers

    d.   none of the above

6.   The largest land forms left by the retreating glaciers were:

    a.   terminal moraines

    b.   hoddy-doddies

    c.   eskers

    d.   kames

Interpretation

7.   We can infer that glaciers had:

    a.   a beneficial effect on the terrain

    b.   a detrimental effect on the terrain

    c.   no effect on the terrain

    d.   irrelevant effects on the terrain

8.   The tone of this article is:

    a.   humorous and entertaining

    b.   inspirational

    c.   objective

    d.   subjective

9.   The personal bias of the author, concerning political convictions, is:

    a.   pervasive throughout his article, greatly influencing the reader

    b.   not obvious in the article

    c.   self-contradictory

    d.   detrimental to the author's message

Main Idea

10.   The main idea of this article is:

    a.   Time and weather changes determine the landscape of our country.

    b.   The Finger Lakes region is named from the eleven lakes formed long ago.

    c.   To understand the varied terrain of the Finger Lakes region of New York State, one must examine the changes in temperature.

    d.   Rivers of snow and ice, and the debris they carried, shaped the present look of the Finger Lakes region of New York State.

Analysis Questions

1. Why are the eleven major lakes in this area called Finger Lakes?

2. The author keeps our attention on this potentially dry subject with the use of vivid images. Identify and discuss some of these images.

3. Describe the makeup and action of a glacier.

4. Why did the waters of the Finger Lakes reverse direction?

5. If a new glacier came into this region today, what do you think would happen?

Exercises

1. Hypothesize a cause for the Ice Age and write a brief article in Wells's style relating it. (*Note:* the author poses four possible causes in the fourth paragraph of the article.)

2. Wells's approach to his subject is straightforward, stressing historical facts. How else might this topic have been presented? Rewrite a portion of the article in a different style or approach.

Man and His Environment

Man has always had problems with his environment because he did not understand it or his responsibilities to it. Owing to this ignorance and lack of concern, his environment has "rebelled" many times, and as a result, man himself has suffered. Belatedly, man has been forced to recognize his responsibility to his environment and the tremendous penalties that his pollution of his world will exact from him if he does not change his ways.

Pollution is not well-defined in scientific terms. Something described as polluted is commonly thought of as being unclean or defiled. For water to be polluted, then, must a substance merely be present that was not present in the original "pure" water? Or must this new substance be present in a concentration that causes the water to be unfit for its intended purpose? Not knowing the original composition of our environment, we are forced to accept the definition of pollution as being that state in which water, air, or soil is unfit for the intended purpose.

Even the phrase *intended purpose* eludes consistent, accepted definition, as exemplified by the struggle to define a unified "purpose" for New York State's Hudson River: the upper reaches of this major river have a much different "intended purpose" than does the river where it flows into the

Atlantic Ocean. A look at the development of standards of water quality throws light on this problem.

In 1965 the Federal Clean Water Act became law. This law required the states to establish standards for all interstate and coastal waters. Nine years later, New York State had succeeded in establishing its standards in a document entitled "Classification and Standards Governing the Quality and Purity of Waters of New York State."

There are six classes of fresh surface water. These include three classes of drinking water and one class each for primary contact recreation (swimming), fishing, and secondary contact recreation (boating). All waters must be suitable for fish survival. Each class is designated for a "best usage," and meeting the criteria for best usage permits all uses under that best usage.

The best usage in the highest class is "enjoyment of water in its natural condition and, where compatible, as a source of water for drinking." This water, class N, is to be clean enough for human consumption with no treatment other than disinfection (required for all public water supplies) and is to be left in a natural state. The classes that follow are AA, A, B, C, and D, the lowest quality water permitted. AA and A water can be used for drinking with sufficient treatment. B water has a best usage of swimming; class C, of fishing; class D, of boating.

In this way the surface waters in the state have been classified, although not without great struggle at all levels of government among special interest groups and lobbyists. The upper reaches of the Hudson River have a higher best usage than does the river as it flows past New York City.

Along with the definition of best usage there are limits set on the concentration of various pollutants (chemical and bacterial) plus the level of dissolved oxygen. These data dictate what may or may not be discharged into that water. Since the Federal Clean Water Act also states that the standards and classifications of waters must be directed toward improvement of water quality, the classification of a water can not give legal permission to degrade quality below that in existence at classification. The result of all this work has been a general improvement of fresh water quality in spite of the presence of areas which some would still term "open sewers."

Have environmental problems grown in magnitude and severity in the last few decades? Unfortunately, it would seem so. The toxicity of modern contaminants has reached a level where small quantities can pollute large portions of the environment. The modern contaminant is not only highly toxic but also complex. Theoretically, there are over 200 different molecular structures that may be found in the complex mixture of compounds we call simply PCBs (polychlorinated biphenyls).

There is another element to the problem. Today we casually talk about nanograms of a contaminant per liter of water or parts per trillion of a pollutant. Our advancing science and technology have given us not only the ability to produce very toxic substances but also the ability to detect minute quantities of such substances that would have gone undetected in the past. "Zero" in this area of study has always been synonymous with "undetectable." As our ability to detect smaller and smaller concentrations has advanced, the purity of what we once considered clean has been brought into question. A recent scare in Louisiana concerning possible intentional poisoning of water supplies is an example. A poison was detected, but further tests showed that the "poison" was in the raw water supply and was considered natural. Low levels of cyanide are permitted in drinking water, even though cyanide is a poison. Indeed, there actually may be several poisons in the water you drink.

Once a pollutant is identified and declared dangerous, the real problems begin. Cleaning up the environment following the release of a pollutant is extremely difficult and expensive. All too often, with our present technology, it is impossible. The presence of PCBs in the Hudson River is such a problem. The PCBs in the river are now in the mud and will be released into the water for years to come. Do we dredge the river? Aside from the tremendous expense involved, we would then face the even more challenging problem of what to do with the mud. No towns or counties along the Hudson want the mud on their land. Could the PCBs be sealed into the mud? So far, there is no answer, except the advice of the State Department of Health that people should eat no more than one meal per month of striped bass caught in the Hudson River. This is not an acceptable solution; yet we find ourselves living with more and more of these problems rather than seeing them solved.

Even when attempts are made to dispose of pollutants satisfactorily, glaring mistakes in judgment have occurred. "Sanitary" landfills, designed to receive all manner of solid waste, have been located in dry areas. In this case, "dry" means land that is well drained. The reasoning for these decisions was: (1) keep the solid waste dry to reduce the decay rate of the biodegradable material, (2) inhibit the movement of contaminants into ground water, and (3) maintain a better working condition for trucks and earth-moving equipment. All seemingly good reasons.

Unfortunately, precipitation falling on the landfill drains through the solid waste, leaching out substances that are highly toxic. Because the soil is well-drained, this polluted water moves unceasingly into the ground water. Millions of tons of solid waste have been legally buried. . . . And this scenario does not even consider the undeniable presence of *illegal* dumps, where there has been no attempt at planning or control.

Even the most careful judgment will be of no benefit if it is based on inaccurate information. Information considered accurate today may be made obsolete by new scientific discoveries tomorrow. As a case in point, we now know that chemical and biological processes transform toxic primary contaminants into secondary substances that are even more toxic. This fact is vividly illustrated with mercury, which was once thought to be inert. Anaerobic bacteria, however, are able to convert metallic mercury into methyl mercury compounds, which are soluble and extremely toxic. There is little chance that this transformation could have been predicted or discovered through research. Without such evidence there would have been no reason to prevent the deposition of mercury and, by implication, other substances in the environment.

From a lay person's viewpoint, there have been too many surprises. We wonder how often these problems could have been avoided. How many times have knowledgeable people compromised the environment by allowing the dumping of dangerous substances? Unfortunately, the advances in technology that have been used to help make our nation strong, have also been misused to make our land less fit for man.

Comprehension Questions

Assimilation

1. Environmental pollution:
   a. could not occur without man
   b. is a new problem
   c. is being resolved
   d. is difficult to define in scientific terms

2. When measuring quantities of a toxic concentration in a substance, "zero" is synonymous with:
   a. none
   b. neutral

    c.   undetectable

    d.   none of the above

3. The author cited an illustration concerning pollution in which of the following places?
   a. the Atlantic Ocean
   b. the Hudson River
   c. the Mississippi River
   d. the Susquehanna River

4. The author believes that pollution problems are a result of:
   a. poor judgment
   b. insufficient correct information
   c. greed
   d. all of the above

Interpretation

5. One writing technique used extensively by Ludington is:
   a. use of dialogue
   b. use of questions
   c. use of hypothetical situations
   d. use of statistics

6. The author's style is predominantly:
   a. formal
   b. slang
   c. informal
   d. colloquial

7. The tone of the article is:
   a. neutral
   b. pessimistic
   c. optimistic
   d. omniscient

8. The author's purpose in writing an article on this topic is most likely to:
   a. solve the pollution problem
   b. refute scientific claims that there is a pollution problem
   c. encourage awareness about the problem of pollution
   d. make a lot of money

9. Our advancing science and technology have given us the ability to do all the following *except:*
   a. produce very toxic substances
   b. detect very minute quantities of a toxic substance
   c. identify toxicity in substances previously considered nontoxic
   d. resolve the landfill problem

Main Idea

10. The main idea of this article is:
    a. Man has always known, but neglected, his responsibility to his environment, until forced to change his behavior.
    b. Man is still unaware of the consequences of his tampering with his environment, mostly because he does not want to change his priorities.
    c. Man has a history of polluting his environment through his own ignorance and carelessness; yet it is man himself who will ultimately suffer most.
    d. The problems man has created in his own environment will most likely never be resolved.

Analysis Questions

1. Pollution is usually considered to be an industrial problem with an industrial solution. Discuss how individuals can add to (or help eliminate) pollution on a personal basis.

2. The question of nuclear disarmament can be discussed from many viewpoints, including national politics, international relations, military science, and ethics. Ludington's concern in his essay is for the environment. How would the question of nuclear disarmament be treated from his point of view?

3. What impact have man-made changes to the environment had on various choices you are making and will make (education, career, where you might live, and so forth)?

4. Ludington states that advances in technology have caused pollution problems for which there are currently no solutions. Does this mean that there should be a slowdown in technology until current problems are resolved? Why or why not?

Exercise

The situation: You are a tax-paying citizen of Midland, Illinois. Your house is one of 30 houses on Lake Lovely, just inside the town limits. Five years ago, a zoning variance was granted to allow a toothpick factory to be erected just upstream from the lake. Now, the lake is no longer clear, and the marine life is dying.

Your response: You are going to write letters to several people. For each individual listed below, describe the *tone* of your letter. Then, choose one individual and write the letter to him or her:

The mayor of Midland

The president of the neighborhood association

The owner of the factory

The state representative of the district

Your best friend, who lives in Chicago

Your 10-year-old nephew, who will no longer be able to go fishing with you there

ROALD HOFFMANN

Two Unfortunate Trends

I would like to express in some detail my ideas on two issues: science education and our scientific relationships with the Soviet bloc.

In a field such as chemistry, 70 percent of the Ph.D. graduates enter industry. Thus, universities train the highly skilled work force that is behind medicine, plastics, photography, synthetic fibers—indeed, every aspect of modern society, everything around you. Universities and industry share a common interest in attracting talented young men and women to the science professions. I'm sorry to say that the great American industry has not done its share in this training process. In a typical good department of chemistry, such as Cornell's, less than 5 percent of our teaching and research support is from industry. Much support is from one or another government source, and a substantial portion comes from the gifts of our generous alumni and from general university funds. There are industrial givers, to be sure, but it is mainly individuals who support us.

Young people are not as attracted to science as they once were. Why? Several reasons come to mind: (1) a growing antirationalist mood in society, manifesting itself through interest in astrology, the occult, and so on; (2) a loss of the perception of science as purely progressive, owing to an emphasis, not necessarily an overemphasis, on the negative side effects of technological development, such as pollution; (3) meager financial incentives to scientific careers; (4) a deterioration in scientific literacy; and (5) a loss of infectious enthusiasm that was inevitable when the exponential, dynamic increase in numbers of scientists leveled off in the past decade. These are a few reasons, among many. I'm sure you can add more. Yet just when it is agreed that we must work to counter these trends in order to assure the future flow of manpower into science, at the same time there are severe cuts specifically in the funding of science education. It doesn't make sense. This is the time to put resources into increasing the scientific literacy of the public and improving science education. We need to train teachers, rejuvenate textbooks, provide creative science programs similar to "Nova" or "Cosmos" on public television, attract students to research through summer research jobs.

I have been speaking about the universities in terms of their teaching function. Let us not forget that in America (unlike France or the Soviet Union, which have alternative establishments for science research) it is in the universities that basic research, the foundation of most applied research, is accomplished. There is no lack of evidence that the basic research already done in universities is being utilized by industry. For instance, the work of mine that was the basis for the Nobel Prize was shown in a recent study to be the research most cited not in the literature of pure chemistry but in journals of applied chemistry.

There is a synergism between education and research at universities. And when universities in general get in financial trouble, as they are now owing to loss of student aid, this is reflected in a general climate of stringency, of budget cuts, of constriction on those people most directly concerned with both education and research. And in constricting times it is difficult to do great research and to excite young people.

Let me turn to another matter: curtailment of scientific exchanges with the Soviet Union and its allies. I have some unpopular opinions to express here. Before I tell you my thoughts, it's important that you know something of my background. My family and I lived under Soviet occupation from 1939 to 1941 and from 1944 to 1945, surrounding a worse Nazi occupation from 1941 to 1944. I was a child then, but I have learned from my parents how things were. In 1960, in the middle of graduate school, I went to the Soviet Union for a year on an exchange program sponsored by the State Department. I have been in the USSR three times since. I speak Russian and am probably one of the few people in the United States who lectures in the Soviet Union on his work in Russian. I have an excellent idea, I think, of the workings (or lack thereof) of Soviet society, and of science and technology in particular. In my research group at Cornell there have worked over the years three Rumanians, two Czechs, one Hungarian, one East German, and two young men from the People's Republic of China. My special background gives me a feeling of great sympathy for the people of the Eastern European bloc countries.

In recent years, scientific exchanges between us and the Eastern European countries have been sharply curtailed. The Carter administration, with the support of Congress, cut exchanges because of the Soviet invasion of Afghanistan; the Reagan administration continued this policy because of the tragic situation in Poland. Our National Academy of Sciences curtailed official exchanges and cooperative research because of the treatment of a colleague, Academician Sakharov. There is substantial private and personal pressure on scientists in this country to break all Soviet contacts because of Russian treatment of refuseniks and dissenters. As a result visits and exchanges in both directions have been drastically reduced.

I think this curtailment is a serious mistake. I think that despite the actions by the Soviets and their allies, actions that you and I disapprove of, it is important to maintain contact between scientists of both worlds, and it is we as much as they who are hurt by the present situation.

In the closed society which is the Soviet Union, every small window that is opened on the West lets in the light of the world, making friends for us. Soviet scientists, the Soviet intelligentsia, are that segment of their society that is most receptive and responsive to our ideas. They have an opening to the West, a sense of being with us, through the open scientific literature. That sense of being with us is reinforced by any American's visit there, by any Russian's visit here.

There is no question that every such visit, in either direction, has official sanction from the Russian side and is used by Soviet authorities in their own official way. Yet they cannot block the personal side of a visit from coming through—the very presence of an American scientist talking freely about his beautiful experiment, using instruments his Russian counterparts don't have, showing pictures of his laboratory—that presence by itself makes more friends, convinces more people of what is right here.

I would also argue on grounds of simple self-interest that it is essential for the security of our country that we have people here with firsthand knowledge of the workings of the Soviet system. The exchanges and joint research programs produce such knowledge. I would urge that we seek the wisdom of people, such as Dr. Armand Hammer, who have shown that it is possible to have meaningful business dealings with the Russians, to our own benefit.

Finally, I think scientists have a responsibility, based on the rational and open tradition of their activities, to keep talking to each other even when the rest of society is disposed to become angry. It is not that we are better people. It's just that we have a base of small talk or shop talk—the facts and excitements of science—by which an angry discourse is turned into polite, friendly conversation. The psychology of communication between people—husband and wife, parent and child, Democrat and Republican, fans of two rival football teams—requires such points of common interest to allow the communicators to bypass anger. It is no different between nations. If we are to achieve a rational and secure plan to end the horrible prospect of nuclear war, we need to keep in touch. Be firm with the Soviets on the level of governmental relations, but let the scientists talk to each other.

Comprehension Questions

Assimilation

1. In chemistry, what percentage of the Ph.D. graduates enter industry?
   a. 30
   b. 50
   c. 70
   d. 5

2. University teaching and research support comes mainly from:
   a. alumni and industry
   b. government funds and alumni
   c. industry and general university funds
   d. government funds and industry

3. Fewer young people are attracted to science for all the reasons below *except:*
   a. little financial incentive
   b. deterioration in scientific literacy
   c. growing antirationalist mood in society
   d. poor teaching available at the secondary school level

4. Methods cited to increase the scientific literacy of the public include all *except:*
   a. improved textbooks
   b. addition of more science programs on TV
   c. replacement of scientific experimentation with more useful work
   d. addition of more summer research jobs

5. According to the article, universities are in financial trouble owing to:
   a. Ph.D.s going into industry instead of teaching
   b. loss of student aid
   c. the recession of the 1980s
   d. decreased alumni giving

6. Dr. Armand Hammer's contact with the Soviet Union is through:
   a. medical research
   b. chemistry
   c. physics
   d. business

Interpretation

7. The author's purpose in giving his personal background is mostly to:
   a. create sympathy for the people of Eastern bloc countries
   b. create sympathy for himself
   c. prove he has unusual knowledge of the situation
   d. increase the number of internationals in his research group

8. The author feels that scientists of opposing nations can and should communicate about:
   a. the psychology of communication between people
   b. how to keep the peace between their nations
   c. scientific topics
   d. political and philosophical questions

9. The tone of the article is intended to be:
   a. neutral
   b. humorous
   c. persuasive
   d. cynical

Main Idea

10. The main idea of this article is:
    a. Scientists of opposing nations, through open contact and exchange of information, can be instrumental in keeping the peace.
    b. Today more than ever our nation must put more resources into scientific education and research.
    c. Contrary to current trends, we must put more resources into scientific education and increase our contact with Russian scientists.
    d. Industry must increase its support of scientific education and academic research.

Analysis Questions

1. Hoffmann was the Nobel Prize winner in chemistry in 1981. How does this knowledge about him influence the impact of his message?

2. Hoffmann addresses two separate concerns in this one essay. Does this add to or detract from the impact of each topic? How?

3. How are the two topics discussed in this essay alike? Different?

4. Hoffmann's discussion about science education touches several immediate concerns of today's college students. Do you agree or disagree with his points? What is your opinion about current trends in science education?

Exercise

There are actually two main ideas in this article. Identify them; then, go through the article to find statements about each topic and list them in two columns. Finally, make two side-by-side concept maps. Indicate where ideas relate or overlap by drawing connecting lines between them.

We Are Not Inferior to the Russians

*I*t is sometimes claimed that by building up our nuclear weapons arsenal we could achieve greater security for our nation. My theme is that we could achieve the opposite: less security. The Reagan government has downgraded the importance of serious arms control negotiations by giving first priority to the addition of many new weapons to the U.S. arsenal (the B-1, the MX, the Trident II) and to the NATO arsenal (the Pershing II and the ground-based cruise missiles). Without these, President Reagan claims, the United States will be caught in a position of permanent inferiority. We are told there is a serious window of vulnerability in our forces. I claim that our strategic nuclear forces are not inferior to those of the Soviet Union.

Let us look at the actual numbers. In intercontinental ballistic missiles (ICBMs) there is rough parity: the Soviet Union has more than we—1,400 compared with 1,050. The Soviets also have more submarine-launched ballistic missiles (SLBMs), but we may count on our side the 144 belonging to the British and French. Our bombers are enormously superior to the Soviets'. A total of 2,030 for us, compared with 2,490 for them is surely not a desperate inferiority. Anyway, what does inferiority mean at this level of numbers?

The Soviets have many more megatons than we have. But this is completely meaningless militarily. If nuclear weapons are ever used in a war, which I hope will never happen, then what will count is not megatons but the number of targets that can be hit.

At the present time, it would be very difficult for a bomber of either country to penetrate enemy territory. Our bombers cannot penetrate the Soviet Union easily because the USSR has installed excellent antiaircraft systems. To counter this, we have introduced so-called cruise missiles—pilotless aircraft installed on top of our bombers—which can be released, let's say, 200 miles from the borders of the Soviet Union and go on to their targets. These missiles are the most accurate weapons anybody has at this time. And there is no antiaircraft device available to bring them down because they fly so close to the ground that they cannot be seen by radar and therefore cannot be targeted.

In my opinion, bombers with cruise missiles constitute one of our two great strategic weapons. The other is the SLBMs.

What really matters is the number of individual warheads—individual bombs, so to speak, that can be carried by our various missiles. And in warheads we are superior to the Soviet Union. At present we have something like 9,000, and the Soviets have something like 8,000—not a big difference, but some difference in our favor. Also important is the fact that most of our attack warheads are located on submarines and there is no way known to detect a submarine reliably. Even if the Soviets could detect one or two, they surely could not detect twenty or thirty, so no possible action of the Soviet Union could disarm all our submarines and thereby negate this main part of our force.

Most U.S. weapons are lodged in the secure submarines. The one-quarter that are lodged in bombers, are almost equally secure: in an alert the bombers can take off, carry their cruise missiles over to Soviet Russia, and launch them there. Some officials have said that our bombers are useless because they cannot penetrate the Soviet Union. That will not be so after cruise missiles are installed, and they are being installed now, having been prepared by the Carter administration.

A point often cited against relying on SLBMs is accuracy: the ICBMs are more accurate than the SLBMs. But why is the accuracy needed? It would be needed only to attack the Soviet missiles in a first strike. But to attack an airfield, a munitions dump, a military staging area—all the locations the Soviet Union would need to follow up an attack on Western

Europe, all the locations that are important for conventional war—pin point accuracy is not necessary. In any case the requisite accuracy will be provided by the cruise missiles.

The window of vulnerability that the government talks about does not exist. It is the Soviet forces that are vulnerable.

Place yourself in the shoes of a strategist in the Soviet Union. He will say, "My God, 77 percent of our forces are in ICBMs. Suppose the United States makes a first strike. They have the accuracy; they could disarm all our ICBMs and leave us with only one-quarter of our forces. And in addition," the Soviet strategist will say, "we know that our submarines are less good than the American ones; they are noisy and can therefore be found." So if ICBMs do become vulnerable, the Russians are much more vulnerable than we. Because our weapons are better distributed and less vulnerable than the Soviets', we are certainly not inferior; we are probably superior to the Soviets in strategic weapons.

This same opinion is held by high-ranking military officials. The chiefs of staff of each of the three services were asked in 1981 whether they would trade their services, their weapons, personnel, missions, ranges, capability, strengths, and weaknesses for the Soviet's counterpart services. Each of the two generals and the admiral said he would not make such a trade.

Most importantly, in a discussion of nuclear weapons the comparison of numbers is meaningless beyond a certain minimum number. Both the United States and the Soviet Union have vast overkill capability. To destroy the other country's important military installations, except for its ICBMs, a few hundred warheads are enough. To destroy the more important industrial plants, another few hundred. And in neither case do the weapons need to have great accuracy. There is no justification for the many thousands of nuclear warheads each of the two superpowers possesses. Superiority or inferiority at these levels has no meaning.

We do not need the B-1 bomber. If we ever need to penetrate the Soviet Union, cruise missiles on our B-52s will do it better, cheaper, and more reliably. Each B-1 will cost $400 million. That $400 million would make all the difference in my field, natural sciences research, between austerity and ample support. And ample support of the physical sciences is the best way to keep us stronger than the Soviet Union. If we need bombers in a small peripheral war, the elaborate electronics on the B-1, which cost so much money, are not necessary. For the same reason, we don't need the follow-up to the B-1, a craft called the Stealth.

The true window of vulnerability is that all of us—the Soviet Union, the United States, and Western Europe—are constantly exposed to the danger of a nuclear war which might kill hundreds of millions of people and would destroy civilization as we know it. This danger is heightened by such statements as "we can survive a nuclear war" or even "we can win a nuclear war." No country can win a nuclear war. There are only losers. On this I want to quote Chairman Brezhnev, who said in October 1981: "It is a dangerous madness to try to defeat each other in the arms race and to count on victory in nuclear war. Only he who has decided to commit suicide can start a nuclear war in the hope of emerging a victor from it. No matter what the attacker might possess, no matter what method of unleashing nuclear war he chooses, he will not attain his aims, retribution will ensue ineluctably."

I am quoting Brezhnev purposely to counter the claim of some influential people in our government that the Russians consider a nuclear war winnable. The main imperative is to make sure that there never is a nuclear war. This must have priority over comparisons of the strengths of nuclear forces (which are, in any case, meaningless). Furthermore, the level of nuclear armaments of both superpowers must be greatly reduced. This is the meaning of arms control.

Arms control is not a favor to the Russians. It is a way to reduce a mortal threat to America and to the whole world. Many secretaries of defense and chiefs of staff have recognized that our defense posture is more secure with arms control than without. Arms negotiations must be undertaken no matter what our relations are with the Soviet Union. In fact, in times of crisis, it becomes even more important to have a good arms control agreement in place.

The arms race has to be stopped. The people devoted to that goal must stand together against the arms race and for real security of the United States and the world at large.

Comprehension Questions

Assimilation

1. The underlying theme of this article is:
    a. nuclear war
    b. arms control
    c. the U.S. vs. the USSR
    d. ICBMs vs. SLBMs

2. Bethe believes that the United States should develop and maintain:
   a. the B-1 and the MX, but not the Trident II
   b. the MX and the Stealth, but not the B-1
   c. the cruise missile, but not the MX or the B-1
   d. none of the above

3. The most accurate weapon at the time this article was written was:
   a. the MX
   b. the cruise missile
   c. Pershing II
   d. the Trident II

4. Concerning the window of vulnerability, Bethe:
   a. agrees with the U.S. Defense Department
   b. believes there is no such window
   c. states that the window ceased to exist after World War II
   d. redefines it in terms of worldwide exposure

5. Comparison of numbers is meaningless for nuclear weapons because:
   a. the numbers keep changing
   b. the numbers are unverifiable
   c. the numbers are already past overkill capacity
   d. the numbers used are incorrect

Interpretation

6. The tone of this article is:
   a. neutral
   b. maudlin
   c. straightforward
   d. devious

7. The reader's agreement with the concerns and opinions presented will depend *least* on the:
   a. clarity of the article
   b. author's reputation and knowledge in the area
   c. reader's personal convictions
   d. author's age

8. Bethe believes that in a nuclear war:
   a. the United States would win
   b. the USSR would win

  c. China would win

  d. none of the above

9. Bethe's attitude toward nuclear war is based on:

  a. his belief that the United States would win the war

  b. his belief that the USSR would win the war

  c. his knowledge and experience with nuclear weapons

  d. U.S. classified documents that were leaked to him

Main Idea

10. The main idea of this essay is:

  a. The security of the United States and the world can be achieved through arms reductions, not through arms buildup.

  b. The Russian window of vulnerability is greater than that of the United States.

  c. Parity of arms must be achieved before reduction can proceed with any real effectivness.

  d. If given the opportunity to switch strengths and weaknesses with their Russian counterparts, the top three U.S. officials would refuse.

Analysis Questions

1. How does the title of this essay set the tone for it? Does the title have a positive effect or a negative one on the reader?

2. Most people have strong feelings about Bethe's topic. How will the reader's own feelings, opinions (schema), affect his understanding and objective consideration of the information and views expressed by Bethe in this essay?

3. Hans Bethe is a Nobel laureate in the field of physics. He was instrumental in the development of the atom bomb in the 1940s and is now a proponent of nuclear disarmament. How does your knowledge of this information affect the credibility of Bethe's thesis in his essay?

4. Do you agree with Bethe that "the arms race must be stopped"? If so, how do you suggest it be done? If not, what should happen next?

5. Bethe states that the United States can rely on bombers with cruise missiles and on submarine-launched ballistic missiles for its defense. Do you agree? Defend your position.

HANS A. BETHE

Exercises

1. It can be said that reading a comparison of facts, figures, and statistics in a text does not have as much impact as seeing such a comparison in chart or table form. Construct a chart comparing the kinds and numbers of weapons attributed to the United States and to the USSR as given in this article. Review both your chart and the text. Which has more impact? Why?

2. What is the impact of the title Bethe chose for this article? Create some different titles, and indicate the effect you think they would have on a reader. (You might try different titles for different prospective audiences—a technical science journal, a popular magazine, the U.S. Congress, a high school text, for instance.)

Why We Are Inferior to the Japanese

*T*oday we hear much about economic competition with the Japanese. We are surrounded by their products: cars and motorcycles on the highways; typewriters, sewing machines, and cameras in our homes. We receive our information through Japanese-built electronic systems. The past 30 years in America have witnessed a remarkable transition in people's attitudes toward Japanese manufactured goods. In the 1950s the label "Made in Japan" was a joke synonymous with shoddy workmanship and low-quality goods. Today this label is the standard of quality against which our own products and those from around the world are compared.

This remarkable transformation and the economic strength of Japan today are the result of many complex factors. A central one is the state of Japanese technology. The Japanese have identified technology as a key to their economic well-being and have made it a national priority that now pervades their society and national policies. Today they aggressively compete in technology and are tooling up for future competition at a rate that leads the world.

Some insight into the Japanese thrust in technology may be gained from an examination of their policies regarding technical manpower. For example, from 1968 to 1980, the fraction of the U.S. labor force represented by scientists and engineers engaged in research and development work decreased by 9 percent.[1] In the same period, that same fraction increased by 70 percent in Japan, by 62 percent in the Soviet Union, and by 75 percent in West Germany. We thus see that in the last twelve years the fraction of the U.S. work force engaged in technology innovation has shrunk, while that in Japan and most other industrialized nations has increased dramatically. If we look at the segment of the work force which is doing only industrial research, we find that in the decade from the late 1960s to the late 1970s this group increased by 72 percent in Japan, by 4 percent in the United States, by 31 percent in West Germany, by 13 percent in France, and by 37 percent in the United Kingdom.

The differences in national priorities for trained manpower are even more startling when one compares yearly trends in the numbers of degrees awarded in engineering. Figures from UNESCO indicate that in 1979, 54,600 bachelor's degrees in engineering were awarded in the United States; this was 5.8 percent of the total number of bachelor's degrees awarded in the United States that year. In the same year, 65,422 bachelor's degrees in engineering were awarded in Japan—20.7 percent of the total number of bachelor's degrees given in Japan that year. In electrical engineering, which is key to much of the future work in microelectronics, computers, and communications, the number of U.S. graduates declined from 17,000 in 1971 to 14,000 in 1977 for a compound annual growth rate of −3 percent. During the same period, Japanese production increased from 15,000 in 1971 to 19,000 in 1977 for a compound annual growth rate of 4 percent. Since 1977, the figures in both countries have increased substantially, but the numbers are larger in Japan. The smaller country of Japan is now turning out substantially more engineering graduates than the United States, and the fraction of its new manpower resource devoted to technology is nearly quadruple that of the United States.

In the United States today serious problems plague the education of engineers. Owing to several factors, which include the decline in esteem for education generally, as well as a shortage of engineers in industry and

---

[1]Most of the statistics quoted in this essay are taken from data compiled in 1980–81 by Stephen Kahne, who was then division director for electrical, computer and systems engineering at the National Science Foundation, Washington, D.C.

the high salaries paid there, many universities are unable to staff their engineering faculties fully. About 10 percent of the faculty positions in electrical engineering in the United States are vacant, and have been so for several years. In 1980–81 there were about three faculty vacancies per electrical engineering department in the United States, and on the average each department hired 1.5 new faculty members during that period. There are about 2,500 open faculty positions in all fields of engineering in the United States, out of a total of 17,000 positions. This is a serious situation because engineering enrollments during the last three years have risen substantially. Increases of 50 percent or more have been recorded in many fields. The result is that today's engineering students are on the average getting a poorer education because the faculty members are overworked and sufficient new faculty cannot be found to fill vacant positions. One reason for this is that the total number of doctoral degrees given in engineering in the United States decreased from a peak of about 3,400 in 1970 to 2,400 in 1979. In addition, the fraction of foreign students receiving American Ph.D.s increased from under 30 percent in 1970 to nearly 50 percent presently. Only about half of these foreign students remain in the United States. There are thus fewer people in the United States receiving Ph.D. degrees in engineering today, at a time when engineering faculties need to be increased in size and industry has a growing demand for doctorate-level people.

It is probable that a major reason for the decline in the fraction of the U.S. work force composed of technical people is the general mistrust of technology which has recently been prevalent in American society and which is fostered by the mass media. Public attitudes of mistrust are encouraged by practices such as the giving of "golden fleece" awards for research projects deemed "unnecessary" by prominent members of the Congress in the United States. In contrast, in foreign countries, awards such as Nobel prizes are given for outstanding scientific contributions. The U.S. media exhibit a tendency toward sensationalism by highlighting accidents, pollution, or technical problems, while ignoring the many benefits advanced technology bestows on daily life and the economy. A further example of the difference in priorities in U.S. and Japanese societies is that in 1979 more than two law degrees were awarded in the United States for every degree in electrical engineering. In Japan the number of law degrees awarded was a small fraction of the degrees in electrical engineering. One high official of a Japanese company is reported to have commented that lawyers are primarily concerned about dividing the pie, while engineers are concerned about making it bigger.

The Japanese thrust in technology is revealed further by comparing that nation's emphasis on research and development (R&D) with that of the United States and other countries. In the United States from 1968 to 1980 basic research as a fraction of the federal budget decreased by 27 percent. It decreased by 16 percent as a fraction of the gross national product. Over the same period in the United States, research and development together decreased by 19 percent as a fraction of the gross national product. During the same period in Japan, research and development increased by 19 percent as a fraction of the gross national product; in the Soviet Union they were up 14 percent; and in West Germany they were up 16 percent. The amount of money spent by U.S. industry on research and development also declined from 1960 to 1979. In 1960 industrial spending on R&D was about 2 percent of the gross national product; in 1979 it had declined to about 1.6 percent. During this same period, industry investment in research decreased by 29 percent as a fraction of the net sales of U.S. industry, and much of the research that was carried on was devoted to new regulatory and environmental requirements.

Besides the general emphasis on devoting economic and manpower resources to R&D and technology, other more general factors support the Japanese technology thrusts. The discipline and productivity of their labor force are two such items. From 1968 to 1978, the productivity of the U.S. worker increased by about 20 percent. During the same period in Japan the average worker productivity increased by nearly 90 percent, the largest increase among industrialized countries. The high Japanese productivity is partially due to the peaceful labor relations that exist there. From 1970 to 1977, the number of man–days lost to strikes per 1,000 employees in Japan decreased from 120 to 40. In the United States, it decreased from 940 to 450, which is still more than ten times the Japanese number. At recent rates of productivity growth, it is projected that four of our international competitors will overtake the United States in production per employee by 1990. These four are Japan, France, Germany, and Canada. Of these, Japan has the highest rate of productivity increase: about 6.3 percent each year. It is generally believed that the discipline of the average Japanese worker and his devotion to his employer are greater than those of the average U.S. worker. Studies show that the Japanese worker has received superior preparation through high school in terms of the discipline imposed by the schooling process. Japanese students spend several times the amount of time on homework in grade school, junior high, and high school years than do American students, and are subjected to rigorous examinations before they can progress from school to school in their educational system.[2] In U.S. society today, there is little general emphasis on the need for rigorous education and self-discipline of young people, in marked contrast to the situation in Japanese society.

Another factor that has promoted Japanese success is a different system of trade and government–industry cooperation.[3] In Japan it is common practice for the government to target specific areas for technological development and industrial domination and to organize companies to achieve these goals. The government also provides a protected home market in which the companies can realize economies of scale and large-volume production and on which they can build a base for a strong export position at low prices. The Japanese financial structure also allows companies to plan for the long term without worrying about short-term profitability. American companies, on the other hand, feel obligated to their stockholders to show reasonable profitability on a quarterly basis, and hence are at a great disadvantage in long-term strategy with respect to a Japanese company that may earn only 1 or 2 percent a year.

William J. Weisz, vice-chairman and chief operating officer of Motorola, Inc., has stated that in America "we encourage individual entrepreneurship, and as a result, we don't develop total consensus, except on very major, critical issues. It takes a long, long time to get consensus in this country, but when it comes the power that is released is awesome. America has an almost unique spirit and capability. When we elevate anything to the proper sense of urgency, we have the ability, knowledge, and willingness to do the job."[4] It is probably true that most of the major progress in technology in

---

[2]For an introductory discussion, see Christopher Lyons, "Made in Japan," *Cornell Engineering* (Fall 1982), p. 9.

[3]See Robert W. Galvin. "Japan Will Dominate the U.S. Market Unless . . . ," address before the Seventh Annual Hyannis Conference of the Communications Division, Electronic Industries Association, June 2, 1982, Hyannis, Mass.

[4]William J. Weisz. "Japanese Competition: American Straight Talk," address before the Electronic Industries Association, April 14, 1981, Washington, D.C.

America over the past forty years has come as a result of considered responses by the country to what were perceived as serious external threats. For example, World War II unified the nation, and the work done then on radar and communications became the foundation for modern electronics. Later on, *Sputnik* unified the country again, and Americans responded with a vigorous space program. The tremendous amount of research that went into this program laid the foundation for today's integrated circuits. These are the building blocks for the computer and information industries on which our future economic progress depends.

We are now at the beginning of another societal revolution which may have almost as much impact as the industrial revolution did. Today's revolution is based on the information-handling capabilities of modern electronics and is built around the computer and communication industries. It is estimated that by the 1990s the electronics industry in all its segments will be the world's second largest industry. The next twenty years will be the age of engineering and technology. Japan presently leads the world in tooling up for this revolution; the United States is far back in the pack in the tooling-up race. Perhaps the current Japanese economic threat is the force that will bring consensus to U.S. society and enable it to recognize the crisis and the opportunity. If, as a result, Americans are able to reorder their priorities to capitalize on these opportunities as they have done in the past, the United States will be able to maintain an eminent position as a world leader. If our society is unable to do this, the United States will begin the economic decline that will herald its end as a world power.

Comprehension Questions

Assimilation

1. In "Why We Are Inferior to the Japanese," the word *inferior* refers to:
   a. technology
   b. lifestyle
   c. government
   d. the arts

2. Japan's present economic strength is attributable to all the following *except:*
   a. excellence of manufactured goods
   b. emphasis on engineering in education
   c. emphasis on short-term profitability in industry
   d. emphasis on research and development

3. The author believes Japanese education to be superior for all the following reasons *except:*
   a. better discipline
   b. rigorous examinations to progress from school to school
   c. more emphasis on the "new math"
   d. more homework

4. The following countries, in addition to Japan, are cited by the author as likely to overtake the United States in production per employee by 1990:
   a. Germany, France, and Canada
   b. Italy, Germany, and Sweden
   c. France and Germany only
   d. Germany and Sweden only

5. From 1970 to 1977, the number of man-days lost to strikes per 1000 employees:
   a. decreased in the United States, but increased in Japan
   b. increased in the United States, but decreased in Japan
   c. increased in both the United States and Japan
   d. decreased in both the United States and Japan

6. According to the author, the key to America's future technological and economic success is in developing:
   a. individual initiative
   b. consensus
   c. change in attitudes in the media
   d. manufacturing capability

Interpretation

7. The organizational pattern employed by the author in his article is:
   a. chronological
   b. thesis–proof
   c. question and answer
   d. cumulative narrative

8. The author's tone is:
   a. humorous
   b. cynical
   c. persuasive
   d. dry

9. The comment by Motorola's William Weisz is included:
   a. for additional facts
   b. to update information already given
   c. for corroboration of the author's point
   d. to offer opposing views

Main Idea

10. The main idea of this article is:
   a. A comparison of the many facets of U.S. and Japanese society clearly shows that Japan's is superior in most of them.
   b. In the past thirty years, Japan's technological position has gone from extremely low to extremely high, which has made Japan the economic leader it is today.
   c. The United States is falling substantially behind Japan in its emphasis on technology, and this lag has serious present and future economic consequences.
   d. Industries in the United States and Japan should cooperate for their mutual benefit, as too much competition will prove detrimental to both countries.

Analysis Questions

1. "Why We Are Inferior to the Japanese" is a provocative title. Do you think Ballantyne's use of this title adds impact to his message? Explain how such impact could be positive. How could it be negative?

2. Ballantyne identifies technology as the key to economic well-being. Do you agree? Why or why not?

3. Reread the statement by Motorola's William J. Weisz, quoted in this article. Is this a valid assessment? Explain.

4. Ballantyne makes frequent use of statistics to support his point. Are they effective? Which statistics in the text are used most effectively?

5. What is the meaning of the "golden fleece" award? Why is that name for the award appropriate?

6. Do you agree with Ballantyne that there is a general mistrust of technology in American society? Why or why not?

Exercise

In a brief paragraph, tell why the title of this passage has considerable potential impact on the reader. Explain how the schema of the reader will influence the impact of the title. (You might create some hypothetical examples of readers with different schemas and indicate their response.)

JEFFREY FREY

Integrated Circuits: The Expanding Technology of Shrinking Structures[1]

*T*he smaller their features, the less they cost. That is the principle behind the research and development effort in integrated circuits that is going on around the world.

Quite simply, the smaller the size of the structures on a single circuit, the larger the number of functions that can be accommodated in a given area—and the smaller the cost per function. The next generation of integrated circuits will have structures with submicron dimensions. Research in this area contributes directly to the compression of integrated circuits and therefore to reductions in their cost.

These results are generally thought to be a good thing. They make possible, for example, computers that are faster and larger, as well as computers that are cheaper and smaller, more economical transmission of data, inexpensive closed-loop control of automobile efficiency and emissions, implantable devices to help the blind perceive their surroundings,

---

[1]Data for this article were collected in 1983.

more reliable washing machines, wireless portable telephones, and electronic transmission of mail. All this technological advancement should also give a boost to the American economy in an increasingly competitive international market.

Industrial Production of Integrated Circuits

To understand this research, we need to understand what integrated circuits are, how they are produced, and why size is such a crucial factor.

A monolithic integrated circuit, designed to perform a specific operation, is a collection of transistors, resistors, and capacitors, all made within a single piece of silicon and interconnected by a pattern of thin aluminum or gold. The individual components are formed by changing the properties of the silicon in selected regions by doping—incorporating controlled concentrations of impurities. Each integrated circuit, or chip, occupies a very small area: in the near future, chips only about one-quarter inch square will contain more than 100,000 electronic components. The components themselves are also very small: with today's technology, an integrated bipolar transistor might occupy an area of three-millionths of a square inch.

Integrated circuits are produced in very large batches. Thousands of identical chips are fabricated at the same time on a single wafer of silicon, usually three or four inches in diameter. This wafer is cut apart after all processing steps and some testing have been completed, thus separating the individual chips. Up to 100 wafers may be processed in a single batch with the use of procedures that are independent of the size or complexity of the individual circuits on them.

The cost of processing a single wafer, regardless of its overall size or the size of the chips on it, is roughly $100; therefore, the cost of each working chip on that wafer goes down as the yield of acceptable chips goes up. Since yield is a function of area-dependent conditions such as defect density in the single-crystal silicon wafer or the extent of dust contamination, the cost per chip goes down with the size of each chip. Alternatively, the cost per function of a circuit goes down as the number of functions that can be incorporated on a chip of a given size is increased.

The Technology Now and Its New Directions

The individual devices on silicon chips are made by altering the properties of the substrate. This is done not only in specified areas, but also at particular depths; the properties of the silicon must be controlled in three dimensions. Local control is achieved by using silicon dioxide—which is easily grown on the silicon—to mask against the selective addition of impurities; the oxide covers the silicon everywhere but where the properties are to be changed. In simple terms, the current procedure is to cut a hole where the impurities must have access to the silicon by etching through the silicon dioxide. The area in which the hole is to be cut is determined by a photographic process that results in a hole being cut in a light-sensitive, acid-resistant film called a photoresist. Where the resist is removed, after exposure to ultraviolet light, the oxide can be etched; where the oxide is etched, the impurities can enter the silicon. The metal patterns for interconnections are created in a similar fashion. Various combinations of masking, exposure, etching, doping, and deposition permit the fabrication of complex, many-layered circuit chips.

Many technological improvements have been made in recent years. Contact printing is being supplanted by the projection of the desired patterns onto the wafer; with this process, the cost of the photomasks (masters for the on-wafer image) is reduced because the masks need not touch the wafer and therefore last longer. As a means of introducing the required impurities, ion implantation has supplanted diffusion, giving greater control of the distribution of impurities with depth and, because high diffusion temperatures can be avoided, resulting in more perfect crystalline properties. Improved working environments have contributed to the reliability of the manufactured products; in modern clean-air rooms, the concentration of dust can be reduced to a level of less than 100 particles per cubic foot of air.

These advances have reduced the size of circuit structures, increased the density of components, and allowed the manufacture of circuit chips with a larger physical size. Ten years ago the minimum width of a line that could be defined in production on an integrated circuit chip was about ten microns; today it is about two. The number of components per chip has doubled every year since the early sixties, rising from about 30 transistors in a 1964 bipolar logic gate to about 100,000 memory elements and transistors in today's 65,536-bit memory. In the past decade, chips have increased in size from about one-tenth to about one-quarter of an inch on a side. Large-scale production has also been aided by increases in the size of wafers; during this same period, they have gone from one to four inches in diameter. Concurrently, the cost per function has declined: for example, from 0.5 cent per bit for a 1,024-bit memory in 1973 to about 0.02 cent per bit for a 65,000-bit memory.

The most recent advances in integrated technology allow production of geometries down to the two-micron level. For geometries of the order of one micron or less, revolutionary rather than evolutionary changes in technology are required. And these changes are coming. For example, submicron fabrication can utilize such techniques now under development as direct electron-beam writing on silicon wafers and x-ray replication of master patterns generated originally by electron-beam writing. Other areas of current research include etching techniques, beam stability, and the physics of submicron-sized devices themselves.

The level of today's best integrated circuit technology is epitomized by the Intel 8021 microcomputer; its 20,000 transistors on a chip about one-quarter inch square provide internal and external control logic, clock timing, a programmable read-only memory, random-access data-storage memory, and input–output ports to a keyboard, a television display, a line printer, or a floppy-disk unit. The chip costs less than three dollars. With new submicron integrated circuitry, the same-sized chip could be furnished with millions of bits of memory for about the same price.

Comprehension Questions

Assimilation

1. A monolithic integrated circuit is:
   a. designed to perform many different operations
   b. a collection of transistors, resistors, and capacitors
   c. constitutes the main bulk of a typical computer
   d. obsolete

2. Integrated circuits are:
   a. produced in large batches
   b. made from an alloy of silicon, gold, and aluminum
   c. produced one at a time on a silicon wafer
   d. none of the above

3. The cost of processing a single wafer:
   a. depends on its overall size
   b. depends on the size of the chips on it
   c. is roughly $500
   d. none of the above

4. Recent technological improvements in individualizing the silicon chips include all the following *except:*
   a. contact printing being supplanted by the projection of the desired patterns on to the wafer
   b. ion implantation supplanting diffusion
   c. improvements in working environments
   d. discovery of a new alloy to replace silicon

5. The number of components per chip has:
   a. doubled every year for almost twenty years
   b. quadrupled since 1964
   c. increased, while the size of the chip has decreased
   d. leveled off in the past three years

6. Changes in wafer size and cost per function are as follows:
   a. wafer size has increased and cost per function has decreased
   b. wafer size has decreased and cost per function has increased
   c. both wafer size and cost per function have increased
   d. both wafer size and cost per function have decreased

Interpretation

7. The author sees the next advance in integrated technology to:
   a. be production of geometries at the two-micron level
   b. be prohibitively expensive
   c. require revolutionary changes in technology
   d. originate in Japan

8. The author's viewpoint is most likely to be that of:
   a. an unbiased, outside observer
   b. a government engineering expert
   c. an engineering expert who is cynical about the new trends in technology
   d. an electrical engineer who is enthusiastic about new developments

9. The author's chief purpose in his introduction is:
   a. to give the historical background of his topic
   b. to defend American technology
   c. to give the reader a perspective on research in integrated circuitry
   d. to describe exactly what integrated circuits are

Main Idea

10. The main idea of this article is:
    a. The key to advancement in the field of integrated circuitry is submicron research.
    b. Cost/benefit analysis reveals that future research in engineering will pay for itself many times over from savings from advances made.
    c. Current technological advancement in integrated circuitry should put the United States back into top position in electronics.
    d. Enhancement of technology of integrated circuitry results in decreased cost and increased function.

Analysis Questions

1. In his introduction, Frey lists several examples of improvements (concerning mail delivery, automobiles, telephones, washing machines) that will result from present development of integrated circuits. Is this a realistic claim? Is it necessary that technological advances be put to practical use by nonscientists to be justified? Discuss.

2. "Computer technology is the wave of the future." Do you agree or disagree with this statement? Comment.

3. How has your life benefited from computer technology?

4. How important is computer literacy? Should it be taught to every student? At what point in their schooling should students be exposed to computers?

5. How can computers assist you in learning math? The sciences? The humanities?

6. What effect will the increasing use of computers have on the United States economy? The world economy? How will it affect employment in the short range? In the long range?

Exercise

Poll your class (or canvas any group of 20 or more students) about their computer expertise: What computers have they used? Have they done word processing? Programming? What software have they used? How about games? (Make up your own questions.) Then, try putting the answers to one or more of the questions in a pie chart or graph. For example, you might indicate what fraction of the whole group polled have done much, little, or no programming.

Profit by Design

*E*ffective engineering designs ultimately produce systems or machines that accomplish the designers' goals. Thus, in the chemical industry, it should follow that successfully designed manufacturing plants produce the desired chemical at the required flow rate and have purities in excess of minimum specifications. Correct? Not necessarily. Although many designs may exist which meet the above criteria, most fail to accomplish the ultimate objective: profitability. All engineering judgments relate directly or indirectly to that reality. And the judgments required to predict accurately the ledger sheets' bottom line rest upon thorough knowledge of chemical-processing technology and of applied economic analysis. Design engineers, in fact, optimize their own careers by branding their minds with this maxim: The business at hand is the business of generating new revenues.

More specifically, the chemical process design engineer repeatedly confronts the following three challenges. The first is the task of using technical expertise to discern which design variables will most dramatically affect the cost of building and operating the processing plant. The second challenge is to reduce to workable equations the often complex and entwined relationship between those parameters and the cost. At this step too much detail is harmful. The third and final challenge is to balance and barter between the inevitably conflicting goals of (1) lowering the investment required for construction of the plant and (2) increasing the profit margin made while operating it. Of central importance here are questions akin to the gardener's dilemma of calculating how many apples he must receive next fall to make up for the vegetables he gives away this summer.

However, the most difficult assignment facing the designer is to handle these three tasks simultaneously on multiple levels. The following example is relatively straightforward but retains some of the multilayering that is encountered in almost all problems of consequence. It thereby illustrates the essentials of designing for profit.

First, a little background information: Much of chemical engineering focuses upon two operations—the chemical conversion of available materials into other substances that are more valuable and the often subsequent need to separate mixtures into purified components. The second operation—physical separation—exemplifies the design procedure and its typical hierarchies. An implied basis is that the substances are more valuable when separated than when in the existing mixture. Then the first design question is, What type of process will most economically achieve the required separation? Each method of separation exploits a physical property difference that exists between the components of the mixture.

Now, the example: Liquid/liquid extraction uses the solubility differences of the components in another solvent. Boiling-point differences lead to distillation as a method of separation. Distillation is frequently less costly because extraction results in two new mixtures, each of which must usually be treated by distillation. If the original mixture, however, contains two components having nearly equal boiling points, distillation may be quite expensive. The designer's quest, then, is to discern the most economically exploitable property difference and to use it to achieve the desired component separation.

Judicious engineering is most needed when that choice cannot be made by a superficial examination of the problem. Then, two or more alternatives must be evaluated at some length before the economically "best" choice can be made. Balance must be kept here: The evaluations should be detailed enough to discriminate accurately between alternatives, yet superficial enough to avoid unnecessary expenditures of costly engineering man-hours on processes that will be discarded later.

To continue the example, we will examine the kinds of "superficially detailed" analyses that are typical for evaluation of the distillation option. The first question to resolve is, What will be the extent of separation? If not specified by purity constraints, it is often economically viable to recover 99 percent of the most valuable component in one of the product streams. In other words, the total costs of product loss and of building and operating the equipment are almost minimized at this recovery. Establishing the extent of separation, however, does not fix the cost of performing it because of a design variable known as "reflux rate." The choice of the reflux rate illustrates the balance between capital investment and operating costs and thus is an important part of the example.

A brief description of distillation operations is necessary to define the concept of reflux before continuing. Distillation systems have three main components: a tall vertical column, which may be filled with irregularly shaped packing; a reboiler/kettle at the bottom, which is used to generate the vapors that emerge from the top of the column; and a condensor to liquefy the product vapors, which emerge from the top of the column. The idea of reflux is essentially to "wash" the vapors before they reach the top of the column by flowing some of the relatively pure liquefied product back down the column. Refluxing not only increases the purity of the vapors but also increases the amounts of liquid that must be boiled in the kettle and condensed in the condensor.

Another means of producing a purer product is to build a taller column. Choosing between column height and reflux rate is the choice mentioned above: capital investment (money spent on the column) vs. operating expense (money spent on steam for boiling and cooling water for condensing). The goal of the designer is to decipher the combination of column height and reflux rate which results in the lowest total separation cost.

How can a present, one-time expenditure be compared to the continuous costs of operation? To grossly simplify, convert the capital expenditure to its equivalent monthly principal and interest payment amortized over the expected life of the project. The capital costs thereby are expressed in dollars per month (or year) and can be added to the utility costs. The total is then minimized with respect to the reflux rate to complete the analysis. Hence, the designer's hierarchy of evaluations for this part of the analysis contains ascendingly layered judgments regarding reflux rate, percent recovery, choice of separation method, and, ultimately, the choice of what products to market.

The scope of the design questions in the example have by necessity narrowed from market choices to operational details of a single unit within a chemical plant, and the relationships between those choices and the profitability of the plant are fairly straightforward. Certain constraints apply, however, which were not accounted for. Environmental regulations, for example, apply to the allowable emission of many materials. This was not considered in the evaluation of the economically optimized recovery.

This kind of "external" constraint, however, is in itself a design variable in a much larger system: Pollution carries with it certain costs to our society. Likewise, overregulation carries with it the costs of stifled economic development. Consequently, regulatory agencies operate on a national scale to balance these costs. The resultant heated battles between industry and government are in essence differing judgments regarding the relative costs and values involved. The difficulties here are compounded by the long lag time between making the choices and paying the subsequent costs—unlike the changes in the operation of a distillation column, where the utility bill is paid every month.

Another area where precise optimums are hard to define is that of worker safety. Accidents occur intermittently, not on regular intervals, and certain health hazards have time lags in excess of ten years. On one hand, if every conceivable danger is eliminated, so is the worker's job. On the other hand, choosing the level of "acceptable" risk, in effect, defines the value of life. And who is qualified to make such definitions?

The designer is concerned with relative value rather than absolute worth. It is the function of the designer—the chemical engineer—to balance all the costs and all the gains so that a particular system will maximally profit by design.

Comprehension Questions

Assimilation

1. The ultimate objective of an effective engineering design is:
    a. purities in excess of minimum specifications
    b. profitability
    c. applied economic analysis
    d. high-level chemical-processing technology

2. Challenges cited by the author that a chemical process design engineer confronts include all of the following *except:*
    a. the task of using technical expertise to discern which design variables will most dramatically affect the cost of building and operating the processing plant
    b. to reduce to workable equations the complex relationship between design variables and cost
    c. to balance and barter between the conflicting goals of the investor and the producer
    d. to produce the desired chemical at the required flow rate at maximum profit, while complying with a constantly growing list of federal rules and regulations

3. Much of chemical engineering focuses upon two operations: converting available materials to other, more useful substances and:
    a. separating mixtures into purified components
    b. distilling the extracted liquids
    c. extracting the liquid solutions
    d. none of the above

4. Distillation is often less costly than extraction because:
    a. the process of extraction neutralizes much of the chemical substances being used
    b. extraction results in two new mixtures that often must be created by distillation
    c. distillation uses water, whereas extraction requires the use of expensive chemicals
    d. distillation can be accomplished by less-skilled workers, who are thus paid less per hour

5. The author characterizes the relationship between industry and government in working out differing judgments regarding relative costs and values as one of:
    a. working "hand in glove"
    b. power vs. authority
    c. quiet suspicion and distrust
    d. heated battles

Interpretation

6. We can infer that the author is:
    a. wary of pollution but not about overregulation

   b.   wary of overregulation but not about pollution

   c.   concerned about both pollution and overregulation

   d.   concerned about neither pollution nor overregulation

7.   Concerning the value of life, the author writes: "And who is qualified to make such definitions?" This question is:

   a.   a rhetorical question, because he does not answer it

   b.   actually a statement indicating sarcasm

   c.   an introduction to a statement of his philosophy

   d.   answered in the preceding paragraph

8.   The formal/technical style of the author is determined by all of the following characteristics *except:*

   a.   complex, high-level vocabulary

   b.   density of information

   c.   many long and/or complex sentences

   d.   technical jargon throughout the article

9.   The author's reference to the gardener's dilemma is a form of:

   a.   allegory

   b.   analogy

   c.   freewriting

   d.   descriptive enumeration

Main Idea

10.   The main idea of this article is:

   a.   All engineering judgments relate to maximum profitability through applied economic analysis.

   b.   The true challenge of a chemical engineer is to compare a present, one-time expenditure to the continuous costs of operation over the life of a project.

   c.   The overriding concerns of the chemical engineer are worker safety and the effects of pollution throughout our society.

   d.   The essence of design is the maximization of benefit and the minimization of detriment, rather than simply the accomplishment of task.

Analysis Questions

1.   Most titles have significance—that is why they are chosen. Discuss the possible reason(s) the author chose "Profit by Design" for this particular

article. Did the title establish any expectations of the nature or main point of the article?

2. The author referred to "the gardener's dilemma." What was the dilemma, and how does it relate to the author's point?

3. The author discusses profitability and "the business of generating new revenues." Explain the influence of such economic concerns on the science of chemical engineering.

4. Define "reflux rate" and explain why it is an important part of the example in the article.

5. Discuss the significance of worker safety. What are the concerns the author mentions? What is the cost, according to the author, of too much emphasis on worker safety? Too little? Do you agree?

Exercises

1. In his article, the author discusses both the engineering aspects of his topic and other aspects, such as the external constraints. Make a chart, with the points directly related to actual engineering facts and concepts on one side of the chart and the other points on the other side. Then consider: Was this task difficult? If so, did making the chart help you to identify and understand the points more clearly? If not, why not?

2. Depending on your previous knowledge (if any) on this topic, you may have had difficulty assimilating and understanding the information. Did the example make it easier to understand? Would seeing the example demonstrated in a laboratory make it easier to understand? Why? Visit a laboratory for one of your courses, or for that of a friend. Analyze the impact the laboratory work being performed has on the learning process of those participating.

"*Genetics Caused That?*"

The answer is usually a resounding "Yes!" especially if the question was with regard to some characteristic of humans, animals, or plants (including bacteria). Every characteristic is caused or influenced by genetics.

We all know that we can blame genetics for our baldness, eye color, blood type, and sex. Did you know, too, that genetics determines human skin color, albinism, hairiness of ear rims, color blindness, and abnormalities such as dwarfism, phenylketonuria (PKU), and Down's syndrome? Animals and plants are under genetic control as well. In fact, the degree of similarity among species and even between plants and animals is remarkable. That is, hair color of *all* animals is determined by genetics. Dwarfism occurs in both animals and plants and is caused by genetics. So, genetics is very powerful.

What is the basis for this science of genetics? For centuries observant people have noted "patterns of inheritance." The Bible tells in Genesis how an enterprising young businessman named Jacob used some important information about patterns of inheritance. He made an agreement with Laban, a sheep owner, to take the spotted lambs and kids from him as pay for tending his flocks. Because, of course, more spotted offspring than pure white ones were born, Jacob gradually became wealthy. We have all observed patterns of inheritance in certain families—"He has the Smith dimple," or "She has the Jones' musical ability."

Gregor Mendel (1822–1884), an Austrian monk, discovered the key to these patterns of inheritance about 120 years ago. He studied garden peas and observed various characteristics such as pod color. When he crossed parent plants with green pods and yellow pods, he noted that all the offspring (the F_1 generation) had green pods. The yellow pods had disappeared! (Can you imagine his initial confusion?) However, when he crossed members of the F_1 generation, he "rediscovered" the yellow pods in the resulting offspring (the F_2 generation). In fact, 25 percent of the F_2 generation had yellow pods. He observed similar results for other characteristics of the garden pea.

Mendel probably examined many hypotheses before he discovered the one that explained the observed pattern of inheritance. Here is the hypothesis that actually worked. (Hence, it is no longer considered to be a hypothesis but accepted as a basic principle.) Characteristics are transmitted from parent to offspring by *genes,* and these genes occur in pairs. The gene that caused green pods was called *dominant* because it dominated, or masked, the effect of the *recessive* gene for yellow pods in the F_1 generation. The recessive gene reappeared in the F_2 generation. It had not disappeared in the F_1 generation: Its effect had just been masked.

Mendel labeled dominant genes with uppercase letters and recessive genes with lowercase letters. This notation can be used to explain the observed pattern of inheritance for seed pod color as illustrated in Figure 4. The outward appearance, or *phenotype,* of the two parents (P) was green and yellow, and their genetic makeup, or *genotype,* was GG and gg. (Note that there are two Gs and two gs: Each pair of Gs (gs) refers to a pair of genes.) Offspring are produced when the reproductive (sex) cells, or *gametes,* of the parents come together to form *zygotes*. An interesting process called *meiosis* reduces the number of genes to one in gametes. Thus, when gametes from two parents come together to form a zygote, the newly formed zygote has a pair of genes. As a result, offspring have pairs of genes: one gene from each parent.

As shown in Figure 4, each parent can produce only one kind of gamete (G or g), because the parents are *homozygotes* (the pair of genes is alike). When these gametes come together to form the F_1 generation of offspring, the resulting zygotes are *heterozygotes* (the gene pair is not alike). The F_1 offspring are all green, and their genotype is Gg—the yellow gene did *not* disappear, but its effect on the phenotype has been masked by the dominant green gene.

F_1 individuals produce two kinds of gametes because they are heterozygotes. When two F_1 plants are crossed, the easiest way to determine the genotypes of the zygotes for the F_2 generation is to make a square table (see Figure 4). Gametes from each parent are placed along two sides of the table, and then one simply fills out the interior of the table to determine the genotypes of the zygotes. The *genotypic ratio* in the F_2 generation is

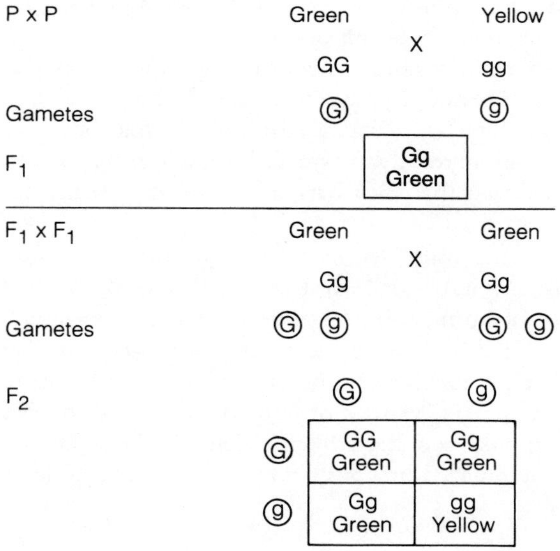

Figure 4.
Illustration of Mendel's cross between parent (P) garden peas with green pods and yellow pods, showing phenotypes and genotypes of the F_1 and F_2 generations and the genetic makeup of the gametes and zygotes.

1GG:2Gg:1gg, but the *phenotypic ratio* is 3 green:1 yellow because the green gene is dominant. So, the mystery of how yellow pods reappear in the F_2 plants has been solved.

Thus, we know the physical basis for the observed patterns of inheritance. We now know that genes occur in *chromosomes,* which are molecules of deoxyribonucleic acid (DNA). These chromosomes occur in pairs in cells of most organisms, resulting in pairs of genes.

The number of chromosomes in humans is 46, or 23 pairs. These chromosomes are very important. For example, they determine your sex. The sex chromosomes are labeled X and Y: If you have two X chromosomes, you are female; if you have one X and one Y chromosome, you are male. Thus, your father determined your sex. Can you determine why?

The number of chromosomes is very important as well. For example, people with three representatives of the twenty-first chromosome have Down's syndrome (commonly referred to as Mongolism). Thus, one extra chromosome produces *many* phenotypic effects.

We know that many human abnormalities and diseases are caused by genetics, and as a result genetic counseling can be provided to prospective parents. For example, if a couple are both normal but have brothers or sisters with six-fingered dwarfism (a recessive form of dwarfism), then they can be advised that they have an 11 percent chance of producing a six-fingered dwarf baby.

The benefits mankind derives from our increased understanding of genetics have inevitably led to the suggestion of practicing eugenics (improvement of humans by selective breeding). However, the question arises as to who would make the necessary choices and decisions. This question and others like it go far beyond the original scientific inquiry into the makeup and characteristics of humans, animals, and plants. Mendel, the Austrian monk who started with a simple observation about garden peas, would be amazed at how far the information he learned has been developed.

Comprehension Questions

Assimilation

1. Which of the following statements about genetics is true?
   a. All physical characteristics of humans, animals, and plants are controlled by genetics.

b. Genetics has been unfairly blamed for causing Down's syndrome and dwarfism.
c. Genetics has a major influence in determining the characteristics of humans and animals but not plants.
d. Color blindness is one of the few characteristics that is not caused by genetics.

2. Gregor Mendel was:
   a. a German scientist
   b. an Austrian monk
   c. a Renaissance man
   d. none of the above

3. Which appear in pairs?
   a. zygotes
   b. genes
   c. homozygotes
   d. gametes

4. The process of meiosis:
   a. is an attribute of medicine that promotes death with dignity
   b. is concerned with the improvement of humans by selected breeding
   c. reduces genotypic and phenotypic ratios in plants
   d. reduces the number of genes to one in gametes

5. Which statement about chromosomes is true?
   a. Humans have 46 pairs of chromosomes.
   b. Chromosomes occur in pairs in all organisms.
   c. Chromosomes are molecules of DNA.
   d. Chromosomes are found in genes.

Interpretation

6. From the article we can infer that one of the following statements is *not* true. Identify that statement.
   a. If you have two X chromosomes, you are female.
   b. If you have two Y chromosomes, you are male.
   c. If you have an X and a Y, you are male.
   d. Your father determined your sex.

7. Concerning eugenics:
   a. The author condemns it.

b. The author is enthusiastic about it.
c. The author does not consider it.
d. The author does not give his opinion about it.

8. The author discusses some specific effects of genetics:
   a. in humans and plants but not in animals
   b. in humans and animals but not in plants
   c. in plants and animals but not in humans
   d. in humans, animals, and plants

9. This article is best described as:
   a. didactic
   b. scholarly
   c. descriptive
   d. humorous

Main Idea

10. The main idea is:
    a. Genetic counseling is one of the primary benefits to come from the study of genetics, although there still remain many questions concerning how it should be used.
    b. One of the most important uses of genetics will be that it will provide a resource for breeding animals for more food for the world.
    c. Much overrated, genetics influences only a few characteristics of some minor species of plants and animals.
    d. Since Mendel's discovery of genetics through studying garden peas over 100 years ago, scientists have learned much about the genetic characteristics of living organisms.

Analysis Questions

1. Explain what is meant by dominant and recessive genes.

2. What is meant by the phrase "patterns of inheritance?"

3. Describe Mendel's work with garden peas. What procedure did he follow, as described in this article? What were the results?

4. Answer the author's question: Can you explain why your father determined your sex?

5. Outside the text of this article, the author has written the following statement: "A thorough understanding of genetics is one reason that U.S. agriculture is so far ahead of the rest of the world. We have developed genetically superior corn, dairy cattle, wheat, beef cattle, potatoes, [and so on] that have been exported to many other countries." Comment, using the information of this article as a frame of reference.

Exercise

Using the author's drawing as a model, construct your own drawing showing the eye color of yourself, your siblings, your parents, and your grandparents (with as much information as you have).

The Biomechanics of Sport

At the 1968 Olympic Games in Mexico City, Bob Beamon set a world long-jump record by leaping in excess of 29 feet. This marvel of human performance has become a popular point of discussion, especially because, to date, the record is still intact. Interestingly enough, it has been discussed not only by physical educators and coaches but also by professionals in the fields of engineering, physics, biology, and medicine. Many questions have been raised about how any individual could jump that far. For example, was the jump aided by the effects of wind? What were the effects of the high altitude at Mexico City? How was Beamon able to create such a high velocity at takeoff to travel so far? Finally, why was Beamon never able to reproduce (or even come close to) his record mark? To make the debate of Beamon's method of long jumping even more intriguing, it has been questioned whether it is possible for a human being to jump farther than the jump in Mexico City. Many professionals feel the answer is "Yes."

This example is only one of many of how scientists have become interested in how to improve human performance in sport. Although the history of scientific inquiry into sport has been brief, much light has been shed on how athletes can "get more out of their bodies." Since the 1950s the study of sport has become so popular that universities throughout the world have created departments of exercise and sport science, and some countries have even initiated sport research centers and institutes. The popularity of the sport sciences in the United States is due largely to the development of the U.S. Olympic Training Center and the success its team of scientists has had in helping our country's athletes. Although several areas of science are included in the training center, one very important aspect is a field called biomechanics.

Biomechanics, technically defined, is the study of the structure and function of biological systems by means of the methods of mechanics. Experts in biomechanics examine the internal (muscle) and external (gravity, wind, friction, and so forth) forces involved in movement and how these forces affect a specific performance in sport. With the increasing awareness of the successful application of human movement analysis by athletes and coaches, the need for an understanding of basic principles of motion has increased. This not only creates the use of improved technology for the coach but also creates a sport–science attitude among the athletes. These athletes become more aware of how their bodies move, what their own force-producing capabilities are, and what movements might cause injury to themselves. The utilization of biomechanics is predominant in many athletic activities, but it has seen a significant increase in the leisure sports as well.

Sport biomechanics deals with an understanding of the techniques involved in sport and the assessment of techniques that can provide an avenue for making an athlete more efficient and effective. The efficiency of a sport performance might be approached from two different viewpoints: (1) to enable the athlete to perform while using less physiologic energy and (2) to minimize the injury potential during high-velocity motion. The effectiveness of performance is governed by how an individual creates force and controls his movement pattern, but most importantly (which in some cases is an unfortunate circumstance), effectiveness is dictated by whether the athlete performed in a way that allowed him to win or lose.

Efficiency and effectiveness of movement involve good form. Identifying proper form, however, is actually quite difficult. Good form is unique to an individual and does not necessarily follow any norms. For example, when Björn Borg appeared on the professional tennis tour in the early 1970s, television commentators proclaimed that because of his unorthodox strokes, he would never make an impact on the game. It is interesting to look back on those comments because Borg certainly did not have any arm trouble while winning five consecutive Wimbledon titles. My point is that although Borg's mechanics were not pleasing to the eyes of the experts, they were, in fact, outstanding in effectiveness.

Another area of concern in sport biomechanics is the stress that is created on various body parts during performance. For example, it is possible to make an athlete extremely effective but forsake efficiency of movement in the process. A pitcher in baseball might be able to throw the ball extremely hard, but could sacrifice control and efficiency of movement, which might yield an injury, either in an acute sense (a sudden trauma) or in a chronic sense (from overuse or extended misuse). Therefore, the sports medicine implications of performance are very important for the biomechanist to understand when dealing with efficiency and effectiveness of motion.

A third and final area of interest to the sport biomechanist is that of equipment design. How tennis racquets, baseball bats, running shoes, hockey sticks, and other sport implements are manufactured reveals a great deal about how performance will be affected. In tennis, for instance, many different materials are commonly used to manufacture a racquet. The advent of racquet materials such as graphite, fiberglass, boron, magnesium, kevlar, and ceramics makes the purchase of a tennis racquet difficult for the layperson. The selection of a tennis racquet is further complicated when one considers the different racquet shapes, balances, flexibilities, and grip sizes. Moreover, the individual has to select from among over 60 types of strings and then choose a tension for the string before the racquet is ever usable. For these reasons the biomechanist must always be concerned with the effects of sport-implement construction on performance as well as the movements of the performer herself.

It is doubtful that Sir Isaac Newton had sport in mind when he discovered the law of gravitation after observing a falling object. However, this law and several other laws of motion have significant application to sport. For example, Newton's first law of motion (law of inertia) plays a large role in explaining how objects move in sport. This law states that a body that is at rest (or in motion) will stay at rest (or continue in motion) until acted upon by an outside force. For example, when a football player hits a blocking sled, a certain amount of force must be exerted before the sled will move. The sled has a specific amount of resting inertia, which must be overcome before it will move. When a coach stands on top of the sled, even more force is required to create movement. Applying the law of inertia, it should be understood that the blocking sled will remain stationary until the athlete creates enough force to overthrow the sled's inertia, thus causing it to move. Likewise, when a tennis ball is struck and flies through the air toward the opponent, it has a certain amount of moving inertia, and only through the effects of gravity and air resistance will it approach the court's surface. If there were no gravity or air resistance, the ball would literally go into space and continue moving until acted upon by some outside force.

Newton's second law of motion (law of acceleration) states that force is equal to mass times acceleration $(f = m \times a)$. It is also a predominant factor in most sport activities. Obviously, there is little that an athlete can do to increase or decrease mass during performance—any weight lost from perspiration is not considered—but the individual can change movement patterns to increase or decrease acceleration. Because this implies that force is directly proportional to acceleration, an increase or decrease in accelera-tion means that a subsequent increase or decrease in force must have occurred. The more force a tennis player generates to swing the racquet, the more the racquet will accelerate. However, the problem that any athlete encounters when attempting to provide more force to a movement is loss of control. And in most sporting endeavors, it should be realized that control is of equal importance, if not more important, than high velocity. The baseball pitcher must throw very hard, but the ball has to be over the plate. Thus, the biomechanist must always be aware of the speed–accuracy trade-off when evaluating human movement in sport.

The law of acceleration also helps to describe another phenomenon in sport, which has received a lot of attention: the cause of injury. Because force is directly proportional to acceleration, it is easily understood that the more force developed, the greater the acceleration, resulting in a powerful movement. However, the law of acceleration also works in the opposite direction. In other words, the greater the acceleration that takes place, the more force is sent into the body of the athlete. For example, the tennis player who feels that the road to success can be traversed only by hitting a heavy topspin on every shot must realize that his arm not only accelerates to hit the ball, but that it also must accommodate the force of impact. This may help to explain why so many of today's young athletes develop sore arms, because they are often taught to perform in a very aggressive manner. There is only so much that the body can handle, either in the acute sense from one very stressful maneuver or in the chronic sense from many repetitions of aggressive movements.

Newton's third law of motion (law of action and reaction) states that for every action there is an equal and opposite reaction. This law is the foundation for virtually all forms of sport activities. For example, every time a baseball pitcher throws the ball toward home plate, much of the force generated comes from the ground in the form of a *ground reaction force.* As the body pushes against the ground (or the rubber on the mound in this case), the ground pushes back with an equal amount of force. To attest to this, watch any baseball pitcher the next time he throws the ball. During the windup, you will notice flexion and a forceful extension at the knee of the support leg. As the knee forcefully extends, a large ground reaction force is created. This is probably the most important part of the entire pitching motion, for without a significant ground reaction force, the pitcher would not be able to make a forceful throw.

The law of action–reaction also helps to explain the sports medicine implications of a sport performance. When the ball hits the tennis racquet, for example, the racquet imparts force to the ball sending it over the net, but the ball creates an *equal and opposite force against the racquet,* which can often be felt in the hand, especially on off-center impacts. The forces encountered by the body can create trauma (that is, tennis elbow) if the athlete continually hits improperly or is not strong enough to withstand the impacts.

Although the previous laws of motion provide basic information about how athletes move, there are other physical principles that play large roles in understanding the biomechanics of sport. For example, once a ground reaction force is created, that force must be transferred from the ground through the body. This is accomplished through two mechanical factors: linear momentum and angular momentum. Linear momentum is equal to mass times velocity *(m × v).* It is generated in a baseball pitch as the pitcher strides forward toward home plate. It takes place in a tennis stroke as the player transfers her body weight forward, and it occurs in football as a defensive lineman accelerates from a three-point stance forward toward the opposition. The body weight (that is, momentum) is transferred forward in a linear fashion.

In many sport performances, the generation of linear momentum is only part of the entire movement. Once linear momentum is transferred forward, there is usually a quick succession of events involving hip and trunk rotation. This upper-body rotation is the angular momentum the body uses to perform. It is this combination of linear and angular momentum that enables athletes in many sports to create sufficient force for optimal movement.

To fully explain angular momentum, a new term must be introduced—the *moment of inertia*. The body's moment of inertia can be defined as its resistance to rotation; angular momentum equals a body's moment of inertia multiplied by its angular velocity. An excellent example of the moment of inertia is a figure skater rotating on the ice. You can visualize the figure skater spinning with arms held out, and the velocity of rotation is quite slow. However, without exerting any additional force, the figure skater can bring the arms in to the body and the velocity of rotation will increase significantly. The moment of inertia of an object is equal to its mass multiplied by its radius squared (mr^2). This implies that the more massive an object is, the more resistance it has to rotation; likewise, the longer the radius of the object, the greater the resistance to rotation.

Another common example occurs when a child picks up a baseball bat or tennis racquet that is too large for her physique. The oversized implement is very seldom swung by holding it at the base of its handle. The child will always "choke up" on the handle to swing it more easily. When anyone chokes up on a sport implement, the radius of the implement is effectively shortened, making the moment of inertia lower and thus making the implement easier to rotate or swing. In essence, it makes overall body motion much easier to optimize performance.

In most sport performances, a rapid succession of events must occur in a systematic manner to transfer force from the ground throughout the body. This transfer of force is crucial to the generation of linear and angular momentum, but the vehicle by which the force is transmitted is the body's linked system. You can actually consider the body as a series of chain links stacked one on top of another that serves two functions: (1) to receive the force generated by the previous segment transferring it to the subsequent body part in the chain and (2) to add to that force so that a summation of all forces generated leads to the final outcome.

Following the initiation of the ground reaction force, the legs generate a certain amount of velocity, and as they reach their peak velocity, the hips begin rotating. As the hips reach their peak angular (or rotational) velocity, the trunk becomes involved, and so on, until the final goal of performance is reached. This can be observed as a coordinated movement pattern. An uncoordinated movement pattern might involve several factors: (1) A body part might be involved in a movement but not be used properly, thus preventing the correct amount of velocity to be reached; (2) a body part could be left out of the movement; and (3) it is possible that the body parts could be used sufficiently but that improper timing between the segments might occur. Therefore, the biomechanist must be aware of the goals in any specific sport performance before a proper analysis of a technique can be made. For example, in tennis the goal of the athlete is to hit the ball forcefully, yet with control. The tennis player does not require the maximum force of a homerun hitter in baseball, but rather enough force combined with optimum control to keep the opponent on the defensive.

Because the body acts as a linked system, it involves a summation of joint forces. The amount of force exerted depends on how many body parts are employed in the movement and how large the force is at each one. Similar to the potential problems noted for coordination, an error in a sport performance could result from a joint being left out in the movement or from all the joints being used, but without optimal force or proper timing.

If a problem occurs in any athlete's linked system, that performer must accommodate her action in some way to perform effectively. A good example of this is throwing a ball. Many individuals have trouble adequately transferring the linear momentum generated by the legs to the angular momentum through hip rotation, causing them to resort to other movement forms when throwing. The most common accommodation of this problem is a forceful forward flexion of the trunk. The problem can be seen by the naked eye if you examine only the specific body part that might be involved. For example, by watching only how the hips of a pitcher are positioned in throwing, you will be able to detect whether they rotate effectively in allowing the athlete to gain a high velocity of throwing or if they seem to be blocked (or prevented from rotation) and the trunk flexes forward quickly. It has been determined that the problem with many of these athletes is that they have never developed a physically mature throwing pattern involving a sufficient amount of hip rotation. It is anticipated that if they were taught proper throwing mechanics, they could begin using this motion when pitching and generate the proper amount of force at ball release.

Many other aspects of sport biomechanics can help an athlete in improving his performance. Indeed, scientists, athletes, and coaches worldwide have become increasingly aware of how movement patterns can be enhanced through use of biomechanical principles. This, combined with new aspects of fitness training, nutrition, and psychology, may create an arena where current world records are soon outdated.

Comprehension Questions

Assimilation

1. Biomechanics is defined as:
   a. the binary forces of mass and velocity applied to mechanical engineering
   b. the study of structure and function of biological systems by means of the methods of mechanics
   c. the sport–science that is most concerned with maximizing performance
   d. the sport–science that focuses primarily on the force-producing capabilities of the human body

2. The three areas of interest in sport mechanics named by the author are good form, stress on body parts during performance, and:
   a. equipment design
   b. force and flexion
   c. the causes of injury
   d. ground reaction force

3. $F = m \times a$ is another way of stating:
   a. Newton's law of inertia
   b. Newton's law of action and reaction
   c. Newton's law of gravitation
   d. Newton's law of acceleration

4. In his discussion of the moment of inertia, Groppel used the following illustration:
   a. a baseball pitcher
   b. Björn Borg
   c. a figure skater
   d. a basketball player

5. According to the author, buying a tennis racquet is complicated because:
   a. there are so many manufacturers from which to choose
   b. there are not enough types of strings to meet everyone's needs
   c. the International Tennis Association continually changes its requirements for racquets for competitive play
   d. the racquets are made from so many different kinds of materials

Interpretation

6. The cause of sports injuries like "tennis elbow":
   a. can be understood through sports biomechanics
   b. cannot be prevented
   c. are mainly due to too much practice
   d. will never be known

7. The author uses what writing technique most effectively?
   a. example/illustration
   b. humor
   c. allegories
   d. statistics and charts

8. The discussion of Bob Beamon's long jump was meant:
   a. to provide an example of what happens when the precepts of sport biomechanics are not followed properly
   b. to provide an illustration that would arouse interest in the article
   c. to provide proof for the author's thesis that injuries can be prevented when proper precautions are taken
   d. to be a teaching example for coaches to use with the athletes under their direction

9. A reader of this article can infer that Groppel's attitude toward the biomechanics of sport is:
   a. that it is interesting, but not practical
   b. enthusiastic
   c. antagonistic
   d. neutral

Main Idea

10. The main idea is:
    a. The methods of mechanical engineering can be effectively applied to all biological systems.
    b. Human performance in sport can be improved through the application of scientific principles.
    c. Proper knowledge and use of the biomechanics of sport can go a long way toward the prevention of athletic injuries.
    d. The successful training of athletes at the U.S. Olympic Training Center has contributed greatly to the popularity of the sport sciences in the United States.

Analysis Questions

1. What does the author mean by the expression "get more out of their bodies"?

2. What are the internal and external forces involved in movement that are studied by experts in biomechanics to see how they affect a specific performance in sport?

3. What is the difference between acute causes of injuries and chronic causes of injuries? Give some illustrations.

4. What are the sports medicine implications of performance, and why are they important for the biomechanist to understand?

5. Several of Newton's laws were discussed in this article. Name them and tell how they relate to the topic under discussion.

6. Groppel drew his illustrations from several different sports. Was this variety confusing or beneficial? Defend your answer.

Exercises

1. There is controversy about the value of learning about and participating in sports in college today. What is your position on this question? Defend your answer in a few brief paragraphs. You may draw on personal experience as well as any factual knowledge you possess.

2. Groppel amplified many of his points through illustrations featuring several different sports. Choose one of his points and think of a different illustration. Write a descriptive passage in which you detail the action taken by the athlete and relate it to the point being discussed.

Nurses' Perceptions of Cancer Patients and Cancer Care

*T*his essay examines in a brief and informal way nurses' perceptions of cancer patients and cancer care and proposes that, however resistant to change they may be, stereotyped perceptions can in time be altered by carefully designed interventions.

In 1960 I returned from a year's leave for graduate study to a faculty position in a baccalaureate program in nursing. I had become much interested in cancer care during my thesis research and was impatient to share my knowledge and enthusiasm by upgrading the undergraduate curriculum in this area. I was surprised and frustrated by the students' stubborn resistance to any study of cancer. I found the nursing students' feelings similar to, but more openly expressed than, the subtle avoidance tactics I had encountered among practicing nurses and medical students.

In trying to deal with this blocking of communication, I used a word-association game, asking: Tell me the first word that comes to mind when I say *cancer,* and we will list all these on the board. Soon two blackboards were filled with such words as death, pain, fear, abandonment, disfigurement, rotting away, hopelessness, dependency, incurability, shortened life, odor, impoverished, and many others with similar negative and frightening connotations. The first two-hour class passed quickly as everyone became involved in adding his or her associations and as we reviewed each one in the light of the most recent research and statistical data about cancer. Our goal was to determine how accurate the beliefs were and where these emotionally loaded impressions had come from. As we compared findings about cancer with findings about other chronic disorders such as diabetes, arthritis, and heart disease, students were able to begin to separate myth from fact and were introduced to many of the major concepts in cancer care. Once some of the emotional associations with cancer were brought into the open and accepted, it was possible to get on with cognitive learning. At the same time it was possible to demonstrate to the students why patients and their families reacted so strongly to the diagnosis.

After these first classroom discussions, I introduced these beginning students to cancer patients in tumor clinics or radiation therapy programs. The students reacted in a positive way to working with people who were coping with cancer rather than dying from it. They found talking with people who had been cured of cancer to be a surprising and gratifying experience.

After the classes in cancer nursing and a week's exposure to care of ambulatory cancer patients, each student responded to an open-ended questionnaire. One question was: In what ways do you see cancer patients as different from other people with chronic diseases? The question was designed to help the students think through their observations as well as to provide information on where the educational experience should be strengthened. Over a period of some eight years I received many responses to that question, but two ideas occurred more frequently than others:

1. Cancer patients often seem to feel trapped. If they want to live any kind of life, they *have* to accept treatment because chances of comfortable survival without treatment are not good.

2. Cancer patients seem to have a different kind of fear, a durable, pervasive fear of an uncertain future.

I was surprised at the number of students who made such mature and thoughtful observations. The change from their original beliefs as expressed in the introductory class, seemed dramatic. I could only guess why this change had occurred. Since there had been no frontal attack on their original beliefs, it seemed that helping them both to increase and practice some of the skills needed in the care of these patients and to expand their knowledge about cancer had been contributing factors.

Some ten years after beginning the course on cancer nursing with undergraduate students, and after having done many short continuing education programs for practicing nurses, we carried out a detailed survey of staff nurses' perceived needs for further education in cancer care. A stratified sample of staff nurses from different types of health care agencies in an eleven-county area responded to a long questionnaire that included a number of questions related to what these nurses saw as the most important activities in the nursing care of cancer patients and which activities were not being adequately carried out in their work settings. The five activities most frequently cited as *both* important *and* not well done were:

1. Helping the patient deal with an uncertain future
2. Helping the patient learn some ways to deal with illness
3. Teaching prevention of cancer, when any measures are known
4. Helping the patient and family come to terms with cancer
5. Dealing with the nurses' personal feelings about cancer

This large group of experienced nurses saw physical care as extremely important, but in general felt that such care was being adequately managed. The nurses felt less secure in providing emotional support and in dealing with their own feelings about cancer patients and about the disease itself.

In addition, we conducted a small pilot study to identify some of the problems that might occur if we opened an oncology unit in the Department of Medicine in the university medical center where I was teaching and practicing. We found strong resistance among the medical nurses to becoming more involved with cancer patients. Their descriptions of how they felt clarified their perceptions of cancer care. They were distressed because many cancer patients die, because others present complex problems that are not obviously responsive to nursing interventions, and because some receive treatments that make them feel sicker. The nurses felt helpless to relieve patients' distress or to allay their fears and were uneasy when patients were assigned to different treatment regimens by randomization in a program that studied the effects of various drugs. These were all serious concerns. But as we discussed them, determining which of the problems were unique to cancer and which applied as well to patients with other chronic diseases, it seemed that other factors were contributing to the nurses' negative attitudes.

We undertook a study of a stratified sample of 100 nurses in the hospital: 40 medical nurses, 40 surgical nurses, 10 ambulatory care nurses, and 10 nurses who had specialized preparation and/or experience in cancer care. Two of the questions we hoped to answer were:

1. Are there differences in nurses' perceptions of cancer patients and other adult patients?

2. Are there differences between nurses' perceptions of themselves and of the nurses best able to care for cancer patients that would account for reluctance to become involved in cancer care?

The results showed no statistically significant evidence that the nurses' responses to the questionnaire were related to demographic factors such as age, length of experience, or type of education.

We were much surprised, however, to find that 96 out of 100 nurses responding held very tight stereotyped pictures of the typical hospital patient and of the typical cancer patient, in spite of protestations that "there are no typical patients." A second surprise was that these two personality descriptions were almost identical, describing (1) a person who was quiet, unassuming, and anxious to conform and (2) a person dependent on others for support and guidance, cautious in new situations, and with a strict sense of duty and loyalty.

Ideal patients were described as friendly, helpful, anxious to please, and interested in others, with some minor variations in less evident qualities. No stereotype was observed for the real-self perceptions of the nurses. However, 8 out of 10 self-perceptions of the cancer nurses correlated significantly with the stereotyped perception of the ideal cancer nurse, as reported by the entire group.

We found that no significant differences existed between nurses' perceptions of cancer patients and of hospital patients in general, and that nurses saw themselves as somewhat less competent and amiable than, but not significantly different from, the nurse they considered best able to care for cancer patients. These findings supported our hypothesis that the above factors alone were not responsible for the nurses' resistance to becoming more involved in cancer care. Based on these findings and on our previous observations, we concluded that this reluctance could be related to their lack of confidence in their own ability to provide adequate care and to their feelings of helplessness in the face of multiple complex nursing problems.

Before recommendations for change can be made, more research needs to be done on the problems stereotyping creates in the health care setting and on the protective functions stereotypes serve for the caregivers. Nevertheless, changes in these perceptions must occur if nurses are to meet one of the most urgent of recent demands—to teach cancer prevention and early detection. The perception of a patient as dependent, compliant, and unable to make decisions will have to change to the view of a person capable of becoming an active member of the health team, capable of changing his or her lifestyle—of exerting some control over his or her environment—if prevention and early detection are to be taught with conviction.

Comprehension Questions

Assimilation

1. The author's primary concern is the resistance to any study of cancer that was demonstrated by:
   a. her students
   b. her immediate supervisor
   c. the administration of the university where she taught
   d. the doctors

2. One technique used by the author in her class was:
   a. role playing
   b. dividing the class into small discussion groups
   c. a word-association game
   d. video demonstrations

3. This technique proved to be:
   a. effective immediately
   b. effective only when the patients were brought into the classroom
   c. effective only when the doctors were involved
   d. noneffective

4. The change in her students' attitudes demonstrated in the questionnaire results are attributed to:
   a. the new curriculum materials
   b. increased knowledge about cancer and practice of nursing skills
   c. holding classes in the hospital rather than at the university
   d. personal experiences with cancer over their lifetimes

5. Almost all the 100 nurses polled:
   a. believed that cancer patients differ greatly from other patients

b. were suffering from burn-out
c. maintained rigid stereotypes of cancer patients
d. believed that cancer patients should be active, decision-making members of the health team

6. Craytor's involvement with nurses' perceptions of cancer care has lasted approximately:
    a. forty years
    b. twenty years
    c. eight years
    d. her lifetime

Interpretation

7. Which best describes the author's position, according to information given?
    a. doctor
    b. hospital administrator
    c. cancer patient
    d. professor

8. The essay's basic structural pattern is:
    a. thesis–proof and narrative
    b. descriptive enumeration
    c. question–answer
    d. spatial and chronological

9. The author aids the reader's grasp of the main point of her article by:
    a. stating it in the opening paragraph
    b. stating it several times throughout the article
    c. ending the article with a personal example that highlights her point
    d. establishing her own credibility before making her point

Main Idea

10. The main idea of this article is:
    a. The curriculum materials concerned with cancer nursing are sadly out of date and must be updated as soon as possible.
    b. Although nurses' perceptions of cancer patients and cancer care are both stereotyped and resistant to change, they can and must be altered.
    c. Cancer patients and their families must be involved in the care, treatment, and decision making of their individual cases, in a team effort with the doctors and nurses.

d. Although several methods and approaches were brought to bear, the negative perceptions of nurses and student nurses toward cancer care and cancer patients remained unchanged.

Analysis Questions

1. What words or images do you associate with cancer? Are they emotionally loaded, as were those of Craytor's students?

2. How important is the patient's attitude in combating disease or other medical problems? What can be done to help patients in this area?

3. How important is the attitude of the caregiver? Doctor? Nurse? Aide? Technician?

4. What is the role of the family in treating a cancer patient?

5. What is your reaction to the nurses' stereotyped pictures of typical hospital patients and typical cancer patients?

6. Imagine that you are a teacher of nursing students and are confronted with complete resistance to the study of cancer care. What techniques would you employ to break down that barrier?

Exercises

1. The author used several questionnaires to help her gather data. Write a sample questionnaire for assessing doctors' attitudes.

2. Try another version of the word-association exercise used by the author with her nursing students: Write down every word that comes to your mind that is associated with the word "cancer." Which of these words are factual, objective? Which are emotional, subjective? Are any of the words due to first-hand or family experience? Which are based on information you have read or heard? Which word associations are stronger—those that were based on experience or those that came from more indirect input? Why?

3. Try the word-association exercise with different trigger or stimulus words. Have your friends try it with the same words and then compare your responses.

The "Apostles' Experiment": A Proof of the Existence of the Supernatural?

*T*oday's intellectual climate is saturated with the antisupernaturalist view that modern science makes unacceptable any supernatural interpretation of existence, from the cosmos to human values. Humanity is seen as an emergence from natural evolutionary forces. Personality is merely a function of a biological organism. All that we were, are, and will become can be explained by natural forces operating through chance over long periods of time. Life as we know it is all that there is. There is no God.

Some who are convinced of the perceived truth of antisupernaturalism have gone beyond promoting their philosophies to discrediting, sometimes unfairly, other points of view. Much in antisupernaturalistic writings has been devoted to attacking the religious miracles inherent in Christianity. Naturalistic explanations for Biblical miracles have been put forth as plausible regardless of whether or not the details of the events as recorded in Biblical documents are contradicted by these explanations. Biblical documents long highly regarded by historians have been dismissed as unreliable. Some prominent Christian leaders have been cast as quacks and reactionaries.

Seasoned observers are aware that movements that seek credibility through discrediting others often cast shadows on themselves. An idea should stand on its own merit. Whenever arrogance is substituted for evidence, intimidation for investigation, one suspects that the view demanding recognition is not as firmly grounded in fact as its proponents would have us believe. Much in the antisupernaturalist argument is presumption. For example, no proponent of antisupernaturalism is qualified by personal experience to substantiate the claim that there is no life beyond physical death.

Today's intellectual mind demands answers to the questions raised by the antisupernaturalists: What proof does Christianity offer for the supernatural? Is there any verifiable evidence that God exists? Does the Biblical record allege any test situations that resulted in observable evidence that uniquely supernatural processes took place? Can experiments be set that would repeat the results of these tests? Can the Biblical interpretations be shown to be superior to the possible alternative explanations or interpretations of the results? Affirmative answers should demonstrate that our understanding of the cosmos will be incomplete if the supernatural has no part in our world view.

To find answers to these questions, I searched Biblical documents for evidence of tests proving the existence of the supernatural. In doing so, I made the assumption that the recorded events actually happened, and I also assumed that those who recorded the events did so honestly. I did not assume that their interpretations of the events were correct. The problems of interpretation will be dealt with later. Note that all quoted material is taken from the Revised Standard Version of the Bible.

A series of events that suggests a supernatural experiment is recorded in The Acts of the Apostles, one of the books of the Bible that deals with the early history of Christianity. Written by Luke, a physician with credentials as a historian, Acts describes what happened when new converts to Christianity received the "gift of the Holy Spirit." This gift has been variously described as an immersion, infilling, baptism, or resting of God's Spirit necessary to fill these converts with supernatural joy, peace, and love, and to give them power to live their Christian faith.

The actions of people involved with these events were in some ways synonymous with the procedures of modern science. First, there was evidence for cause-and-effect logic in the thinking of those connected with the events. This kind of thinking involves the development of hypotheses, which can be tested by repeated experiments to see whether the predictions made on the basis of the hypotheses are borne out. In the case of the Biblical accounts, the hypotheses usually were not stated. It can be inferred, however, from the actions taken by individuals involved with the events whether cause-and-effect logic was a motivating factor. Second, there was a distinct supernatural agent invoked to explain the effect. Either the supernatural agent itself was observable, or the effect of the supernatural agent was observable as a unique manifestation—something that does not normally occur in nature. Third, the events were repeated.

Early church leaders, having received this infilling accompanied by a unique observable expression (Acts, Chapter 2), recognized this relationship between cause and effect. They saw a process that involved an act of the will (the human element) and an act of God (the supernatural element), which was accompanied by an observable expression. They also found that the phenomenon reoccurred with new converts and came to regard the outward manifestation as a sufficient condition that the inward supernatural process had taken place. In a sense they became like scientists as they performed the "Apostles' Experiment." The inferred hypothesis was "if a person satisfies the initial conditions for receipt of the Holy Spirit and if God is sought to fill that person with the Holy Spirit, then that person shall be filled with the Holy Spirit, and we shall observe a unique, outward manifestation of that inward filling."

Luke gave a number of accounts of this baptism of the Holy Spirit. The three examples that follow give evidence for cause-and-effect logic in the actions of these early church leaders as they performed the Apostles' Experiment.

The first example is reported in Acts, Chapter 8. Christianity spread from Israel through Samaria through the proclamation of Jesus' disciple, Philip. Luke reported many alleged miracles at Samaria, even the healing of the paralyzed and lame. An important character in this account was a man named Simon, an occultist who engaged in the practice of magic. Simon had used his techniques to astonish the people and draw attention to himself as someone with special powers. With much to gain from discrediting a fake, Simon attached himself to Philip's movement and, according to Luke, was constantly amazed at what he saw.

Here Luke's account took a curious turn. He reported that it was necessary to send from Jerusalem two other of Jesus' disciples, Peter and

John, who "came down and prayed for them (the Samaritan converts) that they might receive the Holy Spirit. For He (the Holy Spirit) had not yet fallen on any of them. . . ." Apparently, none of the spectacular miracles that "amazed" Simon, nor other activities typical of Christian practice (such as baptism or profession of faith), were taken as evidence that the Holy Spirit had been given. It seems instead that these church leaders were following a hypothesis that looked for a particular manifestation and, regardless of the number of conversions, miracles, and "great rejoicing," the manifestation had not been observed at Samaria.

Upon arrival at Samaria, Peter and John began conducting the Apostles' Experiment: "Then they laid their hands upon them, and they received the Holy Spirit." Apparently, these men observed some phenomenon that permitted them to conclude that the Apostles' Experiment was proceeding with positive results. Evidently, Simon the magician also observed the same results, for Luke recorded, "Now when Simon saw that the Spirit was given through the laying on of the Apostles' hands, he offered them money. . . ." What occurred and what was observed were not recorded. However, the manifestation was observed by onlookers such as Simon, in addition to the church leaders, Peter and John.

The second example of the Apostles' Experiment is recorded in Acts, Chapter 10. Jesus' disciple, Peter, had started a new church at Joppa, about 25 miles west of Jerusalem, and had remained there for some time to instruct the new Christians in their faith. While there, Peter received an urgent request from a Roman centurion located at Caesarea. Six members from the new church at Joppa accompanied Peter on the grueling 100-mile trip north to Caesarea.

Upon his arrival, Peter was asked to present the Christian message to the centurion and his friends, which he began to do: "While Peter was still speaking these words, the Holy Spirit came upon all those who were listening to the message. And all the circumcised believers (Jews) who had come with Peter were amazed, because the gift of the Holy Spirit had been poured out upon the Gentiles also." In the remarks that followed, Luke inferred that the six who came with Peter also had participated in the Apostles' Experiment. The outward manifestation of the supernatural agent acting upon the gathered Gentiles was apparently clearly observed and understood. It was the only sign. The miracles and other Christian activities recorded at Samaria were not suggested to have happened at Caesarea. Furthermore, it was Peter's apparent awareness that the Apostles' Experiment had proceeded satisfactorily that led him to ask, "Can anyone forbid water for baptizing these people who have received the Holy Spirit just as we have?" By the reference "just as we have," Peter implied that what they had just observed was common knowledge to all of the Christians present.

Because Jews did not associate with Gentiles, Peter and his six companions were called to Jerusalem to give an account of his trip before a church council (Acts, Chapter 11). Referring to the success of the Apostles' Experiment, Peter recounted, "As I began to speak, the Holy Spirit fell on them just as on us at the beginning. And I remembered the word of the Lord, how He said, 'John baptized with water, but you shall be baptized with the Holy Spirit.' If then God gave the same gift to them as he gave to us when we believed in the Lord Jesus Christ, who was I that I could withstand God?"

All those assembled allegedly had received the Holy Spirit on different occasions. In his appeal to them, Peter was referring to a common observation that all of them regarded as evidence of the supernatural action of God. Phrases such as "fell on them just as on us" and "gave the same gift to them as he gave to us" were forms of "shoptalk," the meaning of which was understood by the "insiders." Upon understanding that the Apostles' Experiment had been performed successfully upon the Gentiles, those who had opposed Peter were silenced. Knowledge of a unique manifestation at Caesarea—a phenomenon that these church leaders were convinced was evidence of God working within men and women—forced the council to abandon their long-held ethnic prejudice and accept that the Christian message was not intended for the Jews only.

Our third example of the Apostles' Experiment was reported to have occurred at Ephesus, within what is today modern Turkey. In this account the prominent missionary, Paul, encountered about a dozen new believers apparently Christianized by some other minister (Acts, Chapter 19). Paul pointedly questioned them as to whether they had received the Holy Spirit when they believed. Paul was apparently a strong proponent of the hypothesis behind the Apostles' Experiment. He assumed that the new converts could tell when they had received the Holy Spirit. Furthermore, he assumed that he could successfully perform the Apostles' Experiment if necessary to do so. Otherwise, Paul had no rational basis for asking the question.

It turned out that the believers knew nothing about the subject. Paul instructed them, prayed for them, and ". . . the Holy Spirit came upon them and they spoke with tongues and prophesied." Apparently, this observation was sufficient to convince Paul that the believers had indeed received the Holy Spirit. From Luke's account, no additional action was required to satisfy Paul that the Apostles' Experiment had been performed successfully.

These three accounts regarding the beginnings of the Christian movement reveal patterns of thought that were translated into conduct regarding the interface of the natural with the supernatural. It seems that the early church leaders believed that if they sought God on behalf of new converts then the Holy Spirit would be imparted to them. They also apparently believed that this supernatural agent produced a unique outward manifestation that was easily observed. This phenomenon apparently reoccurred with sufficient frequency that these early church leaders came to regard it as typical. From their observations, the hypothesis was developed and verified by the repeated Apostles' Experiments.

Now let us take up the problems of interpretation. Can we be certain that the hypothesis of the early church leaders—the Apostles' hypothesis— gives the best interpretation of the observations? Undoubtedly, many alternative explanations or interpretations of the results of the Apostles' Experiment are possible. *Plausible* alternative explanations, whether true or not, increase uncertainties; they therefore have the effect of increasing our reluctance to accept the original hypothesis. In addition, we are 2000 years, a culture, and a world view removed from the events. We are naturally drawn to the current explanations that are more in accord with today's concepts of reality. We need to consider, however, that the experts of generations in the future and a culture removed from ours might marvel at our confidently held but juvenile concept of the cosmos.

If the Apostles' Experiment was performed successfully only during the first 50–100 years of the Christian Church, we would be left with the problems of uncertainty of interpretation. Furthermore, with the exception of historical curiosity, the issue would be irrelevant to us. However, there are many reports that the Apostles' Experiment continues to be performed successfully. If these reports are correct, there is a way to settle the issue of interpretation: Repeat the Apostles' Experiment!

To repeat the Apostles' Experiment, it is necessary to define the initial conditions. After a review of these and other accounts described by Luke, it is apparent that only three simple requirements must be satisfied. First, the Apostles' Experiment should be performed by a person who has previously been filled with the Holy Spirit. Second, the experiment should be performed upon a person seeking God through Jesus Christ, that is, a Christian. And third, God must be present to provide the supernatural agent.

As one who has received the Holy Spirit through the Apostles' Experiment, I satisfied the first requirement. The second requirement was met by a colleague, a Christian seeking relevancy in his faith. A member of a church that does not teach nor encourage its members to seek the supernatural transformation wrought by the Apostles' Experiment, he was not particularly subject to the power of suggestion in this area. An atmospheric scientist with training from a leading university, he was equipped to observe critically what, if anything, would happen to him during the experiment.

The experiment took place in my colleague's office located on the University of Illinois campus. Following the practices reported by Luke, I took him by the hands and briefly sought God to fill him with the Holy Spirit. The following is his summary of the results of the experiment.

> My baptism in the Holy Spirit provided one of the most joyous and memorable times of my life; yet, despite this, and my training as a scientist to observe the environment and changes in it, I have found it extremely difficult to provide an account of the events that occurred. This difficulty has not been the result of a long delay in recording events (I prepared this account about 36 hours after the events), or an insensitivity to what took place (indeed, the sensations that I experienced are very memorable), but rather a consequence of the almost indescribable feelings, events, and actions that occurred.
>
> As we prayed, a warm "tingling" sensation began to fill my body. This feeling was quite unlike anything I had ever experienced before, reaching through my whole body from the outermost layers of skin to the deepest tissue as it progressed downward beginning at the top of my head. It was as if I was totally immersed in a fluid that could penetrate the very cellular tissue of the body without any resistance, and as it moved downward, the "front" of this feeling was clearly discernible. At the same time, there was a feeling of submission. This feeling intensified, and there began a high-frequency shaking over my body. I had not lost strength. My tongue felt "swollen," yet it wasn't; it was trying to make motions beyond my control. Immediately after this initial experience, I felt a great sense of Christian brotherhood. I could only see beauty in everything. A song of praise just issued forth.

Evidently, the results of this Apostles' Experiment are very similar to those observed by the early church leaders. Certainly, something extraordinary did happen. It was observable to me and was expressible by my colleague. This would seem to verify the correctness of the Biblical interpretation. The existence of the phenomenon does not depend upon differences of culture nor technological sophistication between our world and theirs. Therefore, because it is still occurring—indicating that God is still pouring out His Spirit upon humankind today—the Apostles' Experiment is an indication that the supernatural is as present with us as it was to those who were persuaded to follow Jesus Christ 2000 years ago.

Comprehension Questions

Assimilation

1. The author states that "much in the antisupernaturalist argument is. . . ." :
   a. correct   c. provable
   b. incorrect   d. presumption

2. According to the author antisupernaturalists believe all of the following statements *except:*
   a. Personality is a function of biological organism.
   b. There is no God.
   c. There is life after death.
   d. Man developed through evolution.

3. When the author searched Biblical documents for evidence of tests proving the existence of the supernatural, he assumed that:
   a. the recorded events actually happened
   b. the interpretation of the recorded events was correct
   c. those who recorded the events may have exaggerated or "stretched the truth" to make their points
   d. the events were not recorded until much later than the events actually occurred

4. According to the author a series of events that suggests a supernatural experiment is recorded in:
   a. the Book of Luke
   b. the Acts of the Apostles
   c. the Book of John
   d. none of the above

5. In the article the author gives an account of repeating the Apostles' Experiment. This experience required all of the following conditions *except:*
   a. the presence of God
   b. the presence of a Christian
   c. the presence of non-Christian witnesses
   d. the presence of someone already filled with the Holy Spirit

Interpretation

6. From the article we can infer that the author probably is:
   a. a pastor
   b. a scientist
   c. a missionary
   d. an apostle

7. One of the author's conclusions from repeating the Apostles' Experiment is that:
   a. it could be performed successfully only during the first 50 years of the Christian Church
   b. it could be performed successfully only during the first 100 years of the Christian Church
   c. it can be performed successfully today
   d. it cannot be successfully performed without the presence of outside witnesses

8. The author's bias or point of view is:
   a. that of a scientist but not a Christian
   b. that of a Christian but not a scientist
   c. that of both a scientist and a Christian
   d. not discernible from the article

9. Structural or developmental forms used by the author include:
   a. hypothesis–proof
   b. narrative
   c. descriptive
   d. all of the above

Main Idea

10. The main idea is:
   a. During the early days of the Christian church, the Apostles' Experiment was successfully performed many times.
   b. In today's intellectual and moral climate, the impact of the antisupernaturalist view has been to render the church ineffective.
   c. Through the impact of the media, the church and its leaders have greatly influenced the government leaders of many nations of the world.
   d. Any world view that does not allow for the supernatural cannot give an adequate interpretation of the cosmos.

Analysis Questions

1. In this article we see the tension between a religious or God-centered point of view and a scientific approach. Describe what this tension means to you. How does an individual's personal beliefs affect how he or she would react to this article?

2. "Life as we know it is all there is." Do you agree or disagree? Discuss.

3. The author states that "an idea should stand on its own merit." Explain what he means by that. Can you give an example or illustration?

4. What was the Apostles' Experiment? Describe how it was carried out and the results, as related in the article.

5. In examining the Apostles' Experiment, the author establishes a hypothesis and then sets out to prove (or disprove) it. What was the hypothesis? Was he successful in establishing a proof for it? If so, was it conclusive? If not, why not? Do you agree with his conclusion?

6. The author states that "we are 2000 years, a culture, and a world view removed from the events" of the early church. What does the author mean by this statement? What does the phrase "world view" mean?

Exercises

1. Most of the article is written in the first person. What effect does this have on the reader? Rewrite a few paragraphs in the third person and compare the effect with the original.

2. Consider the section of the article that refers to Simon the magician. Rewrite that section—what happened and his reaction to the situation—from his point of view, that is, in the first person.

COMPARATIVE ANALYSIS QUESTIONS:
PHYSICAL SCIENCES

1. MacNeill and Penfield's discussion of the scientific method included the establishment and testing of a hypothesis. Craytor used questionnaires and other techniques in applying the scientific method to her situation. Describe other similarities and differences in their approaches. Analyze their effectiveness in their own particular situations. Which approach did Achtemeier use?

2. Sagan, Williams, and Achtemeier discuss methods and approaches to scientific discovery. How do their approaches differ? How are they alike?

3. The topic of science education is discussed by Ballantyne and by Hoffmann. What points do they make about this subject? With which points do you agree or disagree?

4. What role, if any, should attitude about individuals play in the practice of medicine? What role does it play in Craytor's article? In Kress's article? In Groppel's article? In your own experience?

5. Clarke and Wells both wrote about natural phenomena affecting our climate. One phenomenon was occasional, rare, and random; the other is regular and ongoing. Identify and describe these phenomena and their effects on our climate.

6. Ballantyne and Bethe wrote about two different topics, yet their titles are obviously coordinated. (Ballantyne chose his title after seeing Bethe's title.) How did each of these titles affect you? What other titles could these articles have had that would have been unrelated?

7. Kress and Leman briefly touch on the topic of human worth and the question of who should determine such values. Discuss their points of view and add your own.

8. Sagan suggested a lack of coincidence in the establishment of the universe. Find this section of his article. What do you think he is suggesting? What do you think his views about the supernatural are? Consider his views in contrast to Williams's or Achtemeier's views.

9. As engineers, Frey and Leman are concerned with both engineering design and technology and with profitability. Compare their treatments of these subjects.

10. Ludington and Wells both wrote about the environment, but their purposes in writing were very different. How does an author's purpose in writing affect his approach to his topic? What effect does his thesis—or even the choice of the topic itself—have on his treatment of the topic?

11. Hoffmann, Bethe, and Ballantyne wrote persuasively about their topics, whereas Groppel, Leman, and Wells wrote expositionally about their topics. What place does persuasion have in scientific articles? Do such articles stop being "scientific"?

12. Both Sagan and Williams refer to Einstein's theory of relativity, and Groppel wrote about Newton's law of action and reaction. Can we understand and benefit from the articles by these authors even though we have never studied these topics?

13. Both Ballantyne and Frey work in the field of electrical engineering. Frey has a narrow subject and takes a technical approach to it. Ballantyne has a broader subject and writes a more general statement. Both articles are written for the same audience—students without previous expertise in the field—yet the articles differ in many ways such as purpose, tone, structure, and presence of bias. Explain some of these differences.

14. Groppel's article discussed how athletes are beginning to understand more of how their bodies function, so that they can increase their effectiveness and decrease possibility of injury. Does genetics, the subject of Kress's article, have a role in Groppel's topic? Explain.

15. Consider the variety of topics in physical sciences. Do any topics surprise you? After reflection, what general statement(s) if any, can you make about all the articles (or their contributors) in this section?

PART III

Social Sciences

The Foundation of Diplomacy

*D*iplomacy ranks among the world's oldest professions. However, like members of another profession often touted as *the* oldest, diplomats have traditionally been held in low esteem both at home and abroad. The stereotyped image of the diplomat clothes him in striped pants and locates him sloshing about on the cocktail-and-banquet circuit—an otherwise honorable person sent abroad to lie for his country.

Nonetheless, diplomacy performs an increasingly vital function in today's complex, interdependent, and strife-prone world. A clear understanding of how diplomacy functions is therefore essential for participants in a democratic, open, pluralistic society such as the United States.

The foundation of diplomacy is communication. The diplomat must function as a two-way channel, both sending messages from the home government and society and receiving for transmission back home messages from the government and society to which he or she is accredited. This proposition seems simple enough until you consider the pitfalls of communicating even *within* your own social environment. Just think, for example, of the first time you tried to thread your way through your school's registration process!

Imagine, then, the problems of coping with the added dimension of communicating between two different languages. We Americans tend to take our brand of English for granted; despite massive waves of non-English-speaking immigrants, our language is still as pervasive as the air we breathe. Indeed, language is a carrier of cultural values in somewhat the way genes transmit physical and personality traits. Different languages embody the different attitudes and values of the societies that speak them. Consequently, *how* a language expresses certain ideas or describes certain ordinary phenomena can provide important clues to the underlying values and attitudes of its society.

In some languages, for example, the reflexive verb form widely employed reflects the reduced role assigned in those cultures to the concept of individual initiative and responsibility. "*Se me cayo*" (literally, "It fell itself to me"), says José in Mexico of the broken vase, whereas Joe in Iowa would more likely say, "Shucks, I dropped it." In the former case, José's language pattern automatically absolves him of responsibility; fate, or the vase itself, was the actor, and José just happened to be present. The Anglo-Saxon language, by contrast, not only inculcates in the individual a strong sense of responsibility for one's acts, but takes equal pains to proclaim the individual's freedom to act.

To cope with this extra dimension of communication, the diplomat, starting with a thorough mastery of his native language, must build on that foundation fluency in not one but several foreign languages. Moreover, his competency must go beyond parrot-style glibness to penetrate below the surface to an understanding of what the foreign words are conveying about underlying attitudes, beliefs, and values of the speaker. Advanced academic training is essential, but full qualification can be achieved only by hands-on experience in a foreign environment. There is no substitute for living, breathing, working, indeed even dreaming, in a second language. I remember vividly the sense of having "arrived" when I had my first dream in Spanish!

Once the diplomat has acquired advanced linguistic skills, the question becomes, *What* does he communicate? Messages from his own country must be conveyed accurately as to both content and emphasis, whether they are official government pronouncements or informal (but significant) messages of the type we label either informed or public opinion. The diplomat must with equal accuracy and with consummate interpretive skill transmit similar messages emanating from his assigned post. This part of the task requires keen judgment to identify those events and trends, sometimes subtle and overlooked by other observers (for example, the media), which carry true significance for the American people and their collective interests. Selectivity in reporting takes on added weight in the context of Washington's bureaucracy. Every hour of every day our government's worldwide, high-speed communications network floods the State Department and other agencies with thousands of messages, each with information believed by the sending mission abroad to be significant and, in most cases, to require urgent attention. Woe betide the diplomat who earns a reputation for clogging these channels with trivia!

What the diplomat must at all costs seek to communicate is the truth—even when, as is all too frequently the case, the truth may be painful to the recipient (or for that matter to the bearer). Consequently, a supplementary art of diplomacy is to find how to convey the truth without giving offense. Whatever the tactic employed, however, the diplomat must be sure the real message gets across. Long practice has developed a standard glossary of phraseology and procedure to sugarcoat the pill. As an example, a foreign request for a loan is seldom refused outright. Rather, our reply will suggest Congress insists on an in-depth review or similar "procedural" delay. Also, on occasion, diplomacy adopts the ancient device of actions that speak louder than words. A classic example of the use of this device in a positive sense was Egyptian President Anwar Sadat's epochal visit to Israel in November 1977. His physical presence before the Knesset said more about Egypt's intentions than the litany of Arab demands and complaints in his speech.

Negotiation is a key element in the practice of diplomacy. Negotiations usually look toward an agreement, either a formal treaty or a simpler executive agreement not requiring Senate ratification. In a variety of negotiating exercises in my own career I discovered the importance of careful advance study in devising a negotiating strategy, particularly to create the right psychological environment. In some cases, as among allies, it may be advisable to lay all one's cards on the table, so to speak, at the outset. Other instances, involving, for example, nuclear disarmament or other national security issues, may require a gradual process of testing to ascertain the parameters of mutual concessions that may eventually lead to an agreement acceptable to both sides. But always, credibility is the key. The diplomat must establish, whether in negotiating or reporting, a solid foundation of credibility by strict adherence to the full dimensions of truth.

Truth in diplomacy, almost inevitably in our kind of open society, bumps into the tangled question of public disclosure. The average citizen instinctively distrusts the diplomat—a distant figure who *chooses* to hobnob with aliens. With every other aspect of our society open to scrutiny by the omnipresent news media, the diplomat's plea for privacy gets little sympathy. Still, professional diplomats are uncommonly unanimous in holding that confidentiality is as essential to their reporting and negotiation as it is to the doctor in his relations with his patients.

In diplomatic negotiating both parties rely on confidentiality to maintain a necessary degree of flexibility because positions taken publicly tend to become rigid and frozen. Among professionals it is axiomatic that when a party to negotiations has recourse to the media, it is a clear sign he is through negotiating. Similarly, in diplomatic reporting, often the most vital information is necessarily obtained in confidence or by clandestine means. Without these sources and the means of preserving their anonymity, at least for a reasonable time, the conduct of foreign relations for a world power such as the United States, most importantly for the maintenance of our national security, would be well nigh impossible.

Since World War II the United States has invested substantially and continuously in developing a corps of world-class professional diplomats, equipped with the language and other skills required in today's complex world. We have seen to it that these professionals acquired wide field experience under sound, disciplined leadership to prepare them for the most demanding jobs both abroad and in Washington. And yet our political leaders still insist on fielding rank amateurs in some of the most critical positions in the diplomatic ballpark. There will always be room—and a welcome from the professionals—for talented amateurs and semipros of the caliber of the late David Bruce or Ellsworth Bunker. But men like these are becoming rare exceptions among a straggling herd of nonentities whose sole contributions too often are to campaign coffers rather than to the welfare of the nation. This is a practice manifestly unwise but even more patently unfair to men and women who have undergone hardships and hazards in working their way up the promotional ladder of a tough, competitive service, only to find the Elysian Fields at the top reduced by 40 percent or more by reason of noncareer political appointments. Imagine the uproar if a President attempted to do the same thing in our military services. Here is an issue of national policy that calls for constant vigilance by an alert public, aware that in peacetime our first line of defense lies in our diplomatic missions, and that diplomacy is an exacting and complex art demanding the dedication, discipline, and decades of experience that can be provided only by a corps of true professionals.

Comprehension Questions

Assimilation

1. The foundation of diplomacy is:
   a. discipline
   b. experience
   c. negotiation
   d. communication

2. The aspect of language most strongly emphasized by the author is:
   a. difficulty in getting competent translators
   b. the length of time it takes to learn a foreign language
   c. the attitudes and social values expressed through language
   d. the capacity to dream in a foreign language

3. One can infer that in diplomacy, what is important is:
   a. the message but not the medium (how the message is conveyed)
   b. the medium but not the message
   c. both the message and the medium
   d. neither the message nor the medium

4. Since World War II, the United States professional diplomatic corps has been:
   a. maintained and developed rigorously
   b. drastically reduced
   c. replaced, for the most part, with political appointments
   d. made obsolete

Interpretation

5. About the author, one can infer that:
   a. despite advanced academic training, he was not able to master Spanish
   b. he believes there should be no amateurs in diplomatic posts
   c. he believes that diplomats must protect the anonymity of their sources
   d. he believes in negotiating through the media

6. The author's attitude toward the profession of diplomacy, as revealed through the tone of this essay, is:
   a. positive
   b. negative
   c. neutral
   d. bored

7. The author's attitude toward negotiation in diplomacy is best represented by:
   a. complete candor and openness
   b. the ends justify the means
   c. credibility based on devotion to truth
   d. total secrecy and permanent anonymity

8. Your own schema concerning this subject:
   a. is nonexistent because you have no direct experience in this area
   b. is irrelevant when reading the article
   c. exists because schema is made up of direct and/or indirect knowledge, plus opinions
   d. should never change

9. The organization of ideas follows a pattern that is basically:
   a. compare and contrast
   b. descriptive enumeration
   c. explanatory
   d. chronological

Main Idea

10. The main idea of this essay is:
    a. Diplomacy is an exacting profession that demands expertise in cross-cultural communication, discipline obtainable only from first-hand overseas experience, and a reputation for accuracy and credibility.
    b. Diplomacy is established on the four cornerstones of communication, negotiation, confidentiality, and public scrutiny.
    c. Rather than leaving diplomacy in the hands of political cronies and other amateurs, this vital profession should be carried out by professional career diplomats trained by the State Department and the CIA.
    d. Diplomacy is a profession that should be open to anyone who would like to participate.

Analysis Questions

1. Is there a conflict between truth and confidentiality in carrying out the profession of diplomacy? Discuss.

2. In how many languages are you fluent? Do you ever have problems communicating in your language(s)? What problems are most likely language-related?

3. What do you think are the most important characteristics of a good diplomat for your country? Why?

4. Do you agree with the author about the importance of professional diplomats rather than politically appointed ones? Discuss.

5. Before his retirement, the author was a career diplomat, his final position being ambassador to Guyana. How does this affect his bias? How does it affect his credibility?

6. What is the "foundation of diplomacy"? Discuss.

7. What is meant by the words "Elysian Fields"?

Exercise

The author refers to "the ancient device that actions speak louder than words" and cites the late Egyptian President Anwar Sadat's visit to Israel in 1977 as an example. Think of an example or situation in your own life when this maxim proved true, or had significance for you, and write about it.

Britain: Summer of '82

Argentina had been brought to her knees. British military might had secured a smashing victory thousands of miles away. No wonder crowds gathered at 10 Downing Street to praise the Iron Lady. Margaret Thatcher, the British prime minister, assured them that Britain was once again Great. Well might she proclaim that as the world marveled at the characteristic thoroughness and determination with which the British recaptured the Falkland Islands. A warm glow of pride enveloped the British in the summer of '82. Seemingly forgotten were the lamentations of scholars, politicians, and journalists over the decline of Britain. Talk about her as "the sick man of Europe," talk of the "British disease" was muted by louder choruses of patriotic self-congratulations. All these symptoms of Britain's difficulties were, for a while, forgotten. Few talked of the devastating riots and pitched street battles of the previous summer. The highest unemployment rate (13.4 percent) since the Great Depression seemed to bother few. An emigration rate of colossal proportions that last year alone saw 235,000 mainly skilled and professional people leave Britain was ignored. The virtually stagnant economy beset with chronic labor unrest was on few tongues.

To be sure, there were signs of life and vitality in Britain other than military prowess to make the prophets of doom and decline seem premature. Britons may have rioted in the streets of Liverpool the previous summer, for example, but they hadn't killed each other. There were, in fact, no deaths in the urban riots. Indeed, in Britain there are no more than 500 cases of homicide and manslaughter a year. In the United States the figure is about 17,000 a year. They may be declining, but the British are certainly happy. Gallup polls constantly show the British as among the happiest people in the world. There are, in fact, one-third as many suicides per capita in Britain as in the much more clearly vibrant country of West Germany. Another sign of vitality is the greater number of Nobel Prize winners per capita in Great Britain than in any other country.

Life goes on in Britain, as it always has, seemingly oblivious to any national crisis. As always the royal family manages to steal headlines with a divorce, a marriage, a birth, or a chat with a psychotic intruder. But isn't this itself a symptom of the British sickness? With real problems of rioting cities, a moribund economy, unemployment and emigration at historic highs, the British preoccupy themselves with the storybook lives of royalty.

Something is surely wrong with Britain. Behind the mood of euphoria (perhaps, indeed, accounting for it) in the summer of '82 lay a much deeper sense of national malaise and stagnation, on the one hand, and a real sense of unrest, discontent, and disorder, on the other. Britain has fallen dramatically from the height of past grandeur in three crucial areas. In economic terms this first and most intensively industrialized nation, once the world's factory, has now a growth rate lower than virtually every other industrialized nation. In the international arena, this former world power on whose empire the sun never set seems now bereft of even moral influence in world politics. And, finally, this nation with a tradition of peaceful continuity, so homogeneous, so usually free of strife, has in recent years been wracked by regional, racial, and social tensions that threaten to break up the nation if not the entire social fabric itself. How shallow then was the euphoria of the summer of 1982. Once again, as throughout history, a people were diverted momentarily from their plight by military victory. Would no one wake from this dream world to see the reality of her sad and sorry state?

At the heart of Britain's problems, and very much responsible for its industrial decline as well as its internal domestic unrest, is economic crisis, a crisis much deeper than the staggering inflation and unemployment rates of today. Britain's economy has for years been slowly grinding to a halt, with a growth rate in recent decades of no more than 2.0 to 2.5 percent a year. In the last 100 years this great home of the industrial revolution has been eclipsed by other industrial nations. In 1890 it was the leader of the pack; in 1980 it was at the end of the line. Why has industrial growth slowed so much more dramatically in Britain than in other nations? What is the cause of the long-term economic decline? Any answer to this question involves looking at three quite different factors: structural, attitudinal, and political.

The structural explanation points to the very fact of England's initial industrial preeminence as crucial in explaining her decline. Assets turn into liabilities. A worn-out industrial pioneer, Britain now confronts a world economy of sophisticated technology with ancient factories and ancient methods. Here, alas, is the paradox of World War II in which, leaving Coventry aside, much of English industry was relatively untouched, especially when compared with the wholesale devastation of French, German, and Japanese industry. These latter were in turn rebuilt and modernized in the last thirty-five years.

But the crisis in the British economy is more than a result of these structural factors; it is also a product of attitudes and values. It was never clear that the British have ever been an industrial or industrious people at heart. To many observers it has seemed that industrialism and industrial values are quite alien to the real spirit and character of the British people. A glance at British literature will reveal how striking the emphasis is on the value of rural life and the desirability of its slower pace. The British, more of whom live in cities than in most countries of the world, don't see themselves as a people of chimneys, railroads, and concrete, but as a country of "green and pleasant lands," of grass, trees, gardens, quaint old villages, and old gracious homes. Preindustrial and nonindustrial values dominate the public consciousness. The cultural ideal is the thatched cottage or the country squire.

Even when one does have to work in industry or factories, the British attitude to work is much less driven by the industrial spirit. The tea break and not exerting oneself too hard are the key. Work is done at a leisurely pace with much less exertion and effort. The British seldom see life as best spent striving, struggling, and forgoing immediate pleasure. The work experience is slower and more enjoyable. The Englishman (manager or worker) feels the quality of human freedom is greater when not working in the restless race of life. In that sense, all Britons (workers and executives) live more the life of the gentleman who doesn't try all that hard. This is quite a civilized (perhaps even a higher) view of human freedom, but it certainly doesn't help productivity.

If one adds to this general attitude toward work Britain's elitist educational values, one sees even more devastating effects on industrial and economic efficiency. The disdain for the manager, the preference for the generalist and for the amateur over the expert, is part of Britain's antiquated educational system. The ideal business executive is not the MBA but the good talker, the "nice chap" with a degree in classics from Oxford or Cambridge. The biases of the educational system are, indeed, crucial. Fewer people go to college and university in Britain than in any other industrial society. Throughout the 1950s and 1960s, for example, no more than one-fourth to one-half of all middle and upper-middle management in Britain had higher education. In America, Germany, France, and Japan, the corresponding figures are all between three-quarters and four-fifths. In turn, those in Britain who do go to university seldom go into industry or business—the BBC, yes; the foreign office, yes; but not industry.

A final area of explanation of Britain's long-term economic decline is the political, by which is meant the preeminent political influence of the City of London and its world-famous bankers. This financial community has in the last 100 years oriented the British economy much more to banking and investments all over the world than to investing and sustaining domestic British industry. British bankers helped create the capital for much of the world's industrial nations, including the United States, in the nineteenth and early twentieth centuries, and are now doing the same for developing nations. But these same financial wizards have paid much less attention to the factories of Britain. As a result, investment in British industrial plants has been sadly deficient. This impact of the financial community is appropriately labeled a political factor because the British banking community influences British politics much more than its counterparts do in other countries, owing to the perennial balance-of-payments problem and the traditional use of sterling for many years as the international currency. It is the political power of English finance itself—not unrelated, by the way, to Britain's social and cultural supremacy—that has diverted English politics from paying needed attention to domestic industry.

We are now witnessing the most profound single social change to occur in Britain in centuries. More than 5 percent of all Britons today are nonwhite. In the midst of its economic decline, Britain has been unable to cope with this vast wave of postwar immigration. The middle classes have ignored these new Englishmen, and the working class has pushed them aside. The unprecedented pitched battles between fascist youth and angry unemployed Jamaicans or Indians, or between both of them and the hapless police, are new and ugly variations on the theme of British decline.

But all this was pushed aside in the summer of '82. A great and glorious war had been fought, and the Royal Navy had been victorious. A royal prince was born. It could have been a typical summer from the nineteenth century. Some talked and acted as if it were. It wasn't.

On the surface all looked well in Britain in the summer of 1982, but beneath the self-congratulations and the good feeling lurked serious and staggering national problems.

Comprehension Questions

Assimilation

1. Great Britain's unemployment rate is:
   a. higher than in the 1950s but lower than the 1930s
   b. higher than in the 1930s but lower than in the 1950s
   c. higher than ever before
   d. none of the above

2. The "British disease" refers to:
   a. political and religious upheaval
   b. a highly contagious new strain of virus
   c. economic distress
   d. military decline

3. Optimistic signs in Great Britain include:
   a. a high number of Pulitzer Prize winners per capita
   b. few cases of homicide and manslaughter relative to the United States
   c. both a and b
   d. neither a nor b

4. The mood in Britain in the summer of 1982 is best described as:
   a. bleak despair
   b. seething anger
   c. euphoria
   d. uncertainty

5. Britain's problems are fundamentally based on:
    a. economic crisis
    b. military decline
    c. moral decline
    d. unemployment

Interpretation

6. Kramnick's tone in this essay is best described as:
    a. appreciative
    b. critical
    c. terse
    d. diffident

7. Kramnick considers Britain's decline from the standpoint of all the following *except:*
    a. labor–management: an inability to come to terms has resulted in stagnation, strikes, and a rift between workers and management
    b. political: London's bankers emphasize worldwide investments over domestic investment
    c. attitudinal: human freedom and the bucolic pleasures are prized more highly than hard-driving industrial fervor
    d. structural: early development, unimproved, led to outdated technology

8. Kramnick's approach to his subject is through:
    a. contrast
    b. chronology
    c. question and answer
    d. humor

9. As shown in the article, Kramnick's attitude is best described as:
    a. very concerned
    b. very optimistic
    c. very pessimistic
    d. neutral

Main Idea

10. The main idea of the article is:
    a. On the surface all looked well in Britain in the summer of '82, but beneath the self-congratulations and the good feeling lurked serious and staggering national problems.

b. Ironically, the very fact of Britain's initial industrial preeminence is the major cause of her present industrial decline.

c. Elitist in its values and antiquated in its system, Britain's educational system has had a negative influence on its economic development and social progress since World War II.

d. Economic decline and social change, political unrest, and educational stagnation have all led to Britain's nickname: "the sick man of Europe."

Analysis Questions

1. The author makes several generalizations about the English as a people concerning their values and priorities. Are they valid? Discuss.

2. What do you think Kramnick's purpose was in writing this essay: to convince the reader of something or to start the reader thinking? Support your opinion with specific references to the essay. Did Kramnick succeed in his purpose as you determined it?

3. What effect will the specific date reference in the title and introduction of the essay have on its long-term significance?

4. Kramnick gives evidence of both vitality and decline in Great Britain. Cite some examples of each and assess their relative significance.

5. Kramnick is not British and doesn't live in Britain. How does this affect his viewpoint about the situation in Britain? About his observations of the British people?

Exercise

The author points out both positive and negative situations and occurrences in Great Britain in 1982. Identify them in a list. Indicate which are positive and which are negative according to the author. Add any positive and negative situations you can think of that the author did not mention, including any that have come about after the summer of 1982. Then, identify which are superficial and which are fundamental.

RONALD G. EHRENBERG

Evaluation Research and National Social Policy: An Academic Practitioner's Perspective

Society has limited resources and many competing uses for them. I therefore take it as being an almost obvious proposition that at any point in time policymakers should strive to maximize the social benefits produced by the available funds they have to spend. This proposition implies that evaluation research should be undertaken either by or for government agencies. Policymakers need to know what benefits are being produced by each social program and the resource costs involved. They need to know which aspects of which programs are working and which programs need to be replaced.

Any evaluation study of a social program can have four possible outcomes, depending on the study's results. First, the study may be challenged by those people who are unhappy with, or feel threatened by, the study's conclusions. Because virtually any study has some methodological deficiencies, and because it is easier to find fault than it is to design and conduct an evaluation, this occurs frequently. Second, if the evaluation is negative, the program may be killed and the funds used elsewhere. Third, the program may be expanded or contracted in scale. Fourth, the program may be modified or redesigned. The option chosen depends on policymakers' values and prior benefits; all four outcomes are consistent, for example, with a negative conclusion about the program's impact. Although evaluation research may itself be value-free, the uses to which the research is put are clearly not.

If the need for evaluation research is so clear, one might question why so few evaluations are done in Washington and why evaluation research is given low priority. One reason is that the rewards accruing to individuals who undertake evaluations are quite minimal. For example, at the highest level of the bureaucracy (for example, the Assistant Secretary level and up), individuals are rewarded for their new initiatives, not for evaluating existing programs. The length of tenure of a typical high-level administrator is less than two years. To make a reputation in such a short time, the executive must do dramatic things that call attention to him or her, not simply monitor and evaluate existing programs. To increase the amount of evaluation research being conducted in Washington clearly requires bureaucrats to have longer tenures in their jobs and to be rewarded for their substantive long-term efforts—not for their flashy short-run initiatives.

The second reason evaluation research does not proliferate in Washington is that many individuals with long-term connections to particular programs feel threatened by the prospect of having their programs evaluated. An evaluation conceivably might adversely affect the level of funding of a program or suggest that the program be restructured. Individuals closely connected with a program often conclude that an evaluation can only do them harm and seek to avoid, like the plague, being subjected to evaluations.

Indeed, this suggests that evaluation studies should be undertaken by *outsiders* who have no vested interests in either continuing *or* killing a program. It also suggests the wisdom of conducting evaluation studies under the sponsorship of agencies other than the operating agency that is running a program.

There are at least three constraints on the evaluation research process that severely restrict the quality and objectivity of evaluations done in Washington. First, the agencies funding the evaluations, even if somewhat removed from the operation of programs, often hope that the evaluations will support their positions on policy issues. For example, during the Carter administration I served as a consultant on a project evaluating the displacement effects of the public employment program component of the Comprehensive Employment and Training Act (CETA) program. The project focused on estimating the extent to which state and local governments used CETA funds to hire employees whom they would have hired even in the absence of the funds.

This evaluation was undertaken by the Urban Institute, a reputable private nonprofit research organization in Washington. This project was not sponsored by the Employment and Training Administration, but rather by the Office of the Assistant Secretary for Policy, Evaluation and Research (ASPER) of the U.S. Department of Labor. Under the Ford administration this office tended to summarize the available evidence on the merits and demerits of proposed changes in legislation or social programs, without taking strong advocacy positions. However, during the Carter administration, ASPER was transformed into a policy advocate and became the prime supporter for the inclusion of a large-scale public sector employment program in the welfare reform legislation then being considered.

Because of this change in the nature of the office, high-level administrators in ASPER had a vested interest in seeing that the results eventually obtained by the Urban Institute evaluation did not cast public employment programs in a negative light. Knowledge of this fact placed the ASPER staffers who were monitoring the evaluation in a difficult position, as their desire to maintain scientific objectivity potentially was tempered by their concern not to undercut their "bosses' baby." In the main, in this case they were able to maintain their objectivity, although after at least one meeting, those of us involved in the evaluation came away convinced they had been overcritical of our methodological approach *because* we found significant displacement effects.

Independent of the merits of the public employment program, agencies sponsoring evaluations should not play such an asymmetric role. The research methodology should be critically analyzed by the sponsoring agency, regardless of whether the results of the study support the agency's prior position. More importantly, this example also suggests that evaluation components of the cabinet departments should be divorced from the policy advocate components. In particular, there should be an office in the Department of Labor that is free to conduct long-run program evaluations without having to get involved in short-run policy advocacy.

The second constraint on the evaluation process is time itself. Evaluations typically have short horizons (one year or less in length) because policymakers want results in time to utilize them during their tenure in office. (Recall that high-level policymakers tend to turn over rapidly.) This time constraint prevents many studies from being given careful consideration during the design stage, which is necessary if a methodologically sound study is to be conducted. Another time constraint relates to the manner in which proposals for evaluations are solicited. The typical request for proposals (RFP) is issued with a three-week deadline, preventing academics from bidding on the contract (does this sound like sour grapes?) and precluding most consulting companies from seriously considering what the optimal method of analyzing the problem would be, thereby further limiting the likely usefulness of the studies.

The third constraint on the evaluation process is that most evaluators are in the evaluation business on a long-run basis and consequently are interested in obtaining future evaluation contracts. They are reluctant to submit analyses whose results are in direct conflict with what they know policymakers want. It is hard for investigators to maintain complete objectivity when they know that reporting certain results will increase (or decrease) the probability that they will obtain future contracts from the same funding agency. That the potential for such a conflict of interests exists was obvious to me in the course of my participation in the Urban Institute's CETA evaluation. This problem again suggests that it would be wise to separate the evaluation office in a cabinet agency from the office that is in charge of advocating policy reform. Evaluation should be done in a neutral environment as much as possible, and the evaluator should not be forced to respond to the wishes of a policy advocate.

Independent of how we structure the process by which evaluation research is conducted in government, one might ask what the role of evaluation research is in public policy decisions. Evaluation research seeks to provide information about the benefits and costs of alternative programs and legislation. It is naive, however, to think that such information will dictate a policy decision in any particular situation or typically even play a major role in the decision for at least two reasons.

On the one hand, evaluations tend to be narrower in scope than what the sponsors of the studies (usually government agencies) really want. What is desired is to know whether a particular program is good or bad, but what is offered typically is an estimate of one of the program's many effects. For example, literally hundreds of econometric studies have focused on estimating the adverse effects of minimum wage legislation on employment. However, only a handful have looked at questions such as, Is the legislation complied with? or Do minimum wage laws reduce the incidence of poverty?—questions that surely must be addressed in any complete evaluation.

On the other hand, policymakers' decisions are based on a complex set of factors that are not restricted to the way the program is operating, but often hinge on political considerations. Because of this, all one can hope is that evaluation research will provide some information on the workings of the programs and that this information will allow such decision makers, who are at the margin, to make more informed decisions. Anyone who conducts evaluation research with the anticipation that his or her evaluation study will, *and should,* automatically be transferred into policy recommendations will perpetually be frustrated and should probably find an alternative occupation.

Some distinguished academics and policymakers, such as Harvard's John Dunlop, a former Secretary of Labor, have argued that the benefit/cost ratio for evaluation research is zero. The argument proceeds along the following lines: Evaluation research uses resources, but it rarely influences decisions, so its benefits must be close to zero. As such, the benefit/cost ratio for conducting evaluations is close to zero, and it is a waste of resources to undertake the studies. This evaluation of evaluation research suggests that society needs less of it rather than more.

I draw the opposite conclusion. Rather than eliminating such studies, one can increase their benefit/cost ratio by increasing their benefits via utilizing them more in policy decision. It is incumbent upon academic economists who accept policy positions in the federal government, as Dunlop did, to increase the extent of rationality in the policy decision process by making more use of these studies.

Comprehension Questions

Assimilation

1. According to the article, evaluation research should be undertaken to:
   a. enable program supervisors to hire the right people to implement the program
   b. enable program supervisors to be changed without affecting the program itself
   c. enable policymakers to conduct cost/benefit analysis
   d. facilitate proper record keeping

2. Evaluation research is:
   a. value-free, as are the uses to which it is put
   b. not value-free, but the uses to which it is put *are* value-free
   c. value-free, but the uses to which it is put are *not* value-free
   d. not value-free, nor are the uses to which it is put

3. The length of tenure of a typical high-level administrator is less than:
   a. nine months
   b. one year
   c. eighteen months
   d. two years

4. Evaluation studies should be conducted by:
   a. the director of the program under evaluation
   b. the person who hired the program director
   c. an outside agency
   d. none of the above

5. The author discusses which set of problems confronting those conducting evaluation research:
   a. time, bias
   b. bias, cost
   c. cost, time
   d. time, cost, and bias

6. Sponsors of studies often find evaluations to be:
   a. too broad in scope
   b. too narrow in scope
   c. too expensive
   d. too time-consuming

Interpretation

7. The author believes that the benefit/cost ratio for evaluation research:
   a. is higher than one would rightfully expect
   b. is zero
   c. should be increased through greater utilization
   d. should be decreased by eliminating waste and duplication

8. Concerning his own bias, the author:
   a. made no attempt to hide it

b. unsuccessfully tried to hide it
c. successfully hid it
d. eliminated it altogether

9. The author's structural organization of his subject is best characterized as:
a. chronological and spatial
b. descriptive enumeration
c. comparison and contrast
d. illustration and quotation

Main Idea

10. The main idea of the article is:
a. Benefits of evaluation research studies should be maximized through greater utilization when planning national social policy.
b. The federal government spends too much time and money on evaluation research studies, which, all too often, are unnecessary.
c. Evaluation studies should be conducted by academicians who have no vested interest in either maintaining or eliminating the program under evaluation.
d. Although national social policy has changed greatly under the last three presidents, it has not been improved.

Analysis Questions

1. Ehrenberg refers to himself as an academic practitioner. How would his topic be approached by a cabinet official? A clerk in a social security office? A government economist?

2. Ehrenberg maintains that evaluation must be done properly, and without bias, to be both fair and useful. Apply this view to faculty grading of students. To student evaluation of faculty. To evaluation by one's peers on a jury.

3. How can the results of evaluation studies be translated into public policy?

4. If you headed a delegation to overhaul the social security system, how would you proceed?

5. The author uses the phrase "sour grapes" in the article. Explain the meaning of the phrase in this context.

Exercise

Ehrenberg uses many pivotal words and phrases (for example, on the other hand), which help guide the reader through the text, much like road signs help a driver of a car by warning him of a change in direction, change in safe rate of speed, and so on. Go through the article and underline all of the pivotal words and phrases you can find. How effective are they in clarifying Ehrenberg's writing?

Incentives and Self-Regulation

*I*n 1776, while America was seeking its independence from Great Britain, another revolution of equal importance was occurring in the philosophical field. The year 1776 also marks the birth of the modern discipline of economics, heralded in the publication of Adam Smith's *An Inquiry into the Nature and Causes of the Wealth of Nations.* Although a great deal of that book is devoted to showing that a country's wealth consists of the energies and abilities of its people, contrary to the then-popular mercantilist notion that a country grows rich by accumulating gold through trade with its colonies and other powers, its most important contribution is in quite another realm. Surprisingly, Adam Smith's greatest contribution lies in showing the importance of selfishness.

Why is this doctrine revolutionary? To understand, we need to see what Adam Smith was concerned with in trying to describe the economies of Britain and Europe in the late 1770s and to see how selfishness plays a role. Today, a modern economist would say that Smith was concerned with resource allocation, the process that decides how much labor and machinery will be devoted to the production of particular goods and services, which, in turn, are consumed by individual households. Smith concluded that prices did the job and that producers' and consumers' responses to prices were the key to understanding the interrelationship between the different sides of the market. In doing so he made two astute observations that have assured his place in history. The first is that selfish interest—the desire to maximize profits on the part of firms and the desire to buy the highest quality products at the best price on the part of consumers—explains the response of each to changing prices in the marketplace. The second is that this interplay, based on personal objectives, actually leads to a socially desirable or best outcome. In a justly celebrated passage he wrote:

> But it is only for the sake of profit that any man employs a capital in the support of industry; and he will always, therefore, endeavour to employ it in the support of that industry of which the produce is likely to be of the greatest value, or to exchange for the greatest quantity either of money or of other goods.
>
> But the annual revenue of every society is always precisely equal to the exchangeable value of the whole annual produce of its industry, or rather is precisely the same thing with that exchangeable value. As every individual, therefore, endeavours as much as he can both to employ his capital in the support of domestic industry, and so to direct that industry that its produce may be of the greatest value; every individual necessarily labours to render the annual revenue of the society as great as he can. He generally, indeed, neither intends to promote the public interest, nor knows how much he is promoting it. By preferring the support of domestic to that of foreign industry, he intends only his own security; and by directing that industry in such a manner as its produce may be of the greatest value, he intends only his own gain, and he is in this, as in many other cases, led by an invisible hand to promote an end which was no part of his intention. Nor is it always the worse for the society that it was no part of it. By pursuing his own interest he frequently promotes that of the society more effectually than when he really intends to promote it. I have never known much good done by those who affected to trade for the public good. It is an affectation, indeed, not very common among merchants, and very few words need be employed in dissuading them from it.

The implication of Smith's observation is even more remarkable when converted into common parlance. If an economy left to its own devices acts in the social good, then any attempt to improve its workings is really interference, or meddling, which will only do more harm than good; thus laissez-faire or hands off is the best policy. After centuries of royal decrees, government attempts at control, clamor by labor guilds and foreign traders for government-granted monopoly, and so on, freedom of the marketplace was decreed in 1776.

The view that firms *should* seek to get as much profit as they are able, and that consumers *should* seek to sell their labor at as high a price as they can and purchase goods to satisfy their own selfish needs, requires detailed explanation. Smith considered the problem in Books 1 and 2, covering over 150 pages of print. In barest essentials the argument is that increased preference for a good by consumers leads to increased sales, which in turn cause the market price for the good to rise. In response to higher prices, producers see the opportunity for greater profits. They increase production of the good, demanding in turn greater resources of labor, machinery, and land to produce it, until the greater quantity being supplied satisfies the demand at the new price. The factors that go into making the good are therefore shifted from other uses and receive higher rewards for their services as required by the greater output of the good in question. Thus firms acting to increase their own profits have supplied what the consumer wants. The consumer, by expressing his desires through purchases for his own use, creates a signal that causes those desires to be satisfied. High prices act as signals in the other direction also, telling consumers that a product is costly and that they should conserve on its use in favor of cheaper substitutes. Repeating this story for all the markets in the economy, producers and consumers are led to do the right thing to enhance total welfare, even though no single individual or authority acts to ensure it. Of course, I do not mean that corruption, false representation by firms, shoplifting by consumers, and so on should be allowed. Injustices and frauds must be prevented, and selfish interest must operate within a particular framework.

Because the desire of firms for profits and the desire of consumers for personal satisfaction are coordinated through prices, Smith opposed the creation of the government-condoned monopolies and labor guilds that were prevalent in his day. Such monopolies do not treat prices as outside their control because, as the only seller, they know they can increase prices within limits to their own advantage. As long as there are many separate sellers, competition among them prevents any one from taking advantage of the buyers by charging an improperly high price. If one did, other firms would preempt its sales at a lower price. Competition therefore means that each firm must take prices as outside its control. Similarly, competition among many buyers prevents any one from taking advantage of firms by lowering the price. Competition is the "policeman" that keeps selfish interest in check and allows the market to work.

Viewed from this perspective, the marketplace is a remarkable institution, springing from the natural desire of individuals to trade, produce, and better their own lot, and having the inevitable effect (if allowed to operate properly) of coordinating everyone's actions to achieve the social good. Prices and competition are essential components of its proper functioning.

Since Adam Smith's time we have learned much more about how economies work and are better able to describe how the choices of all firms and consumers fit together to promote aggregate welfare in what is called general equilibrium. Smith, however, built on timeless foundations, and his insights are visible today in the growing edifice of the field he founded. Today, as in 1776, the principle of selfish interest operating through the marketplace, with the strictures of competition to guide it, acts as if "led by an invisible hand" to achieve the common good.

Comprehension Questions

Assimilation

1. The invisible-hand doctrine as it relates to selfishness, states that:
    a. the existence of market prices and profits leads to selfishness on the part of firms and consumers
    b. the marketplace is like an invisible hand that stops the selfishness of firms and consumers
    c. the marketplace coordinates the selfish actions of firms and consumers to accomplish the social good
    d. the social good is not the intention of firms and consumers, who are interested only in their selfish ends

2. According to Adam Smith, an example of an affectation is:
    a. charity to the poor
    b. trade for the public good
    c. advertising for the support of charities
    d. nonprofit institutions

3. What does Adam Smith consider a country's wealth to consist of?
    a. the energies and abilities of its people

b. the sum of its money, valuable metals, and jewels

c. only the gold it acquires through foreign trade

d. the size of its export surplus

4. What is the mercantilist doctrine?
   a. National greatness consists of a country's ocean-borne trade and merchant fleet.
   b. The route to national wealth is through encouragement of imports.
   c. National wealth lasts only as long as a country has colonies.
   d. The acquisition of gold through foreign trade is the route to national wealth.

5. What is the "policeman" of the marketplace?
   a. selfishness
   b. competition
   c. government
   d. high prices

6. Which correctly describes what Adam Smith is opposed to?
   a. monopolies but not labor guilds
   b. profits by firms but not self-interest on the part of consumers
   c. selfishness by consumers but not profits by firms
   d. none of the above

Interpretation

7. What does laissez-faire mean, as used in this article?
   a. a state of competition between firms and consumers
   b. government licensing of trade
   c. selected government control of the marketplace
   d. no government control of the marketplace

8. What do higher prices tell a competitive firm to do?
   a. usually nothing, since their inventories are gone
   b. take advantage of consumers by cutting back on sales
   c. produce more in order to increase profits yet again
   d. enjoy the easy profits and use the time to prepare for times of low prices

9. The author's tone is:
   a. emotional
   b. expository
   c. wry
   d. interrogative

Main Idea

10. The main idea of this article is:
    a. The marketplace, if let alone, will always do the right thing in terms of social good.
    b. Although things have changed considerably since 1776, laissez-faire was not a bad policy at the time of Adam Smith because of the invisible hand.
    c. The invisible-hand doctrine is an old idea going back to the earliest times, which Adam Smith wrote down in 1776.
    d. Today, as in Adam Smith's time, the selfish interest of firms and consumers are coordinated through the marketplace to achieve the common good.

Analysis Questions

1. What would Adam Smith say about abuses in the marketplace? Is government intervention always helpful? Ever helpful? Ever harmful? Give examples.

2. Government-granted monopolies in trade were instituted to deal with a perceived need to encourage foreign trade. Adam Smith contended that the cure was worse than the problem. Assess his position.

3. Grinols uses a theoretical-historical approach to the subject of government regulation in the marketplace. What other approach might have been used? (See Kahn's article.)

4. Do you think Adam Smith would change his views today?

5. What does the author mean by the phrase "importance of selfishness"?

6. Compare the writing style of Adam Smith in the quoted passage with Grinols's in his text.

Exercises

1. Metaphors and analogies add interest, originality, and colorfulness to this article. Go through the article and underline those you find. Identify each one and describe the impact of its use.

2. Consider an industry such as the automobile industry. When is government intervention needed? When is it not needed or desirable? (How about pollution-control devices? Body design? Prices? Big vs. small cars?) Write your conclusions in a brief position paper to be presented to (choose one): an industry official, a government official, or a labor union official.

ALFRED E. KAHN

Using the Market in Regulation

Government regulation is under fierce attack these days along its entire front. One has only to hear the claim, for example, that it is responsible for all the problems of our automobile industry, or other such fatuous observations that I refrain from further identifying, to understand how great the threat really is. Where would the auto companies be now, one wonders, were it not for the mandated fuel economy standards, about which they complained so bitterly?

But that doesn't mean the criticisms are baseless. Underlying the attacks are two basic complaints: regulation is excessively costly and excessively coercive.

We in government have no choice but to believe that if we meet the criticisms of regulation that are valid, we will be in the best possible position to repel the ones that are invalid.

The most striking way in which we can meet the legitimate complaints is simply to deregulate in the many cases in which the government has intervened to protect private parties from the discipline of the competitive market. Where competition alone can effectively protect the public, this is clearly the proper remedy. I am proud of our deregulations or substantial deregulations, during just the last seven years, of airlines, motor carriers, railroads, financial institutions, and communications, not to mention the related, but different, cases of crude oil and natural gas.

In the many cases in which competition cannot be trusted to do the job, much can still be done to reduce the cost and intrusiveness of regulation. One of the most heartening recent developments is the increased willingness of regulators to experiment with innovative techniques to do just that. The recent report of the Regulatory Council to the President provides an encouraging summary of 376 such experiments.

Significantly, many of these techniques use or stimulate the market. Because markets leave the requisite cost/benefit comparison to the people directly involved, who have every incentive to make the proper economic choices, they simultaneously achieve the twin goals of regulatory reform I have already identified: imposing only costs that are justified by benefits and minimizing coercion.

I recall a discussion at the Civil Aeronautics Board before I became chairman of how to handle the vexing problem of airline bumping. The good lawyers assembled debated at length what would be the fairest basis for setting priorities among potential bumpees: first to reserve, first to buy tickets, first to check in. For every proposed criterion of equity, it soon became clear, there was an equally valid counterconsideration.

At my first meeting on the subject, I suggested (following Professor Julian Simon, among others) that the real problem was the involuntary selection of the passengers to be bumped, and that there could not be any objection if the bumpees were permitted to select themselves in response to economic incentives. Airlines engage in overbooking because it pays. It makes perfect sense, then, to require them, when bumping becomes a necessity, to offer whatever monetary compensation is necessary to induce the requisite number of people to give up their seats voluntarily. The result will be economically efficient and uncoercive.

As the Regulatory Council's report shows, there are many other situations in which regulators are experimenting with ways of achieving the requisite protection of the public merely by setting up the framework within which the market can do the actual choosing. Where, for example, it is necessary to ration portions of the limited radio spectrum, or the right to land at crowded airports at peak hours, or the amount of pollutants that may be emitted, innovative regulators are evaluating proposals to auction off the rights or distribute them more randomly while allowing people to buy and sell them freely.

Similarly, it is now almost unanimously accepted that if we ever do have gasoline rationing, we should permit free purchase and sale of the ration coupons. Such a system has the critical virtue that under it every single gallon of gasoline that anyone uses has to be worth at least as much to him as it would be to someone else, to whom he could instead choose—voluntarily—to sell the coupons.

These cases illustrate yet another closely related principle that innovative regulators are adopting: make the rules as general and nonprescriptive as possible while still achieving the ultimate purpose. A corollary of this principle is a preference for specifying ends rather than prescribing means: leave it to the regulatees to figure out the lowest-cost method of achieving the prescribed performance standards. The classic example is the Environmental Protection Agency's bubble policy, which sets overall limits on air pollution for plants, rather than specifying exactly what emissions are allowed from each source or how control is to be achieved. The du Pont Company estimates that the bubble will cut its costs of complying with the Clean Air Act by $81 million annually.

But the rules do require—and their progressive adoption reflects—a changing attitude. Traditional regulators tend to be compulsively neat. They want things to be done the right way, and they have a compulsion to prescribe that way. It is only by disciplining themselves, like the House of Lords, to "withhold their legislative hands," wherever this would be consistent with the ultimate objectives, that regulators are going to preserve the defenses we have been erecting in the last decade or two of the public health and safety, of workers on the job, and of consumers in the marketplace.

Comprehension Questions

Assimilation

1. The word *market* in the title of this article, "Using the Market in Regulation," refers to:
   a. a store handling one particular kind of goods
   b. consumer protection law
   c. regulatory council
   d. competition

2. According to Kahn, government regulation is:
   a. beneficial but not vital

    b. too intrusive
    c. cost-effective
    d. capricious

3. Recently, substantial deregulation has been:
    a. costly
    b. unfair to the consumer
    c. beneficial
    d. lacking

4. Overbooking by airlines should be:
    a. increased
    b. eliminated
    c. balanced by appropriate monetary compensation
    d. examined by the Regulatory Council to the President, not the Civil Aeronautics Board

Interpretation

5. In the article, Kahn identified his viewpoint with:
    a. the federal government
    b. the academic community
    c. the House of Lords
    d. none of the above

6. Complaints about regulation refer mainly to:
    a. cost and intrusiveness
    b. the Environmental Protection Agency and the Civil Aeronautics Board
    c. the economic marketplace
    d. reform and legislation

7. Concerning his own bias, the author:
    a. allows it to show
    b. eliminates it
    c. is neutral about the topic, thus has none
    d. hides it

8. The author's approach to his topic is mainly:
    a. historical
    b. advisory
    c. sarcastic
    d. pessimistic

9. To make his point, the author relies considerably on:
    a. current trends of thought
    b. experience
    c. the guidance of leaders of the auto and airline industries
    d. none of the above

Main Idea

10. The main idea of this article is:
    a. The automobile and airline industries, through Alfred E. Kahn's assistance, have led the way in reducing needless regulation.
    b. One of the most important duties of government is to protect the consumer from industry and big business.
    c. Government agencies should be looking for ways to reduce the cost and intrusiveness of regulations by using market forces to achieve their goals.
    d. Federal government regulations should undergo cost/benefit analysis to determine whether they should be subject to gradual reduction or elimination.

Analysis Questions

1. Do you find Kahn's article convincing? Would you if you owned General Motors? Nissan Motors? The corner grocery store? A new solar energy business?

2. Kahn gives an example of uncoercive regulation of the airlines with respect to bumping. Think of an instance where the government is presently employing coercive regulation and offer a noncoercive alternative.

3. Kahn states that excessive government regulation has been costly to the American economy and its consumers. Name some examples. How did these excessive regulations come about?

4. This essay includes several current examples of the author's points that add to its effectiveness. Will these same examples render the essay obsolete in the near future? What other approach could have been used to avoid this problem? Would it have been as effective? How can a writer resolve this dilemma?

5. Kahn's use of the first person allows him to write about experiences he had in influencing government policy. How does this add to his credibility? To the interest level of the article?

Exercise

Have you ever been "bumped" from your reserved seat on an airplane? Using the first-person approach, write about your experience: what happened, your reactions, and so forth. If you have never had the experience, create a hypothetical one.

Profiting from the Past:
The Antique Marketplace

*B*uying and selling antiques for profit happens in elegant galleries, small family-operated shops, private homes, suburban malls, at auctions, at shows, at flea markets, and through the mail. While certain areas of the country and even specific neighborhoods in some cities have been identified with the antique business, the enthusiasm for collecting antiques, and consequently the location of sellers, know no regional boundaries. During the two decades before the early sixties, the consensus among collectors was that the finest antiques in America could by and large be found only in New York, Boston, Philadelphia, and Washington, D.C. Since the sixties, that consensus has collapsed. These days antique shops, operated by owners who travel all over the country to find high quality and good buys, are located in small cities and rural areas as well as in the large metropolitan centers. Auction houses in the country are often called auction barns and may actually be found in furniture stores, houses, and garages.

The market for antiques is for many dealers an international one. The most esteemed magazine in the business, *Antiques,* regularly features "Letter from London" and "Letter from Paris." Stuart Slavid, a proprietor of the Boston shop The Den of Antiquity, located in the heart of the prestigious Beacon Hill area, also has an office in London, England. Specializing in English and oriental porcelain and pottery, including Wedgwood, and in decorative accessories, Slavid and his father moved to Charles Street from the suburbs in part because of Boston's superior accessibility to international markets. "When we were located near Wellesley, we often missed people from overseas who were just here for the day," he explains. "Now I can easily meet them at the airport and bring them to Charles Street."

Some antique dealers are generalists, selling everything from agate glass to scriveners' desks. Generalists are more likely to sell through a shop, but even those who do not specialize in particular antiques may notice that certain customers prefer certain types of merchandise. The cooperative on Charles Street was praised by some of its customers for carrying "everything imaginable." Still, about 75 percent of the jewelry the shop sells is earrings, and a large number of the earrings go to college students. George Tedder, whose furniture, stained glass, china, lamps, and mirrors are displayed in an elegant old house in Saint Augustine built around the turn of the century, and formerly used as a tourist home, says that young people are more interested in furniture because they need it most. "Young people also go heavily for leaded items: leaded glass, lamps, and shades, for example," he muses.

Such information about the relationship between types of antiques bought or preferred, and demographic variables such as region, occupation, age, income, and so forth, can be used by antique dealers to market their goods more profitably. Slavid emphasizes the importance of demographics in direct marketing. Stuart and his father, Leslie Slavid, have been using the mail to market special antiques for about thirty years. They carry many items that have some type of association with William Shakespeare. Once they employed a direct-mail company to secure lists for use in selling the Shakespeare items. Although the lists were too broad, including all English and drama majors everywhere, and thus had to be culled, once narrowed down, the lists were useful.

Suppose a hypothetical antique gallery knows that most of its clients who buy antique art earn over $40,000 a year, are in the forty- to fifty-year age range, and are college graduates. The gallery also knows that its best local customers come from the area of town in which the gallery is located. By matching collectors' addresses and profiles with demographic data from the census, the dealers can increase their ability to target potential collectors. Whenever the time comes for a special showing, the gallery can mail brochures not only to loyal clients but also to others in geographic areas with high concentrations of persons in the forty- to fifty-year age bracket, in the $40,000-per-year income range, and with college educations.

Tedder, the Florida antique dealer mentioned above, says that his customers' occupations and ages are varied, ranging from young attorneys to old store clerks. The most dependable buyers, according to Tedder, are the solid middle class. "Some of the women who work in dress shops," Tedder says, "will buy an antique for $50 down and $50 a month." He has never had a problem with their paying.

The antique business spills over into a variety of other businesses. Emily McAdoo owns the Wandering Eye, a "retrospective" boutique in Cambridge that is a link between fashion and antiques. She carries some Edwardian children's clothes and some Victorian clothes that are true antiques. Often antiques are sold at a decorator's gallery or in an oriental rug store. Still another illustration of this diversity is Elder's Bookstore in Nashville, Tennessee: the store specializes in old books, but antiques are included as a sideline. When antiques are sold along with other merchandise, it is often worthwhile to do a survey to discover whether the customers who buy antiques have the same demographic profiles as the other customers.

Demographic trends are expected to make a difference in the antique market of the future. It is no secret that the baby boom generation, now in its family-forming years, is a major determinant of market trends. Its members constitute such a large segment of the U.S. population that anything they decide to buy will be in great demand.

The rising divorce rate may also help the antique business because it is one of a number of trends, including the aging of the population and a lower birth rate, that have led to smaller and more numerous households. The fact that households are increasing faster than the population means that more household items and furniture may be purchased; some of the housewares and furniture will come from antique dealers. More divorces may also mean that more property will be on the market, increasing circulation of antiques.

Greater geographic mobility, another current trend, makes it less likely that children and members of the extended family will be living close by when death comes to aged parents. Thus antiques may be more likely, in some cases, to be sold rather than kept in the family as in the past, especially in families where the value of antiques is not appreciated.

In the past, antique dealers often felt that it paid to advertise only in periodicals strictly limited to the subject of antiques and to concentrate on meeting potential collectors at shows and auctions, because the best customers are those already knowledgeable about antiques. As the market opens more to private consumers, and the auction boom draws newer collectors into the action, a willingness to target groups demographically similar to veteran collectors may increase. If doctors tend to buy furniture for investment, for instance, and clerical workers, including secretaries, buy jewelry for beauty, as a Boston dealer in antique jewelry claims, subsequent advertisements and mailings need to take this information into account. It is a good bet that dealers will be cautious about relying too heavily on chance when statistical tools are available for the planning and decision making necessary to the marketing process. Many dealers have already learned that demographics is just such a tool.

Comprehension Questions

Assimilation

1. Before the 1960s, the finest antiques in America were available:
   a. in New York, Philadelphia, Boston, and Washington, D.C.
   b. in certain auction barns east of the Mississippi
   c. in Paris and London
   d. virtually everywhere

2. Today, the finest antiques in America are available:
   a. in New York, Philadelphia, Boston, and Washington, D.C.
   b. in certain auction barns west of the Mississippi
   c. in Paris and London
   d. virtually everywhere

3. According to one dealer, young people are mainly interested in:
   a. jewelry and period clothes
   b. furniture and leaded items
   c. oriental rugs
   d. art reproductions

4. Demographic trends cited for their positive impact on the antique business in America include all the following *except:*
   a. the baby boom
   b. increased geographic mobility

c. larger families
d. increasing divorce rate

Interpretation

5. The focus of this article is:
   a. the European influence on the American antique business
   b. what makes some antiques more valuable than others
   c. how to make a fortune buying and selling antiques
   d. current trends in the antique business in America

6. One may infer from this article that antique dealers:
   a. rely mainly on location for their success
   b. can use demographic tools to increase their business
   c. are superstitious and regard Lady Luck as vital to their success
   d. prefer direct marketing to galleries

7. One writing technique *not* employed by the author is:
   a. to end the essay with an amusing anecdote
   b. to pose a hypothetical situation as an example
   c. to include quotations from major antique dealers
   d. to compare today's antique marketplace with that of the past

8. The author's bias in this essay is best described as:
   a. skeptical of the influence of demographics in this business
   b. seeing the marketing of antiques as more of an art than a business
   c. convinced about the benefits of statistical tools
   d. negative about the current diversity in the antique business

9. The tone of this article is best described as:
   a. insistent and persuasive
   b. emotional and overstated
   c. low key and matter-of-fact
   d. vague and self-contradictory

Main Idea

10. The main idea of this article is:
    a. An appreciation of the relationship between demographics and the antique business can lead to more profitable marketing of antiques.

---

b. There is a great fortune to be made in the antique business for the entrepreneur who is in the right place at the right time and who has the courage to take risks when necessary.

c. Success in the antique marketplace is due to a combination of good furniture, solid background and training, superior location, and an impeccable reputation.

d. As the American antique business has diversified and spread, the European influence on it has declined.

Analysis Questions

1. What should the title contribute to an essay? What other title can you think of for this particular essay?

2. Stuart Slavid's shop in Boston is named The Den of Antiquity. What makes this a good name for an antique business? What other appropriate names can you create?

3. What trends are cited by the author as having a positive influence on today's antique business? Can you think of any others? Can you think of trends that have a negative influence?

4. What is meant by the word *demographics?* What businesses other than the antique business would benefit by demographic information? How would they benefit?

5. Do you have any interest in antiques or in the antique business? Did this article add to your interest or information? Why or why not?

6. Many informational articles begin with a brief tracing of some history on the topic, just as this article does. Why is this a good technique?

7. The author cites several examples of combining antiques with other items in one business. Name them. Can you suggest any others?

Exercise

Brief anecdotes that are amusing or engage the reader's attention often make good introductions to informational (or educational) writing. In 200 words or less, create such an anecdote to introduce this essay. (A hypothetical incident can be a good start!)

Righting Writing, in Business

*I*f you glance through the "Help Wanted" sections of the business newspapers these days, you will see a widespread concern with communication abilities: "good writing and speaking skills needed," "must have excellent written, oral, and interpersonal skills." These requirements appear not just for jobs traditionally associated with communication—public relations, sales, personnel. They are now being sought for positions previously associated with quantitative abilities—finance, accounting, and operations. At the same time businesses are looking for new employees who can write and speak well, they are also hiring consultants to train middle- and upper-management persons, as well as technical and professional staff members, in these skills. The ability to communicate has always been a prerequisite for those at the top and for those who represent the organization to such outside groups as clients, the press, and the government. But it has only recently become critical for people throughout the organization who may be communicating only with other employees. Why are businesses suddenly concerned with communication skills, and particularly with writing?

The answer lies in the ways on-the-job writing has deteriorated and in the advances in communication technology that have made this deterioration an urgent problem. Indeed, big business has joined the teachers, grammarians, and columnists in bemoaning the inability of the educated to write clearly and concisely.

How has writing deteriorated? Much attention has been paid lately to the role of television and the public school curriculum in causing writing problems. Certainly where television replaces reading, young people are less exposed to examples of good writing and to a variety of writing styles. They don't see the written word as a source of pleasure or as something that can be manipulated for particular results. And certainly the question of who is supposed to teach students how to write has been pushed progressively higher—into the colleges and even the graduate schools. In fact, most of the top MBA programs in the country today have some type of writing course for their students. The decline in the study of foreign languages has also contributed to the problem. One of the best ways to get a sense of the structure, logic, and plasticity of English is to learn a foreign language. Whatever the cause, when written English loses its familiarity it becomes a type of artificial language, divorced from spoken English. The writer is no longer sure of the rules or options open to him.

If you add to this initial insecurity about writing the layers of conventions that have developed in business writing, you begin to see the seriousness of the problem. Business writing, like other types of styles, both changes and retains vestiges of the past. For many years "correct" business style was legalistic in tone. Here is a passage from Edith Wharton's short story "The Spark" describing a conversation between two businessmen in the 1860s:

> "How the devil shall I say: 'Your letter of the blankth came yesterday, and after thinking over what you propose I don't like the looks of it'?"—"Why, say just that," I would answer; but he would shake his head and object: "My dear fellow, you're as bad as I am. You don't know how to *write good English.*" In his mind there was a gulf fixed between speaking and writing the language. I could never get his imagination to bridge this gulf, or to see that the phrases which fell from his lips were "better English" than the written version, produced after much toil and pen-biting, which consisted in translating the same statement into some such language as: "I am in receipt of your communication of the 30th ultimo, and regret to be compelled to inform you in reply that, after mature consideration of the proposals therein contained, I find myself unable to pronounce a favourable judgment upon the same."

This dilemma still arises today. Many people think that "good" writing is stiff and formal, and that direct, conversational English is inappropriate.

Another type of "false" language began to appear several years ago with the spread of computers and computer jargon out of the information systems ghettos and into the mainstream. Soon everybody who wanted to seem savvy affected the high-tech tone: "The interface impact will be optimized by the maximization of input and thruput." Although nobody likes to read that type of writing, people struggle to produce it. They expect that their readers expect it and that the simple and direct version won't sound as important.

Business organizations breed conformity, and when writers who are unskilled to begin with sense the universality of the legalistic or computerese models, they tend to cling to those forms. The impetus to pry the writer loose, to restore plain English, comes from both without and within: from without, in legislation and court cases requiring that documents directed toward consumers be written in clear, understandable English; from within, in technological developments that have allowed ever-increasing amounts of material to be generated at ever-increasing rates.

Virtually all types of organizations have acquired photocopiers and word processors. Now many organizations are installing electronic mail systems. These systems eliminate such intermediaries as typists, photocopiers, and traditional mail delivery, and thus increase both the quantity and rapidity of internal communication. Although communication technology is designed to increase productivity, it contains traps for the writer and the organization. First, the easier it is to compose and transmit material instantly, the less likely the writer is to revise and improve the work. Second, the easier it is to send copies to everyone, the more likely people are to be inundated with junk mail. Third, the more numerous and diverse the readership, the harder it becomes for the writer to be clear, direct, and specific. The writing becomes lengthier, to fill in all the background and cover every contingency. The tone becomes impersonal and jargonesque.

Faced with a glut of unreadable material, businesses are rightly becoming concerned with writing skills. But the skill must now be defined more broadly. Good business writing is not merely knowing how to string sentences together correctly. It is also the ability to know whether to write, when, and to whom. Otherwise the efficiency of the generating and delivery systems is offset by the amount of time people waste trying to decipher large amounts of marginally relevant material.

Businesses have responded to the communication problem in a number of ways. One strategy is, not surprisingly, the quick fix: a consultant, in-house trainer, or videotaped instruction module teaches writing to the maximum number of people in the minimum amount of time. This strategy has two weaknesses. The first has to do with the skill itself. Good business writing is not the product only of good grammar and organization, but also of good thinking, good manners, and good sense. It's the habit of seeing the needs of the reader first, the habit of regarding language as a tool to be manipulated thoughtfully and deliberately. These things cannot be acquired in a few days, particularly when they must replace old habits. The second flaw in the quick-fix strategy has to do with the nature of organizations. Even if the participants in such workshops master good writing skills, they are still confronted by a confusing scene when they try to apply these skills on the job. "Yes, that sounds better, but my boss won't like it, my colleagues won't take me seriously." The people with whom they are communicating—upward, downward, and sideways—may not have received such training. The writer is then still in doubt about how to handle the array of preconceptions about "good" business writing. And he or she may well lapse into the stilted, wordy, bureaucratic style for camouflage.

Another strategy some businesses are adopting is to set a limit on the length of internal writing: one-page memos or short reports. If this forces the writer to weed out extraneous matter, it may be effective. To the extent that it is an artificial limit, however, it may not teach the writer anything about improving the quality of the work. Certainly one page of poor writing is a chore to comprehend, particularly if brevity is achieved through a dense pack of telegraphic prose.

Finally, businesses are making a serious effort to acquire these skills with new hires, especially those headed for managerial functions. They are not only specifying these skills in job announcements, but also putting pressure on undergraduate and graduate business programs to teach them. Some companies even require job applicants to submit writing samples as part of the interview process.

There is no quick and easy solution to the problem of employees who communicate poorly. But it is encouraging that writing is now included under the rubric "people skills," the complement to analytical and quantitative skills. It is important to recognize that the good writer is not a mere wordsmith. He or she is a diplomat as well, sensitive to the uses of the document and secure enough, and able enough, to serve those uses in plain English. Businesses need to ensure that the quality of material they generate is as high as the quantity. The productivity gains in communication technology should allow people timely access to the material they need in readable and even enjoyable form.

Comprehension Questions

Assimilation

1. Business's concern with communication skills has only lately become needed by:
    a.   top management
    b.   public relations
    c.   employees who communicate only with other employees
    d.   employees who communicate with government agencies

2. Those cited in the article who complain about the lack of ability to write clearly and concisely include all the following *except:*
    a.   teachers
    b.   politicians
    c.   big business
    d.   columnists

3. According to the article, the increasing role of television and the decreasing role of reading in students' lives contribute to writing problems because:
    a.   students are less exposed to examples of good writing
    b.   students become more prone to violence
    c.   students have a shorter attention span
    d.   teachers and students watch different television programs and therefore have little basis for communication with each other

4. Why does Rosen include the quotation from "The Spark"?
    a.   It includes an excellent illustration of her point.
    b.   It relates a true historical occurrence that reinforces her point.
    c.   It is an example of clear business writing.
    d.   It is an example of computer jargon in business writing.

5. Computer jargon in day-to-day communication is viewed by the author as:
    a.   false language
    b.   necessary

    c.   easy to read
    d.   dying out

Interpretation

6.   Rosen's style is predominately:
    a.   narrative
    b.   jargonesque
    c.   expository
    d.   technical

7.   Rosen's bias is most likely:
    a.   probusiness
    b.   antibusiness
    c.   progovernment
    d.   antimonopoly

8.   Rosen's tone is:
    a.   cynical
    b.   concerned
    c.   sarcastic
    d.   pessimistic

9.   Rosen's attitude toward "people skills" is most likely that:
    a.   they are just another name for qualitative skills
    b.   they fit best under analytic skills
    c.   they are a current fad but will not last
    d.   they are necessary

Main Idea

10.   The main idea of this article is:
    a.   The problem of poor writing in business has been considerably alleviated by the increasing use of electronic mail systems.
    b.   The solution to poor communication skills in business is neither difficult nor long, but is in fact more simple than people think.
    c.   Good business writing is the result of proper grammar, good organizational skills, and a readable style.
    d.   Concerned by the deterioration of business writing in an era of rapidly expanding communication technology, the business community is acting.

Analysis Questions

1. How have developments in communication technology exacerbated the problem of decline in writing competency in business?

2. What approaches (other than those cited in the article) could business take to solve the problem of poor writing or other communication skills?

3. If you had to explain or defend a point, would you prefer oral or written communication, to speak or to write? Why?

4. How can a word processor make writing and editing easier?

5. How comfortable do you feel about your ability to communicate effectively when you write? What are you doing to enhance your ability and confidence in this vital area?

Exercises

1. Refer back to the passage from "The Spark." Now, try your hand at writing a memo in three different styles: informal, everyday English; stilted, overly formal English; and computer-type jargon.

2. Write a brief letter to your parents in which you tell them you must add one course and drop another. Give your reasons for doing so. Now, rewrite the information as if it were a business memo to your advisor. Which is easier for you to write? Why? Describe the difference between your approaches to the two forms of communication.

The Goal of Undergraduate Education: Can Colleges Serve Adult Students?

Your mom has just announced that she plans to go to college to earn a degree. Your initial reaction may be dismay and disbelief as you are suddenly confronted with the terrible potential inconvenience this may entail for you. Who's going to do the cooking, the cleaning, the running of errands, and all the other things everyone depends on Mom to accomplish. However, once you have recuperated from these most discomforting thoughts, you may begin to ponder the motivation for what seems to you such a rash and atypical decision for a person your mom's age. That decision is not unique. On campuses across America a change is taking place that is viewed by many as a revolution in education. The traditional youth-filled undergraduate classroom is becoming a thing of the past. Patricia Cross notes that whereas until recently most adults on campuses were college employees, middle-aged and even elderly persons are now enrolled in colleges to obtain degrees.[1] These persons, referred to as *mature students,* are usually twenty-

---

[1] Patricia Cross, *Adults as Learners* (San Francisco, Jossey Bass, 1981).

four years of age and over, and have, upon completing their initial cycle of full-time education, spent some years in activities other than education. Some entered the work force immediately after graduation from high school. Others started college but dropped out before getting their degrees. Many women married and raised families.

Although mature students constitute a new population for college classrooms, their arrival has revived an old and unresolved controversy. Just as you may seriously question your mother's motives for attending college, the presence of mature students has caused faculty and administrators to further debate what the purpose of college education should be. There are two sides to the argument. One side claims that a college's only goal should be the training of students' minds through a liberal arts education. The other faction maintains that college should prepare students for the world of work. According to a recent study, this argument flares anew each time a new population is admitted to college. [2]

The long history of this controversy is evidence that there are no easy and clear-cut answers. Any argument forwarded by one side is quickly countered by an equally valid statement from the opponents. Even though the issue never completely subsides, its intensity varies at different times. Here we will consider some of the reasons why the matriculation of mature students has renewed the controversy.

Many colleges are caught in a dilemma. The demographic or societal factors that drive many adults to seek higher education promote the view that college should prepare a person for work or a career. A college that believes its mission is to train minds is tempted not to try to attract a population that wants what it feels college is not intended to provide. If sentiments are so strongly against what mature students want out of college, why do colleges feel they must accommodate this group?

For the first time in American history, there is a larger number of adults than of younger age groups in the population. According to the National Center for Educational Statistics, the United States is becoming a nation dominated by persons in their middle years. There has been a shift from domination by persons under fifteen years of age to domination by those between twenty and thirty-nine. The effect of the high birth rate from

---

[2]Carnegie Council Series, *Mission of the College Curriculum: A Contemporary Review with Suggestions* (San Francisco, Jossey Bass, 1977).

1947 to 1958 is that the individuals born during this baby boom are now between twenty-nine and forty-one years of age and are participating in education. In addition, the educational level of the adult population is higher. Patricia Cross notes the well-substantiated fact that the more education people have, the more they want. As recently as 1940, only half the adults in the United States had completed elementary school. Now the majority of adults in America have completed high school.

Unfortunately for education, the baby boom was followed by a baby bust. Thus, while the number of adults is growing, colleges are faced with a dwindling number of students between seventeen and twenty-one years old. For many colleges, keeping their doors open means attracting adults to participate in education; therefore, they cannot ignore mature students.

But colleges are oriented toward shaping for society the young and inexperienced. Educating or training the mind is seen as the continuation and maintenance of the integrity and excellence of the universities established during the colonial period in America. These early colleges were basically four-year institutions that provided liberal arts instruction. They offered what were thought of as the tools of learning: logic, mathematical skills, languages that cultivated a facility for communication while disciplining thought and reason, and basic principles that could be drawn from what was known about mankind. They believed education should be based on academic disciplines because the great intellectual disciplines not only exemplified ways of thinking, but fostered the moral training and value development needed by the young. However, these opportunities for higher learning were limited to the upper classes, to the children of wealthy and influential families. Free, public education did not yet exist; elementary and secondary education was private and costly.

Colleges began to change when public education became available and more students desired to continue their education after high school. The initial resistance to extending higher education to a larger population decreased when practical subjects such as agriculture and engineering were added to the curriculum. This move raised the floor of minimal learning for more people. In addition, the industrial revolution created a demand for specialists and managers with a higher level of education than that which could be obtained in secondary schools. At this point rewards for having attended college, in terms of greater opportunities and higher salaries, became more widely recognized. The seeds of older adults' desire to attend college were planted during this time, although half a century passed before their wish was granted.

Other events have furthered the changes begun during the industrial revolution. During the 1960s, the inequality between the opportunities available to persons with and without access to a college education resulted in social pressure on institutions to broaden their student bodies to create a more diverse population. This accelerated the trend from elite to mass education. The concept of universal access to college became dominant as education came to be perceived as the equalizer of opportunity. John Gardner claims that a college degree is now regarded as the best means of establishing one's worth and is seen as the key to happiness, self-respect, and increased confidence.[3] Adults who desire socioeconomic mobility for themselves are thus turning to colleges to realize this dream.

In the modern technological world, society expects colleges to prepare individuals for the complex jobs of today and the future. Thus, the American people have assigned high priority to career preparation as a function of college. There has even been a trend toward upgrading occupations by requiring a college degree as a condition of employment, irrespective of the candidate's occupational performance. Students in general, and mature students in particular, are responding to such shifts in manpower demands by seeking out colleges to prepare them for this new situation that has developed in the labor market. According to social critic Ivan Illich, college has become virtually a prerequisite for high attainment in America's eyes: now the only positions available to those without it are jobs classified as unskilled labor. Thus, a college education is firmly associated with upward mobility, market value, and self-esteem.

Older adults are reacting to the situation that exists in the larger society. Do colleges have a responsibility to respond by providing education that is not designed solely to mold the young?

What really underlies the dilemma colleges face in the controversy about liberal arts education versus education for the world of work is what John Gardner has described as unidimensional thinking. Are the two goals of developing the mind and educating for a career mutually exclusive? Earlier it was stated that the mission of the first American colleges was to provide a liberal arts education. In reality, this education was designed to prepare the participants for work. When Harvard and William and Mary first

---

[3]John W. Gardner, *Excellence: Can We Be Equal and Excellent Too?* (New York, Harper and Row, 1961).

opened their doors, their purpose was to prepare young men for the ministry. For this profession a curriculum that consisted of classical studies was appropriate. In today's complex world, other studies have become more appropriate. As the debate continues over what the goal of college education should be, perhaps professors and administrators will begin to consider how their institutions can best help adults meet societal demands through a college experience that is relevant *and* that stretches the mind through excellence.

Comprehension Questions

Assimilation

1. Mature students are defined in the article as:
   a. those who have left their studies and are now returning to school
   b. those students who are over twenty-one
   c. those students who are pursuing their education past the bachelor degree level
   d. those students who are interested in career education rather than the traditional liberal arts courses

2. The *Mission of the College Curriculum* was the subject of a:
   a. Carnegie study
   b. Cornell study
   c. Mellon study
   d. MIT study

3. The reason for the increased number of adults going to college is attributed largely to:
   a. unemployment
   b. demographics
   c. computer technology
   d. divorce

4. The tools of learning taught by early liberal arts colleges included all *except:*
   a. languages
   b. logic
   c. mathematical skills
   d. geography

5. The original purpose of Harvard University was:
   a. to educate the elite

b. to prepare young men for the ministry
c. to provide formal education for the future leaders of our country
d. none of the above

6. The author cites in her article all the following *except:*
   a. John Gardner
   b. Patricia Cross
   c. Andrew Carnegie
   d. Ivan Illich

Interpretation

7. The author's style in her introduction is:
   a. formal
   b. slang
   c. colloquial
   d. none of the above

8. The author's tone is:
   a. satiric
   b. didactic
   c. objective
   d. impatient

9. In examining bias or viewpoint of this article's author, it would be *most* helpful to know her:
   a. educational experience
   b. political affiliations
   c. race
   d. income

Main Idea

10. The main idea of this article is:
    a. College administrators and teachers will face tremendous changes in the years ahead owing mainly to demographics and societal changes in attitudes.
    b. A college education is firmly associated with upward mobility, market value, and self-esteem.
    c. The enrollment of mature students in colleges and universities has revived an old controversy over what should be the role of undergraduate education.

d.   The purpose of higher education in colleges and universities has changed from liberal arts to career preparation, through the influence of mature students.

Analysis Questions

1.   How does the fact that a "college education is firmly associated with upward mobility, market value, and self-esteem" reflect on American culture in the twentieth century?

2.   How do the needs of mature undergraduate students differ from those of other undergraduate students? How are they alike?

3.   What effect will opening the college experience to a more diverse group (age, socioeconomic) have upon our society?

4.   Burris discusses two different goals for college education. What are they? Which goal seems more valid to you? Why? Can they be effectively combined? Should either goal be given priority by administrators?

5.   Why are you in college? Has your purpose changed at all since you matriculated? Comment.

6.   Define *liberal arts education* and discuss the relevance of this term. Are you getting a liberal arts education? Should you be?

Exercises

1.   Make a list of all college courses you have taken or are presently taking. For each one, identify whether it is directly career-related or more to "train the mind." Indicate any overlap.

2.   The introduction focused on the student whose mother is returning to college, that is, the *student's* questions, reactions, and concerns. Rewrite the introduction to focus on the student's *mother's* questions, reactions, and concerns.

"So, What Are You Planning to Be?"

*I*n our society we have considerable help with decision making—advertising directs us to certain products, financial experts advise us as to how to spend and invest money wisely, nutritionists enlighten our understanding of foods. The array of decision-making assistance could continue almost indefinitely.

One area in which many individuals are not assisted is *career* decision making. Somehow we expect that when a person with reasonable intelligence reaches the age of eighteen, a basic education provides preparation for career decision making. Many of today's public high schools do offer career planning in conjunction with vocational education; in these same schools there is probably no hint of the need for career planning associated with the college-preparation study program. The suggestion is that only students contemplating direct entry to the work force need to consider career planning. College-bound students frequently enter the higher-education arena without the tools to make decisions that are important in career choice. For substantiating evidence, consider the number of students in any specific institution who make two or more major curriculum changes.

We all behave as though the three components of age, intelligence, and education yield a "magical" result of career direction through appropriate decision making. But do they? Isn't it curious, then, that on the average, individuals change jobs or careers a minimum of seven times? Equally puzzling is the realization that an estimated 70 percent of the labor market represents individuals professionally engaged in areas for which there has been no formal schooling. It seems that even college graduates find that their degrees are not "magical" decision makers either! I propose that it is appropriate to contemplate the need for investment of time and attention to decision making about careers and the mastery of an effective job search.

This investment could be initiated with a lecture on career development theory—the notion that individuals pursue self-awareness (interest/ability assessment, values clarification, values prioritization, definition of preferred work places, and analysis of functional skills)—before they are ready to engage in the higher-level career development tasks of decision making and launching the job search.

First, let us consider appropriate assessment of abilities and interests. Many college graduates believe that a college degree is the entrée, or "passport," to employment. Yet there is a component that is missing—the student's grasp that within almost *any* degreed area, various sets of skills and interests are advantageous. An example follows.

A degree in health education may involve broad academic preparation, but each student must decide on which subset of skills and interests to focus within the global context:

Degree: Health Education
Job: Operating a health-information program
Useful skill: Administrative and organizational skills

Job: Counseling teenagers at a health clinic
Useful skill: Human relations skills

Job: Writing/disseminating public health information
Useful skill: Technical writing skills

Equally as relevant as the focus on interests and skills is the need for articulation of values. This includes both values clarification and values prioritization. Attention to an honest assessment of values may result in the basis of a sound career decision. The impact of values on career decision making is exemplified in the following actual career counseling case.

A man who had been a successful teacher for eight years decided the money in real estate justified quitting teaching. After a year in real estate, it became clear that real estate held no promise for him. Remember, the reason (value) for the job change was money. This young man then sought counsel in writing a résumé for a job search. When it was explained to him that a résumé is the *final* stage of the job search and that there was work to do before it was written, he expressed impatience. The need to deal with values, interests, and abilities was reiterated. Nevertheless, all he really considered was the résumé and the immersion into the job search.

In a few weeks I received a jubilant telephone call saying that he had landed a job as a manager in a fast-food chain with considerably more pay than he had earned in teaching or real estate. Weeks passed before another contact was made. Now it seemed that inherent in the job was a work schedule that included nights, Sundays, and Saturdays—conflicts were arising in the young man's life. He had *valued* time with church activities and his two young sons, including coaching their teams. With his present job schedule, none of the activities could be pursued.

These were more than mere activities, however: they reflected personal values. When a job is in conflict with personal values, stress is usually the result. Both practical experience and research studies from industrial psychologists reveal this reality. Had this individual given some time and attention to values at the onset, the entire career-planning process would have been illuminated: The result would have been a savings of time and energy, as inappropriate decisions and job switching could have been avoided. It is significant to note here that the young man has returned to teaching.

To some, the focus on planning, assessment, and articulated decision making may appear ponderous and unnecessary. These individuals may identify with the example of the young man wanting only a résumé. Nevertheless, the critical issue is that few individuals are prepared for the job search until the stages of awareness and information have been traveled. One needs only to seek the employer's perspective or to read a list of "most commonly asked interview questions" to realize the need for self-awareness and planning. Interview questions are most often directed to the applicant's grasp of her skills, interests, and goals plus her compatibility with the job description. They are less often concerned with technical issues. If the number one question that employer/interviewers pose is, "What is your objective in applying for this job?" the answer from the applicant had better be more than "the money" or "I need a job." Employers reading résumés are looking more for a sense of what interests and skills an applicant offers than simply a list of degrees and places of employment. Individuals who have not identified their own skills and interests are not prepared to present them credibly to an employer. Job candidates, both young and old, who invest the time and effort to engage in career decision making find a sense of direction and assurance that inspires confidence in the final stage of the career development process—the job search itself.

Because this discussion of career decision making is based on a developmental scheme (that is, level number 1 should be attained before number 2), it should be noted that self- and career awareness are the ideal base for continued decision making. Again, preferably this would occur at the secondary school level, but—almost categorically—it does not. Therefore, when an individual begins the career decision-making process—no matter what the chronological age of the individual—it is imperative to begin with self-awareness.

Career planning provides a sense of direction for the student who is unsure of which academic preparation area, for the graduate who is unsure of career pursuit, for the individual who wishes to redirect his career, and for the adult who has been out of school and the work force and wonders if resumed study and training are necessary. Learn the process! The result will be illuminating and worthwhile. After all, because the average American *does* change jobs seven times, learning the process can be a lifetime asset.

Comprehension Questions

Assimilation

1. According to the author, assistance in making decisions about one's career:
   a. is begun at the junior high or middle school level
   b. is often done in high school only for those planning to go on to college
   c. is often done in high school only for those planning to go to work directly after graduation
   d. is not done at all

2. On the average people change jobs:
   a. nine times
   b. seven times
   c. five times
   d. four times

3. The author refers to self-awareness in all the following areas *except:*
   a. interest and ability assessment
   b. values in retirement planning
   c. values clarification
   d. analysis of fundamental skills

4. The author's case-study example revolves around:
   a. a young man in teaching
   b. an older man near retirement
   c. an older man who is self-employed
   d. a young man who is laid off from his job

5. According to the author, employers give *most* consideration to:
   a. the education of the job applicant
   b. the previous employment record of the job applicant
   c. the "right" degree achieved by the job applicant
   d. the interests and skills of the job applicant

Interpretation

6. The author believes that a significant reason for people changing jobs as often as they do is:
   a. the general switch from industrial jobs to service jobs
   b. that people do not know how to make wise choices in this area
   c. that people are never satisfied with their income level
   d. the continual rises and declines in the economy

7. The person described in the author's case-study example:
   a. left his first job because he was bored
   b. left his first job because of family responsibilities
   c. did not get the job he wanted because of a poor résumé
   d. returned to his original line of work

8. We can infer that the *best* time to do career planning is:
   a. while still in high school
   b. approximately one year after taking your first job
   c. approximately three years after taking your first job
   d. whenever your employer offers seminars or training in this area

9. The author's tone is best described as:
   a. sarcastic
   b. heavy

    c. persuasive

    d. complimentary

Main Idea

10. The main idea of this article is:
    a. Any student in college who is unsure about academic preparation should undergo career planning before making decisions.
    b. Values clarification is the first and most important step in wise career planning.
    c. Choosing the right career has significance that carries over into one's physical and mental health, one's relationships with family and friends, and one's sense of satisfaction and self-worth.
    d. Career planning is as necessary for college-bound or already degreed individuals as for those who plan no college training.

Analysis Questions

1. Define "values clarification." Give examples.

2. What career-planning assistance was available in your high school while you were a student there? What is your opinion of it now? What do you think *should* have been available?

3. What career planning have you done? How has it affected your academic choices and performance to date?

4. The author points out the importance of making an assessment of one's skills, interests, and abilities. Make such an assessment of your own skills, interests, and abilities; then, tell how they have (or have not) influenced your career planning and academic goals and choices.

5. What does the author mean by the word *self-awareness?* Apply this word to yourself.

6. The author makes the following statement: "When a job is in conflict with personal values, stress is usually the result." Explain this statement. Give examples, either real or hypothetical.

7. Has the author convinced you of the necessity of career planning for yourself? Why or why not?

Exercises

1. Make a chart listing all the steps in career planning cited by the author (interest and ability assessment, values clarification, values prioritization, and so on) on one side and then your own responses to these categories on the other side. Describe how such a graphic representation of this information increases your awareness of it.

2. The author described a case study of a man who made poor career choices due to lack of appropriate career planning. Create a hypothetical case study of your own. Write it first from the point of view of a counselor in career planning, following the example in the text; then, write it from the perspective of the individual going through the process. Choose a case in which the individual makes inappropriate choices due to lack of (or poorly carried out) career planning.

3. Follow Exercise 2 with this change: Create a case in which the individual makes appropriate choices due to proper career planning. Trace through all the steps necessary for such career planning.

Change and Continuity in the Lives of American Women

*I*n 1800, the average American woman bore more than seven children during her lifetime. Today, the average woman has two or less. In 1800, a woman's life expectancy at birth was about fifty-five years; today it is about seventy-five. In 1800, the typical woman did not experience independence until she was widowed, for she went directly from living in her parents' house to living with her husband. Today, the vast majority of women live independently of their parents and work for wages prior to their marriages, and many women remain in the labor force throughout their lives, even when they have small children. (The 1980 census showed that over half the mothers of children under six were employed and that only 17 percent of American households consisted of a wage-earner father, a mother "in the home," and children.) The changes in the basic circumstances of women's existence over the past two centuries have thus been vast. What has caused those changes?

Although many factors have influenced women's lives, three stand out as the most important: industrialization, contraception, and economic instability (often caused by war). This essay will briefly examine each in turn.

The industrialization of the United States in the nineteenth century measurably altered women's experiences because the first factories took over work that had traditionally been done by women: the production of cloth. In colonial America, women—especially teenage girls—devoted much of their time to preparing wool and flax, then spinning those fibers into thread and weaving them into cloth. When textile manufacturing establishments were founded in New England in the 1820s, rural women were accordingly freed from an enormously time-consuming task. It was appropriate, then, that the first American industrial labor force was composed of those young rural women who were no longer needed at home to manufacture cloth; they moved into the factories to perform the same function by supervising machines. That early phase of industrialization lasted only until about 1850; after that, immigrant families took the farm girls' places in the factories. But women continued to be affected by industrial expansion because the development of better lighting (first oil, then electric lamps), modern food processing (the tin can, then freezing), more efficient cooking and heating devices, electrification, refrigeration, washing machines, and so forth progressively reduced the amount of time they had to spend on housekeeping chores. That in turn allowed them to spend more time on other things and especially on childrearing.

In the colonial period, a woman's obligations to her children and her household tasks often conflicted with one another. Because she became pregnant, on the average, every two or three years from her marriage until her fertility ended in her mid- or late forties, she was either pregnant or nursing most of her adult life. Indeed, she usually had dependent children in her household until she or her husband died. Given the magnitude of her responsibilities—not merely cloth production, but also cheesemaking, candle and soap making, cooking, baking, cleaning, milking, gardening, food preserving, and even cider making—she had little time for any children over the age of two.

How then were the older children raised? For the most part, they were reared and educated by their older siblings or by their mother's unmarried younger sister, who might live in the household for a time before her own marriage. (There were few schools, public or private, to help with upbringing or education.) Mothers were generally unhappy about their inability to spend time with their older children; the surviving sources show that they loved their youngsters and regretted the many hours they had to devote to household work.

One therefore sees why such women might well have wanted to limit the number of children they bore; with fewer children, they could spend more time with each one and take greater care in childrearing. But no one understood women's menstrual cycles, and the only certain method of contraception known was sexual abstinence. Nineteenth-century Americans tried such means as coitus interruptus (withdrawal), vinegar-soaked sponges inserted in the vagina, prolonged nursing of a previous child, abortion, and other less effective methods. By such means they cut their fertility in half during the course of the century, without access to such modern methods as the diaphragm, the intrauterine device, the pill, or even the condom (which was used in the nineteenth century to prevent the spread of venereal disease, but was not normally used for contraception). By 1900, American women were bearing an average of only 3.5 children each—a dramatic contrast with the figure just 100 years earlier. That such reduction in childbearing was achieved without much contraceptive knowledge is a clear indication of the strength of American women's determination to limit their fertility.

Had it not been for these first two developments—industrialization and contraception—the third, war and economic instability, could not have had the effect it did. For what has happened in the twentieth century is that women, freed from burdensome household tasks and nearly constant pregnancy, have been able to enter the employed labor force when required to do so. When large numbers of men have been away serving in the armed forces, as they were in the two world wars, women have stepped in to fill their jobs in factories. When their husbands have been unemployed (as they were in the 1930s and also in the early 1980s) or underpaid (as black and other minority men traditionally have been), women have gone to work to increase the family income. In addition, the development of coeducational high schools in the late nineteenth century (previously, advanced education had been open only to young men) and of women's and coeducational colleges meant that young women finally received the sort of training they needed to find jobs in the new white-collar sector: as secretaries, nurses, teachers, librarians, and social workers. Although in the first half of the century women tended to drop out of the labor market when they married, more recently they have continued to be employed throughout marriage.

Thus, as was indicated at the outset, the patterns of women's lives have shifted dramatically during the past two centuries. But one might well ask how deep-rooted those changes are, for there are many elements of continuity in women's lives. For example, Americans still believe that a woman's primary responsibility lies in the home, in the care of her husband and children. Even though a majority of American women are in the work force, our society tends to regard them as aberrations, as temporary workers. We do not assume that women should work for wages, as we assume men should. Working women and nonworking men appear to be abnormal. We often ask, Can a *woman* combine marriage and career? But we never ask, Can a *man* successfully combine marriage and career? That could be an important question to consider, since we know many marriages have foundered because of conflicts with a man's job obligations. Yet men are never forced to confront the issue directly; women encounter it constantly. And that at a time when, as we have seen, American women have fewer responsibilities to household and children than they have had at any other time in our history. What, other than tradition, is the reason for arguing that woman's place is in the home, when that home contains two or three children at most (and they are in school much of the time) and a variety of labor-saving devices?

Tradition in the manner of gender roles is extremely strong. It can be seen everyday in television commercials and in newspaper and magazine advertisements that continue to portray women as homemakers and mothers, men as breadwinners. It was clearly evident in the anti-ERA campaign led by Phyllis Schlafly, herself a professional woman with a career, who built a political movement around Americans' fears that the Equal Rights Amendment would bring major changes to traditional gender roles. Among her most effective points, for example, were charges that the ERA would destroy marriages and deprive women of advantages in the event of divorce, and that the ERA would force women to serve in combat in future wars. Both drew on a long history of sex-role divisions to raise questions about an unknown, more sexually egalitarian, future. The hold of traditional gender roles is also illustrated whenever employed women express guilt about not being able to spend more time with their children or not being there when their children come home from school. Why, in such circumstances, should an employed mother feel any more guilty than an employed father? Why is he never the one to express such thoughts? Again, the answer lies in traditional definitions of male and female roles in this country, definitions that have changed little over the past 200 years.

So we are left with a dilemma. Which has been more important: the changing circumstances of women's lives or the unchanging attitudes about women's lives? I leave the answer to you.

Comprehension Questions

Assimilation

1. Norton cites statistics concerning American women's life expectancy, independence, and number of children in order to highlight the fact that their lives have:
   a. changed for the better
   b. changed for the worse
   c. changed
   d. not really changed at all

2. All the following factors of influence on women's lives are cited and discussed by the author *except:*
   a. increased divorce
   b. industrialization
   c. contraception
   d. economic instability

3. From 1800 to 1900, American women's childbearing rate:
   a. decreased slightly
   b. increased slightly
   c. decreased by half
   d. decreased by about one-third

4. What development in the late 1800s led to increased job opportunities for women?
   a. war and recession
   b. discovery of scientific methods of contraception
   c. coeducational high schools and colleges
   d. none of the above

5. American society, according to the author, regards American women in the work force as:
   a. temporary workers

b. deserving of pay equal to that earned by their male counterparts
c. feminists
d. the norm

Interpretation

6. One would expect the author to be:
   a. in favor of the ERA
   b. against the ERA
   c. neutral about the ERA
   d. ignorant of the ERA

7. In making her points, the author effectively uses what technique(s)?
   a. contrast
   b. descriptive enumeration
   c. thought-provoking questions
   d. all the above

8. The author's bias is probably most influenced by her:
   a. sex
   b. occupation
   c. education
   d. family

9. The basic mode of development of the author is to:
   a. employ subtle humor in unexpected places
   b. guide the reader to a prestated conclusion
   c. raise several points and leave the conclusion to the reader
   d. make effective use of individual examples of specific women's viewpoints and situations

Main Idea

10. The main point of the article is:
    a. The lives of American women have changed for the better in the last 200 years.
    b. American women's lives have not changed as much as American men's lives have changed.
    c. The lives of American women have actually changed for the worse in the last 200 years.
    d. American women's lives have changed dramatically since 1800—or have they?

Analysis Questions

1. Norton ends her essay with a question. Is this an effective device? Would a different kind of ending have been more effective?

2. On the basis of this article, do you consider Norton to be feminist? Are you a feminist? Explain your answers.

3. Contrast this history of American women's role in society with that of women of another country or culture.

4. Describe the ERA. What is good about it? What is bad about it? Can there be an objective answer to these questions?

5. How would you answer the question that ends the essay?

Exercise

This essay presents an historical perspective on the role of women in American society. Finish the essay by writing about what should follow—that is, Where do we go from here?

Egalitarian Relationships: The Sex-Role Revolution Begins at Home

*A*s everyone is supposed to know, there has been a sex-role revolution in this country during the past fifteen years. The typical American family with the husband at work and the wife at home with the children is no longer the typical American family. With 46 percent of all married women with children now working outside the home, the "typical" family now represents only 17 percent of all American households. The enrollment of women in the professional schools of law, medicine, and business, which used to be almost exclusively male, is now around 40 percent. And surveys show that women seniors in college have career aspirations that are virtually identical to those of the men, with both sexes now anticipating dual-career marriages.

But the true nature of America's sex-role revolution was conveyed to us most clearly one night when we were dinner guests at the home of a married couple, a sociologist and a social psychologist. While dinner was being prepared and the table set, the husband, the sociologist, gave us an incisive Marxist analysis of the oppression of women throughout history, showing how societal institutions have conspired to keep them in their place. After dinner, while the dishes were being cleared and coffee prepared, he continued, explaining the steps necessary to bring about change. It was a brilliant sociological analysis. We would have liked to have heard a social-psychological perspective on the issue, too, but because of the many dinner-related tasks to be attended to, his wife didn't have time to join our discussion.

And it was at that moment that the true nature of the revolution became clear to us: it has been only half a revolution. The role of women has changed, but not yet the role of men. Accordingly, upper-middle-class women have now joined their blue-collar sisters in holding a job outside the home while retaining their traditional duties inside the home. They have joined their "revolutionary" sisters in the Soviet Union where, after a hard day at work, the wife prepares dinner and gets the kids ready for bed while the husband reads *Pravda*. A dual-career marriage apparently means a marriage in which the wife has two jobs!

Nor is this just a pattern of the older generation. A survey of juniors and seniors in our classes at Cornell reveals that although virtually everybody now believes in equal pay for equal work (100 percent of the women and 90 percent of the men), the sexes still diverge when asked about equal housekeeping duties in the home: 99 percent of the women approve, 81 percent of them strongly; 86 percent of the men approve, but only 46 percent do so strongly. Male support is even softer for equal child-care responsibilities between the partners: 98 percent of the women approve, 78 percent strongly; only 57 percent of the men approve at all, and only 29 percent approve strongly.

Many of our women students appear to assume not only that their careers will proceed like those of the men around them, but that they will proceed with the active support and cooperation of at least one of those men. Our survey suggests that a woman had better administer a question-naire of her own before committing herself to one of those men.

Of course, an increasing number of young people claim to be seeking fully egalitarian relationships. Some of them cite examples such as the following:

> Both my wife and I earned college degrees in our respective disciplines. I
> turned down a superior job offer in Oregon and accepted a slightly less
> desirable position in New York where my wife would have more opportuni-
> ties for part-time work in her specialty. Although I would have preferred to
> live in a suburb, we purchased a home near my wife's job so that she could

have an office at home where she would be when the children returned from school. Because my wife earns a good salary, she can easily afford to pay a housekeeper to do her major household chores. My wife and I share all other tasks around the house equally. For example, she cooks the meals, but I do the laundry for her and help her with many of her household tasks.

Without questioning the happiness of such a marriage or its appropriateness for many couples, we can still legitimately ask if the marriage is, in fact, egalitarian. Have the hidden assumptions about the woman's "natural" role really been eliminated? There is a very simple test. If the marriage is truly egalitarian, then its description should retain the same flavor and tone even if the roles of the husband and wife are reversed:

> Both my husband and I earned college degrees in our respective disciplines. I turned down a superior job offer in Oregon and accepted a slightly less desirable position in New York where my husband would have more opportunities for part-time work in his specialty. Although I would have preferred to live in a suburb, we purchased a home near my husband's job so that he could have an office at home where he would be when the children returned from school. Because my husband earns a good salary, he can easily afford to pay a housekeeper to do his major household chores. My husband and I share all other tasks around the house equally, For example, he cooks the meals, but I do the laundry for him and help him with many of his other household tasks.

Somehow these two marriages sound different, and yet only the pronouns have been changed to protect the powerful. Certainly no one would ever mistake the marriage just described as egalitarian, and it thus becomes apparent that the ideology about woman's "natural" place unconsciously persists even in the thinking of people who believe they have rejected it. It is true that a wife gains some measure of equality when she can have a career of sufficient importance to influence where the couple lives. But why is it the wife who automatically seeks the part-time position? Why is it *her* housekeeper rather than *their* housekeeper? Why *her* household tasks? And so forth throughout the relationship. Such is the subtlety of the hidden assumptions about the woman's role in our society.

A truly egalitarian marriage, of course, would give both partners' careers equal priority, and the division of labor in the home would satisfy what we like to call the "roommate test." The labor would be divided just as it is when two men or two women room together in college or set up an apartment together. Errands and domestic chores are assigned by preference, agreement, flipping a coin, alternated, given to hired help, or—perhaps most often—left undone.

It is curious that today's young people, so many of whom live precisely this way prior to marriage, find this kind of arrangement within marriage so foreign to their thinking. Surely if a white male college student set up an apartment with a black male friend his conscience would not blithely let him assume that the black housemate was to handle all the domestic chores. But change this hypothetical black housemate to a female marriage partner and somehow the student's conscience goes to sleep. At most it is quickly tranquilized by the comforting thought that "she is happiest when she is ironing for her loved one."

Because our survey indicates that there are no longer many happy ironers around, perhaps our male students would also be well advised to administer a questionnaire of their own before selecting a mate. In any case, the current incompatibility between the women's aspirations and the men's expectations cannot be sustained for very long.

Something—someone—will have to give. Perhaps the second half of America's sex-role revolution is coming.

Comprehension Questions

Assimilation

1. According to this article, the proportion of married women (with children) who work outside the home is:
    a. 17 percent
    b. 44 percent
    c. 46 percent
    d. over half

2. A survey among Cornell students revealed that male and female responses differed *most* concerning:
    a. equal pay for equal work
    b. child-care responsibilities
    c. housekeeping responsibilities
    d. decision-making responsibilities

3. The Bems' position is most correctly stated as:
    a. the women's role has changed, but the men's role has not changed

b. the men's role has changed, but the women's role has not changed
c. men and women of the older generation have not changed their roles, but those of the younger generation have changed
d. college-educated men's and women's roles have changed, but noncollege-educated men's and women's roles have not changed

4. The survey among Cornell students revealed that women felt the most strongly positive about:
   a. equal pay for equal work
   b. equal child-care responsibilities
   c. equal housekeeping responsibilities
   d. equal decision-making responsibilities

Interpretation

5. The Bems' inclusion of a man's statement, followed by that same statement with the roles of the husband and wife reversed, is an example of:
   a. descriptive enumeration
   b. compare–contrast
   c. thesis–proof
   d. cumulative narrative

6. The "roommate test" is:
   a. an actual test given to roommates in college to ensure compatibility
   b. an actual test given to college roommates by each other to ensure equal division of responsibility
   c. a hypothetical test conducted by college counselors to measure success in matching roommates
   d. a method of measurement used by the Bems concerning equal division of labor between spouses

7. The Bems believe that when two people marry:
   a. the husband usually assumes that his wife will take care of household chores
   b. the husband and wife share equally in responsibilities of the household
   c. the husband should provide the income, while the wife takes care of the house and children
   d. none of the above

8. The bias of the authors is that they are:
   a. for egalitarian relationships
   b. against egalitarian relationships

    c.   neutral about egalitarian relationships

    d.   for egalitarian relationships, yet believe they will never come about

9.   The Bems would classify which of the following tasks as those being traditionally performed by the wife:

    a.   budgeting and bill paying

    b.   maintaining the car

    c.   taking care of errands

    d.   preparing income taxes

Main Idea

10.   The main idea of this article is:

    a.   The second half of America's sex-role revolution will be harder to achieve than the first half.

    b.   In America today, there is an incompatibility between women's aspirations and men's expectations.

    c.   America has actually experienced only half a sex-role revolution in the past fifteen years; the role of women has changed, but not yet the role of men.

    d.   America's society is still characterized by sexual and racial inequality, but progress is being made.

Analysis Questions

1.   The Bems use subtle sarcasm and humor throughout their essay. Find some instances of this and discuss their effect on you.

2.   The authors make a major point of predicting disillusionment for the married woman of the future. Do you agree with their assessment? Why or why not?

3.   Do you believe in egalitarian relationships as described by the Bems? Has this essay affected your viewpoint on this subject? How? If not, why not?

4.   What experiences have you had that the Bems would have cited as evidence for their thesis? How about the reverse?

5.   The impact of the Bems' viewpoint on your own viewpoint can be most accurately stated as:

    a.   none, because you already agreed

b. none, because you strongly disagreed and still do
c. some, because now your viewpoint is closer to theirs
d. a lot, because you used to disagree, and now you agree

Exercises

1. The authors suggest that women and men should administer questionnaires to prospective mates to determine compatibility of expectations. Draw up such a questionnaire. (You might even try it out on some of your friends and classmates. If you do, how do your results compare with the results obtained by the authors?)

2. Make a list of the various child-raising, housecleaning, cooking, bill-paying, yard-maintenance, and car-related tasks that are performed routinely and often by couples. For each task indicate the following:
    a. Who typically performs this task
    b. Who should perform this task
    c. Which tasks you would choose to perform in a fair arrangement with a mate
    d. Which tasks you think *you* would be expected by a mate to perform

Alternatives to a Deficit Model for American Families and Children

I believe that developments in the structure and position of the American family over the past several decades are about to change direction—slowly, but surely.

I am aware that the evidence is against me, as recent census data clearly show. For example, the age at first marriage has been postponed once more. The increase in households composed of unrelated persons has again taken a marked jump, and not only with respect to members of the opposite sex living together. Also increased is the number of persons living alone—the main demographic change in American society. The decrease in extended families has continued, and the number of children in single-parent families is still increasing. Working mothers are now the majority rather than the minority. And in 1977 the United States became first among industrialized nations in the rate of teenage pregnancy.

These have been the trends roughly since 1948, but they have been accompanied by another, more recent development, about which there are fewer data. I refer to the much-publicized decline in scores on the Scholastic Aptitude Test and the fact that this is not limited to the college-bound: various testing programs have shown the same thing, despite the efforts of our most ingenious statisticians to make it go away.

The most disturbing figures are those on juvenile delinquency. The census has now been forced to include younger age ranges in order to cover the drug traffic, homicide, and, of course, school vandalism and violence. Literally, the handwriting is on the wall.

Yet I say all these things are going to change, going to turn around. What's the basis of this prediction?

Let me first put myself out on a limb and say that I mention the data on young children and the data on families in the same breath because it is my best judgment that there is a lawful relation between all these disruptive trends in the lives of families, on the one hand, and the disarray in the lives of children, on the other. I am implying that there will be a change in what's happening to families that will in turn be reflected in—among other things—higher reading scores on the part of kids.

How can I arrive at such a simplistic answer to such a complex set of phenomena? Let me begin by suggesting that the process of human development can be thought of as a Ping-Pong game between an adult and a young child—joint reciprocal activity between two people who have an irrational attachment to each other. I propose that this is the basic way in which human beings become human. The process has its roots in a biological reality, a period of dependency during which a child learns basic motivation skills. Here the dyad is absolutely fundamental. Therefore, if there has been a breakdown in the functioning of developing human beings, it must somehow reflect a breakdown in that dyad.

Now I begin to become a little less orthodox. I have already indicated that I regard the dyad as a basic structure for human development, but now I suggest that there is an even more fundamental unit than the dyad. Without it, the dyad can't continue: the Ping-Pong game gets fouled up. That unit is a three-person system. For the dyad to function, it has to be validated by some third party. Dyadic interaction between a child and an adult is both rough and rewarding. It is a complicated, highly skilled game, especially tough on grown-ups. You need somebody on the outside who will say, "Hey, hang in there. Give 'em the backhand. Let me spell you for a while." Furthermore, I suggest that three-person systems are important in any setting, not just within the home, but in any setting in which there is a growing human being—and a growing human being is anybody, of any age. There is a functional utility to having three parties involved, so that the two who are engaged in the major action can have the blessing of the third. By "blessing" I mean something to help the relationship along, such as the neighbor who meets you on the street and says, "I saw your son today; what a wonderful young man." In short, a three-person system is important because it enables the dyad to work.

Not only does this principle apply within any setting, such as home, day-care center, or school classroom, but it also applies in relations *between* settings. The evidence is not in, because we do not do those kinds of studies. But I am persuaded that one of the reasons the American school has become a major breeding ground for alienation is because it has been placed outside the community. The only way you can get there is on a bus on which no one is allowed to ride except the kids; and the only adults allowed in school are those with masters' degrees. School is an isolated island.

I'm suggesting that it is difficult for a school to teach these days—not because we do not have dedicated teachers, not because we do not have superb instructional materials, not because we lack or fail to apply excellent principles of teaching and learning—but because school is isolated. What is happening in the school doesn't determine whether a child learns; the existence and nature of interconnections between the school and the other settings in which the child lives its life are what make school worthwhile.

If the classic triad within the home is the mother-father-child triad, what is the analogue in the three settings outside the home? Clearly the family is one. Clearly the day-care center/preschool/school is another. The third, and in my view the most critical in terms of what happens to families and children in this country in the next decade, is the workplace.

Why do I say the workplace? Here, for once, there are some data, coming out of a pilot study we carried out in five countries. We used an interview to identify the sources of stress and support perceived in the environment of families with young children. We simply asked parents what were the circumstances in their lives that made it easy or hard to be the kind of parents they wanted to be. It turned out that the most intensive, but not the most pervasive, was money.

The second and more pervasive source of stress was conditions at work, especially time schedules. "How can I work out a schedule so I can be there when my kid comes home from school?" "I wish I could take sick leave when my child is ill." These are the things parents talked about.

Toward the end of the interview, we asked, "What about you yourself? Is there anything about you as a person that makes it easier or harder for you to be the kind of parent that you want to be?" Interestingly enough, people who described themselves as irritable or tired tended to be the same people who were not able to get satisfactory child-care arrangements.

Conversely, people who liked themselves and their kids were also happy with their child-care arrangements. We can't prove causality from these kinds of associations, but they are suggestive.

I propose that the capacity of any setting to foster human development depends on the degree to which that setting is supported by other settings in the society. When such support is not provided, the original setting begins to squeak and fall apart. I suggest that this is what has been happening in our society—in the case of families, in the case of schools, and in the case of neighborhoods.

How come we have let the social fabric fall apart to this extent? One answer is that we have focused our attention elsewhere. We have been busy doing other things, such as working overtime. Another answer has a longer history. As Alexis de Tocqueville pointed out more than a century ago, we are a very individualistic society. It is hard enough for us to get connected in the family, let alone to connect families with anything else. We are independent. We are a nation of immigrants who were rebels in their homelands, who could not tolerate interference there, and so came here, to "do our own thing," as we say. There is a lot of strength in that, and that's what made our nation great. But there is a point of balance in these matters, and I am suggesting that we have gone beyond that point.

Closely related to the concept of individualism is another American predilection. Locating the sources of problems "out there" is not our way. In our view, fault lies within the individual. If you succeed, congratulations; we knew you had it in you. And if you fail, you didn't have what it takes. Today we have built a whole industry on this principle. We find a learning disability in just about everybody. Even if you don't succeed in finding a learning disability, that's all right, because if the child is not the problem, then it's the parent who is not doing things right. If it is not the parent, then it's the group that has been deprived. In every case the task is to diagnose the problem and then try to correct it. This is the deficit model.

Yet I have said I see a prospect that this will turn around. Where do I get that notion? I get that notion from another observation of Tocqueville: that in addition to being individualists we are also pragmatists. If something doesn't work, we look at facts; then we set ideology aside, and say, "Hey, something's got to be done." To be sure, we often make it only by the skin of our teeth. But there is that pragmatic point when we finally say, "I don't want to do this, but I guess I have to." I believe I see that happening in relation to families. I have a keen sense of this because, for the past two decades, I've tried to get people interested in learning about the family. In recent years, the problem has been reversed: everyone wants to hear about the family. What has happened? In my judgment it's quite simple. We are pragmatists. We see that something isn't working and are prepared to correct the situation.

What can we do? The line of argument I have been developing suggests that the systems that work most dramatically for human development are the informal ones. In a formal system you have to be professional. You can't be irrational. But meeting the needs of children requires an irrational commitment. You've got to say, "This is my kid, and he's the greatest kid," even when he isn't the greatest kid. In fact, it's absolutely essential for the development of the kid. You can't do that if your relationship is professional. You have to have informal systems. There is one around invented some time ago. It's called the family; it's informal and irrational and meets kids' needs very well.

But it isn't enough. You have to have additional informal systems to support that original informal system. Those are called neighborhoods, social networks, connections, songs you sing together. I submit that we, being pragmatists, are discovering the cash value of the irrational, and it's bringing us together and getting us interested in these questions. Remember the statistics are still where I said they were. But I think our pragmatism is finally turning us around—by the skin of our teeth!

For the past dozen years I have been saying things have to get worse before they can get better. My message today is that things have gotten so bad now that we can feel conscience-free to do something about them.

Comprehension Questions

Assimilation

1. The author believes that the position of the American family is:
   a. in a state of complete disarray
   b. about to change direction
   c. improving constantly
   d. hopeless

2. Recent census figures cited in the article refer to all the following *except:*
   a. the increase in number of the children in single-parent families
   b. the increase in number of unemployed families
   c. the increase in number of people living alone
   d. the increase in number of working mothers

3. The process of human development is compared to:
   a. a dance
   b. a custom
   c. a game
   d. a melody

4. The most pervasive form of stress on the family, according to the study cited by the author, is:
   a. money
   b. divorce
   c. working conditions
   d. poor health

5. Bronfenbrenner defines a growing human being as:
   a. preschool-age child
   b. adolescent
   c. anyone under the age of twenty-one
   d. anybody, any age

6. A three-person system is important because:
   a. it replaces the dyad
   b. it enables the dyad to work
   c. it allows a third party to replace the parents
   d. it allows a role for the grandparents

Interpretation

7. The author believes that our attitudes are changing because we are:
   a. practical
   b. knowledgeable
   c. idealistic
   d. imaginative

8. The author's tone is best characterized as:
   a. optimistic
   b. cynical
   c. bleak
   d. angry

9. Bronfenbrenner's bias, as revealed in the article, is profamily and:
   a. antigovernment
   b. pro-games and sports
   c. antipragmatism
   d. pro-support systems

Main Idea

10. The main idea of this article is:
    a. The disruptive individualistic trends in today's society must be changed in order that our culture, as we know it, can endure.
    b. In the case of divorce, the presence of the father or some other third party, such as a relative, friend, or neighbor, is vital in order to support the mother–child dyad.
    c. Although our schools have dedicated teachers, superb instructional materials, excellent principles of teaching and learning, they cannot succeed without interconnectedness between the school and other settings in which the children live out their lives.
    d. The current formal diagnosis–prescription approach to families should be replaced by irrational, total commitment to the child, worked out within the family, with support from outside informal systems including the neighborhood, child-care center, school, and workplace.

Analysis Questions

1. The author names two ways in which excessive individualism has weakened our social fabric. Do you agree? Explain.

2. What is the deficit model?

3. Comment on Bronfenbrenner's views about the family.

4. Do you think Bronfenbrenner's optimistic attitude toward his subject is warranted? Discuss.

5. Consider the questions of paternity leave, child-care centers at places of employment, and government-subsidized child care from Bronfenbrenner's perspective. How about your perspective?

6. Tocqueville considered midnineteenth-century Americans to be both individualistic and pragmatic. What would he say today?

Exercise

Figure 5 is one concept map of this article. Add any points, examples, and connecting lines between ideas that will make the map an even better study tool. Or, if this map is not helpful to *you,* try constructing one of your own.

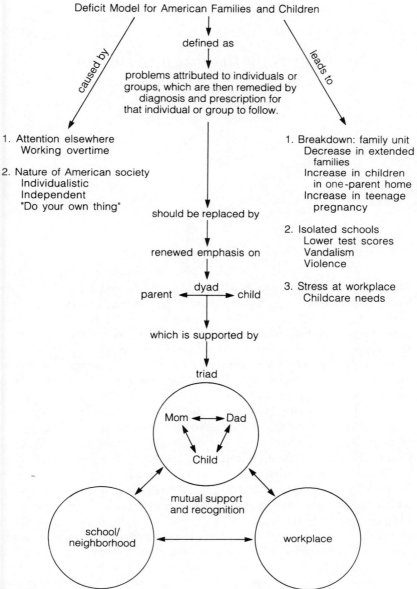

Figure 5.
Concept map of a deficit model for American families and children.

Exorcising the Nuclear Demon

A t the dawn of the nuclear age, Albert Einstein gave us this warning: "The unleashed power of the atom has changed everything save our mode of thinking, and thus we drift toward unparalleled catastrophe." Almost forty years have passed since then, and mankind is closer than ever to fulfilling Einstein's dire prophecy. We have not changed our way of thinking in the least. We still believe that more and better weapons will make us safer. We still picture ourselves at high noon, pitted against the bad guys. Our government even talks about waging a "successful nuclear war."

Today the facts are even more awesome than Einstein could have imagined. The United States and the Soviet Union possess a total of 16,000 strategic nuclear warheads, each one thousands of times more devastating than the bomb dropped on Hiroshima. Strategic weapons are long-range, capable of traveling thousands of miles in minutes. In addition, each superpower has 15,000 to 20,000 tactical (short-range) nuclear weapons, which are not included in disarmament negotiations. Numerous other countries, most of them with considerably less stable governments than that of the USSR, have or are developing nuclear weapons as well. Already capable of building them, for example, are Brazil, Argentina, Israel, and South Africa. Soon to have the capacity are Iraq, Pakistan, and Libya, among others. There is continuous and rising risk that nuclear weapons will fall into the hands of irresponsible leaders or even terrorists.

Comparing the Hiroshima bomb with sophisticated modern systems is like comparing a musket with a machine gun; yet that is our only basis for speculation about what the results of use would mean. Everyone knows what happened at Hiroshima. When the bomb fell, there was a tremendous flash of light, so hot that the eyes of those looking at it were burned in their sockets. Many people were reduced to ashes in the furnace of this flash, which was followed by hurricane-force winds that flattened all buildings for miles around. The blast was followed by a fire storm and finally by darkness, as the mushroom cloud rose 40,000 feet in the air, blotting out the sun. Few doctors were left alive to aid the people with agonizing burns who managed to reach the hospitals left standing, which soon overflowed. As everyone also knows, the explosion was not the end of the devastation. Radiation took its toll weeks, months, and years later.

Megaton means having the explosive force of one million tons of TNT. All the bombs dropped by the United States on Germany and Japan in World War II add up to two megatons. Today, just one of the larger nuclear warheads in the arsenals of the United States and the Soviet Union surpasses that measure ten times, and many warheads can be carried on a single missile. Clearly, a small number of missiles could reduce our cities to rubble. Horrifying as that thought is, however, it is not what worried Einstein.

By "the unleashed power of the atom" he meant the fission and fusion releasing radiation. The invisible particles can travel hundreds of miles carried on the wind and penetrate many thicknesses of material, even steel. A single particle of radiation can damage the nucleus of a living cell, with the result that the cell begins rapidly multiplying. These are the cancers doctors agree can be caused by radiation: cancer of the blood, lung, thyroid, breast, stomach, lymph glands, and bone. A result of numerous nuclear explosions would be the production of nitrous oxide, which would destroy much of the ozone layer, so crops could not grow. In addition, genetic damage and mutations could cause new kinds of diseases and world-wide epidemics. Severe ecological imbalance and drastic changes in climate would take place.

The author now pauses to allow the reader to examine what he or she is thinking and feeling. Very possibly, dear reader, you are about to repress the above information. This numbing is a common phenomenon encountered by supporters of nuclear disarmament. It is extremely difficult for the mind to accept the fact that mankind can destroy the earth, and right now. The paralysis of such repression partially explains why we've done so little to combat the menace of nuclear war. But there are other reasons, some rather sinister. Irrational as it may seem, the fate of the planet has become a political matter.

The military budget in 1980 was about $133 billion; for 1983 the administration's request is $258 billion. Even that figure doesn't include all military costs, some of which are hidden in the funding for other departments, such as the Department of Energy. To give an idea of the magnitude of the sum, federal funding for elementary and secondary education totals $3 billion. So we would do well to look closely at who profits from defense spending.

The Department of Defense contracts with private firms to design and produce armaments systems. Most contracts are not awarded on the basis of competitive bidding, however. They are made exclusively with one of the few giant corporations, such as General Dynamics, McDonnell Douglas, or Lockheed, making it difficult to enforce cost controls. Often the original price estimate for a product is doubled or tripled in the final cost. In turn, the corporations supplying weapons are dependent on the Pentagon for business, creating a common interest: expanding the defense budget. This highly interdependent association between the military and the giant corporations is what President Eisenhower called "the military–industrial complex."

In his last speech before he left office in 1961, Eisenhower warned the American people of the dangers of such an alliance. "This conjunction of an immense military establishment and a large arms industry is new in the American experience," he said. "In the councils of government we must guard against the acquisition of unwarranted influence, whether sought or unsought, by the military–industrial complex. The potential for the disastrous rise of misplaced power exists and will persist." The sounding of such an alarm by a political conservative and a military man should have been heeded. It wasn't. Today the military–industrial complex is firmly entrenched and very, very powerful.

In many ways the economy of the United States has become dependent on military spending. About half our scientists and engineers are employed by the military and related industries, as are millions of other Americans. Corporations that make up the nuclear industry influence politicians through massive lobbying, and politicians compete intensely for defense spending in their districts. This continues in spite of the fact that our economy would prosper better by following the example of countries with very small defense budgets, such as Germany and Japan. With no military spending to speak of, Japan has emerged with one of the most successful of modern economies. In fact, the Japanese have beaten us in many markets. This is partly because their talented scientists and technicians have not been drained off into arms production.

We come now to the specter of Russia. Advocates of the arms race claim we have to produce ever more and better weapons to keep the Russians from infecting the world with communism or reducing us to submission with nuclear blackmail. Let's suppose this simplistic view of the world— good guys and bad guys—is accurate. Suppose the Soviet Union did launch a first strike against us. According to MIT professor Henry Kendall, even if all our land-based missiles were destroyed, and most of our bombers and submarines, the thousands of nuclear warheads remaining would suffice to wipe out every city in Russia. And vice versa. In fact, each superpower has enough weapons already to wipe out the human race. Whether or not the Russians are out to get us, more nuclear weapons won't make any difference.

Conjuring up the specter of Russia, rapacious and evil, is a wondrously effective way to silence calls for arms control. But the greatest enemy of American democracy—of civilization itself—is our own nuclear arsenal and the men who promote it.

Our only hope for a future lies in drastic reductions in the nuclear arsenals of the United States and the Soviet Union. The age-old conviction that the more weapons you have, the stronger you are, dies hard. We aren't so different mentally from the Americans of 1776 or the Europeans of 1200 or even the Romans of 200 B.C. But our technology—our capacity to destroy the whole world—is very new and different. Somehow we must adjust ourselves to this and change our way of thinking. Who knows? The unleashed power of the atom may make war obsolete.

Comprehension Questions

Assimilation

1. Radiation causes cancer by:
   a. traveling great distances
   b. inducing cells to multiply
   c. resulting in severe burns
   d. thickening the ozone layer

2. Strategic nuclear weapons:
   a. are mostly used for chemical warfare
   b. are short-range, able to travel hundreds of miles
   c. are not included in disarmament negotiations
   d. are long-range, able to travel thousands of miles

3. The most difficult obstacle to public outcry against the arms race is:
   a. fear of war
   b. loss of jobs
   c. psychic numbing
   d. reluctance to sound disloyal

4. President Eisenhower warned that:
   a. the military–industrial complex threatens democracy
   b. Americans must fight totalitarianism
   c. our armed forces were in jeopardy
   d. the military–industrial complex is costly

5. Heavy defense spending means that Americans:
   a. maintain their economic leadership
   b. rely on giant corporations for economic strength
   c. have to tighten their belts
   d. lose ground to competitors with small military outlays

6. Picturing Russia as evil is useful for:
   a. competing for Third World markets
   b. silencing protests against the arms race
   c. protecting free enterprise
   d. taking a tough stand on disarmament negotiations

Interpretation

7. The writer of this article would probably prefer:
   a. a freeze on nuclear weapons
   b. international negotiations to limit nuclear weapons
   c. immediate dismantling of most nuclear weapons
   d. development of an antiballistic system

8. A possible benefit of nuclear weapons according to Mattes is that:
   a. arms negotiations will ease tensions
   b. they're so destructive nobody would ever use them
   c. a nuclear war would be over in a very short time
   d. they may make war obsolete

9. The author implies that:
    a. religious people believe in Armageddon
    b. Russia will not be able to compete with free enterprise
    c. private profit is a major reason for American government support of the arms race
    d. Israel will use nuclear weapons in the near future

Main Idea

10. The main idea of this article is:
    a. If we don't change our way of thinking, civilization is likely to be destroyed in a nuclear holocaust.
    b. American democracy is threatened by political corruption.
    c. The more weapons you have, the stronger you are.
    d. The United States and the Soviet Union must negotiate a mutual, verifiable limitation of nuclear weapons.

Analysis Questions

1. How do the author's style and tone contribute to the essay's effectiveness?

2. The element of fear plays a strong role in the issue discussed by the author. In her view, of what should we be afraid? Do you agree? Why or why not?

3. Why has mankind not been able to rid the world of war?

4. Mattes states that "the greatest enemy of American democracy is our own nuclear arsenal and the men who promote it." Assess this statement. What facts confirm it? Deny it?

5. In a democracy, criticism of government is not evidence of disloyalty. Comment, with respect to this essay.

6. How would this topic have been approached by an army general? A school teacher in the Soviet Union? A religious leader? Without reverting to stereotypes, can we really know? Discuss.

7. According to Mattes what is a possible outcome of nuclear weapons?

Exercise

This essay raises several provocative issues. Write a response to at least one of them.

Elective Death and the Hospice Concept

Modern medicine possesses an impressive arsenal of treatments and intervention strategies to protect and preserve human life. Surgery and drug therapy are among the best known intervention strategies and are widely accepted by the public as appropriate. Such intervention is expected in acute non-life-threatening illnesses. Even more powerful technological intervention is expected in situations where life is threatened. The availability of lifesaving equipment, such as the respirator, is critical to emergency rooms and trauma centers around the country. But the successes of our medical technologies have contributed to an expansion of their use, even into areas for which they were not intended. We find increasingly that equipment and techniques designed to save lives in crisis situations are being used to prolong lives in situations where no crisis exists, as in the case of the terminally ill. The effect often is to forestall death rather than to prolong life.

In the case of a terminally ill patient, the use of massive lifesaving interventions must be questioned and the patient's right to choice of treatment respected. This must be so even if the patient's choice is no treatment at all, which amounts to elective death. A distinction may be made between suicide and elective death. Suicide literally means "self-murder" and involves the element of intent; that is, the suicide engages in some activity known to result in death. Often, too, the suicide is a physically healthy person, albeit a despondent one, whose suicidal act itself is a cry for help. Elective death involves the decision by an already dying person not to undergo further medical intervention. The result of exercising this choice is death as the illness progresses through its usual course. In an elective death situation, the patient continues a regimen of pain relief therapy as needed.

The medical model of efficient, objective treatment of illness is particularly unprepared for the patient to exercise the elective death choice. The health care team is trained to save lives and to relieve suffering, often with the aid of technological interventions. Some physicians even maintain the attitude that they must never give up their efforts to cure a patient and that they must fight on the patient's behalf to the very end, using whatever means are necessary. The problem with this attitude is that it can lead merely to a temporary postponement of the dying process, as respiration and circulation are mechanically maintained while consciousness and meaningful existence have ceased.

Delivery of health care is institutionalized through our hospitals, and hospital routine leaves little time to talk to patients about dying. In fact, the effort to maintain a glimmer of hope for the patient's survival often results in a conspiracy of silence in which little is said to the patient about his prognosis, and "awkward" questions from the patient are evaded or ignored.

Yet the information explosion of the last decade has reached patients, future patients, and health care teams alike. Laymen are aware that machines can maintain bodily functions for an indefinite period; ordinary people are concerned about spending their last days in a vegetative state; responsible citizens are increasingly expressing a desire to spare relatives the anguish and cost of a protracted terminal illness; and, importantly, people seem to embrace the notion that for each of us there is a time to die, and that obstructing the inevitable can be distasteful, perhaps even irreverent. As a result, a growing segment of the population is turning away from hospitalization, with its intervention strategies, during their final days, and turning instead to the old notion that family and friends, providing care in familiar surroundings, can be appropriate. Such therapy is embodied by the hospice concept.

Hospice is a program in which care and supportive services are provided to dying patients and their families. Usually an interdisciplinary team works with the dying patient, family, and friends to provide palliative care (medical relief of pain), comfort, and companionship. The patient is aware of his condition and is made as comfortable as possible, but no heroic intervention efforts are used. The hospice patient must have accepted the fact of impending death and elected not to undergo additional curative efforts. Hospice is for patients with weeks or months left to live, not years. The objective of hospice is to make the patient's last days as comfortable as possible. Four basic principles are at work in hospice that serve to distinguish between hospice and hospital:

1. The patient and the family are considered to be the unit of care; the patient alone is the unit of care in hospitals.

2. An interdisciplinary team assesses not only the physical needs of the patient, but also the psychological and spiritual needs of both patient and family; in contrast, hospitals focus treatment on specific illnesses of the patient.

3. Pain and collateral symptoms associated with the terminal illness and its previous treatment are controlled, but no heroic interventions utilized; hospitals intervene routinely.

4. Bereavement follow-up is provided the family to help with their griefwork and emotional suffering; hospitals are not concerned with bereavement follow-up.

Although the hospice concept is not a new one, it certainly represents a major departure from the kind of thinking about death that has contributed to the growth of medical centers and hospitals over the last half-century. It is estimated that over two-thirds of all deaths in the United States occur in hospitals. While much of medical technology has focused on ways to save or prolong lives, hospice eschews medical intervention for the terminally ill. Such a perspective raises many questions, which cut across religious, legal, even scientific boundaries. Is medicine playing God by prolonging life? Do individuals have a right to die, free of medical intervention? What is death and when has it occurred? But perhaps the most fundamental question is whether or not it is right to allow individuals to die when medical technology can keep them alive. Those who choose hospice over other forms of institutional care provide an emphatic answer. To them, length of life is not the only consideration. They recognize that there are costs associated with prolonging the life of the terminally ill which go beyond monetary concerns. They acknowledge that artificial life maintained by extraordinary means offers them nothing. And, importantly, they have elected to be a part of the decision-making process that governs the nature of their final days. In fact, some hospice candidates are apt to challenge the medical profession regarding its role during the terminal period. When there is no chance of surviving the illness, some patients want to be in familiar surroundings, such as at home, and without further medical intervention.

The dilemma is that our society attaches such importance to the sanctity of life that a conflict with individual liberty can develop. Our health care system, like our legal and judicial systems, is based on the fundamental issue of preservation of life. Yet principles of individual liberty give rise to the right to privacy and to informed consent regarding medical treatment. Exercising these rights means that a person can elect to receive no treatment or to receive a form of treatment that will alleviate pain, but not attempt to cure. As unsettling as it may be, the terminally ill patient electing to forgo medical intervention is electing to die. What was once a matter between physician and patient has become a legal issue as well. For example, legal challenges to the notion of elective death may be brought by well-intentioned institutions or individuals. But the right to choose or to refuse treatment seems firmly ingrained in common law. So the real dilemma may be the cognitive dissonance accompanying the knowledge that a person may choose certain death over medical intervention and uncertain life. The growth of hospice programs may serve to reduce such dissonance and accentuate the futility of intervention in many cases, while also emphasizing that patients can maintain a sense of control over their lives even in the terminal phases. Personal care, alleviation of pain, and familiar surroundings can do much to make one's last days more tolerable. As families and institutions become more familiar with hospice programs, we can expect the dissonance generated by the notion of elective death to give way to the humanitarianism engendered by the hospice concept.

Comprehension Questions

Assimilation

1. Hospice is a program that:
   a. allows the patient to choose when to die
   b. provides palliative care, comfort, and companionship

    c.   emphasizes hospitalization over home care for the terminally ill

    d.   helps to make dying easy

2.   Some modern medical technologies are inappropriate for the terminally ill because:

    a.   such equipment was designed to save lives in a crisis, not to prolong the existence of the dying

    b.   health insurance does not cover their use with dying patients

    c.   the terminally ill cannot make reasoned decisions

    d.   doctors can always find a better use for the technology with patients who are not dying

3.   A main objective of hospice is:

    a.   to eliminate hospitalization for cancer patients

    b.   to make the patient's last days as comfortable as possible

    c.   to stop physicians from playing God

    d.   to emphasize the sanctity of life over all else

4.   The conspiracy of silence mentioned in this article refers to:

    a.   the routine by which doctors and nurses communicate with each other

    b.   the fact that a dying patient's physical condition is confidential

    c.   evading or ignoring the patient's questions about his condition

    d.   the withholding of information about the cost of certain medical treatments

5.   Powerful technologically based medical intervention is expected:

    a.   whenever a physician agrees to treat the patient

    b.   for all terminally ill patients

    c.   for non-life-threatening situations

    d.   in critical, emergency room situations

6.   In an elective death situation:

    a.   the wishes of surviving family may overrule those of the patient

    b.   the patient continues a regimen of pain relief therapy

    c.   the patient's vital systems must be mechanically maintained for twenty-four hours

    d.   the physician should not be asked "awkward" questions

Interpretation

7.   One can infer that Collins believes that the real dilemma of elective death is:

    a.   medical

b. legal
c. societal
d. scientific

8. The author's approach to this subject is best characterized as one of:
   a. cynical despair
   b. flippancy
   c. adamant didacticism
   d. reasoned debate

9. This author believes that hospices are:
   a. a humanitarian alternative for terminally ill patients
   b. more cost-effective than hospitals
   c. the closest thing to institutionalized murder
   d. more likely to keep patients alive than hospitals

Main Idea

10. The main point of this article is:
    a. Elective death and suicide differ in name only.
    b. Terminally ill patients have a right to elect the kind of medical treatment they will receive, even if they choose palliative rather than curative care.
    c. Doctors are expected to prevent suicide regardless of the will of the patient.
    d. Terminally ill patients often require massive medical intervention on their behalf.

Analysis Questions

1. The concept of elective death has many ethical, religious, economic, legal, and other implications besides medical. Choose one area and comment.

2. Should hospice programs be financed through medical insurance? Through government assistance? Comment.

3. In such phrases as *sanctity of life*, *quality of life*, and *preservation of life*, the word *life* can be interpreted in different ways. Or can it? Discuss.

4. How do one's own beliefs on this topic influence one's understanding of the author's treatment of it?

Exercise

The author developed his ideas for this article through a basic structure of problem–solution. Identify the problem and the solution. Now, create an outline and write a rough draft for another article on this topic with a developmental structure that is chronological; narrative; question/answer.

LARRY I. PALMER

Understanding the Medical Malpractice Crisis

Malpractice has become a battle-ground for physicians and patients, dominating most of law's interaction with medicine and, allegedly, driving up the overall economic and social costs of health care in the United States. The fear of lawsuits is believed to be the cause of "defensive medicine"—the practice of physicians ordering tests or procedures to protect themselves from potential lawsuits rather than to meet patients' particular health care needs.

Patients and their legal advocates counter with allegations that physicians have been given too much license. They also allege that modern physicians are trained to treat the disease only, rather than the well-being of the "whole person." They argue that the possibility of a lawsuit protects the patient in his interactions with modern medicine and its various practitioners. In their view, malpractice suits are a necessary corrective to physicians overstepping their appropriate social role.

If, however, we were to ask the protagonists in this struggle to define "malpractice," they would probably offer complex models of the way in which law and medicine should *not* interact. Curiously enough, almost all of their examples would focus solely upon the physician–patient relationship. Physicians often assert that law, under the doctrine of informed consent, now requires that a litany of useless information be given to patients. In contrast, patients and their advocates often describe physicians as a self-protective guild, which fails to police incompetence and often uses an authority derived from science to deceive patients through silence or misinformation.

One cause of the confusion about the nature of malpractice is the assumption that the legal doctrine of informed consent actually leads to greater patient decision-making authority and presumably greater patient protection. The difficulty with trying to understand malpractice from this perspective is that it is too narrow. What is needed is a broader perspective that takes account of the social context of modern medical practice and the role of law as it relates to that context.

We need to understand the causes of negligent medical practice to which malpractice rules are responsive. These causes can include a physician's incompetence, the obsolescence of methods or materials, and the inherent risk of new, highly technical and intrusive forms of medicine. Our efforts to understand these and other causes, and to design social systems to prevent them, should be placed within the larger context of economic and social trends affecting the actual practice of modern medicine.

The first of these trends involves governmental efforts to control health care costs through health care planning and incentives provided by Medicare and Medicaid. Although a significant body of data has been collected on the health care system, correlating this data to the alleviation of the medical malpractice crisis has yet to be systematically explored.

The second of these trends is the widespread dissatisfaction with the education of modern physicians and the corresponding call for a more humane approach to patient care and policy issues surrounding health care. Implicit in the public debate about why patients sue physicians for medical malfeasance is the notion that the manner in which modern physicians and their patients interact is responsible for the apparently increasing tendency to resolve disputes through litigation. If this is correct, changing the nature of physician–patient transactions could lead to a decrease in malpractice litigation. Unfortunately, one method of prevention—educational reform—has not been part of the national malpractice debate. Physicians need to know more about the social forces that encourage their patients to sue. Attorneys need to know more about the inherent risks in the complex, highly technical forms of modern medicine.

Physicians who call for a system that would prevent patients from suing them in all but the most blatant instances of negligent care have assumed that a philanthropic vision of their professional roles is sufficient to answer all ethical questions. In so doing, they disregard the transformation of individual conceptions of health, life, and death that occurs in response to cultural changes. Physicians have yet to realize that these changes, caused in part by progress in biomedical research, will require them to make radical alterations in their conceptions of the roles they perform in society. When the physician had just a few modes of intervention, patients were more willing to accept and believe in her as a healer/god. With the advent of new drugs, complex diagnostic techniques, and more sophisticated modes of intervention, patients have shifted their faith to technological tools and no longer treat the physician as someone akin to a religious figure. The malpractice suit, then, is the symptom, rather than the cause, of the problem of discontinuity between physicians' conceptions of their social role and the changing expectations of the society around them. Too often, proposed legal reforms are designed merely to allow physicians to hold onto their philanthropic view of themselves rather than seek a new vision of the modern healer.

A recent set of proposed legislative reforms, designed to stem the rise of physician malpractice insurance premiums in New York State, illustrates how the current legal debate centers on symptoms rather than causes. During the negotiations among the New York Medical Society (representing physicians), the governor, and the legislative leaders, physicians insisted that the legislature limit the amount of damages that patients could recover for "pain and suffering." This proposed legislation was seen as a means of reducing potential damage awards and thus slowing the rise in malpractice premiums. In proposing this limitation, physicians were apparently viewing illness and its consequences from what they considered to be a scientific perspective. They thought it was perfectly reasonable to propose that an objective amount of pain and suffering resulting from any medical misadventure could be determined in advance and thus fixed by the legislature. From their perspective, the jury's authority to assess the amount of pain and suffering in each case appeared irrational and unjust.

In rejecting this particular request, the governor argued that the proposed limitation would be unfair to the victims of medical accidents as compared to victims of other kinds of accidents, which carry no such limitations. For example, the amount of money for pain and suffering that a victim of an automobile accident can receive is set by juries in individual cases rather than by the legislature. Significantly enough, physicians apparently did not realize that their proposed reform, if adopted, implied a wholesale reform of the American legal system of accident litigation.

One key issue that legislatures must face is the possibility of organizational liability rather than individual professional liability. Claims against physicians could be transformed into claims against the hospital for failure to properly supervise physicians. This is particularly true when physicians are using intrusive and innovative treatments, such as artificial heart transplants, which from a broader perspective could be called experimental. In such a legal change, the hospital would be viewed as more representative of the social institution of medicine than the individual physician. In a recent reform, for example, the New York legislature adopted such an approach by requiring hospitals to provide a certain amount of malpractice insurance coverage for physicians who practice in their facilities.

The most profound discovery likely to emerge from legislative examination of ways to reform malpractice is the discontinuity in the way in which we finance health care in the United States. Many of the "large claims" of malpractice involve situations that in other Western countries are covered by either national health insurance programs or other forms of social insurance. This does not suggest that the United States must move toward some form of national insurance. Rather it suggests that our present method of financing health care delivery does not cover the social and economic costs of all cases, including cases of medical misadventure, regardless of whether anyone could be said to be legally at fault.

Allowing patients to recover damages in malpractice litigation, when properly understood, plays a vital role in our attempts to control the practice of modern medicine. There may, however, be aspects of the malpractice system in need of reconstructive surgery if not reform. In considering such reforms, legislatures would do well to shift their focus from the physician–patient relationship to the larger social context, and to assess whether "defensive medicine" is a result of the malpractice system or of other forces.

Comprehension Questions

Assimilation

1. Progress in biomedical research has caused:
   a. patients to have more trust in their physicians

b. physicians to take too many chances
c. increased specialization and thus higher costs
d. patients to have more trust in technology and less in physicians

2. The practice of "defensive medicine" is usually attributed to:
   a. physicians' fear of lawsuits
   b. the new technological advances in medicine
   c. physicians' holistic view of medicine
   d. the influence of recent educational reform

3. As a perspective from which to study malpractice, the legal doctrine of informed consent is:
   a. too narrow
   b. too broad
   c. suitable
   d. never used

4. One way the government has tried to control health care costs is through:
   a. eliminating Medicare
   b. reducing Medicare
   c. health care planning
   d. installing national health care insurance

5. The author states that the cause of the malpractice problem is:
   a. best understood in the changing social context of modern medicine
   b. found in the doctrine of informed consent
   c. due to problems in the physician–patient relationship
   d. due to the lack of a national health insurance program

Interpretation

6. The author's attitude toward a national health program is that:
   a. it is necessary in the United States
   b. it would be a mistake in this country
   c. it is very expensive to install but would result in savings over the long term
   d. it often covers large claims of malpractice in other Western countries

7. The author approaches his topic:
   a. from a historical standpoint
   b. objectively, citing the views of physicians, attorneys, and patients

c. from the point of view of a physician
d. in a light-hearted way

8. The author names and examines two kinds of trends that affect the practice
of modern medicine, as follows:
a. social and economic
b. religious and social
c. economic and educational
d. religious and financial

9. One can infer that the author believes that:
a. malpractice suits are the cause of the problems in modern medicine
b. malpractice suits are totally unnecessary
c. malpractice suits are necessary in some cases
d. malpractice suits will delay medical advancement

Main Idea

10. The main idea of the article is:
a. The key to the malpractice problem will be found in the doctrine of informed consent, rather than in new legislation or large lawsuits.
b. The malpractice problem is just one of many problems between physicians and attorneys, caused by the lack of a national insurance program in the United States.
c. Policymakers will find meaningful solutions to the malpractice problem by considering the larger social trends affecting modern medicine, rather than by simply trying to modify the doctrine of informed consent.
d. It would be unfair to impose restrictions on the amount of damages that patients can recover for "pain and suffering" as a result of an automobile accident.

Analysis Questions

1. The malpractice problem causes much disagreement between physicians and attorneys. Is the article written from the medical perspective or from the legal perspective, or is it perfectly neutral? What evidence do you find in what the author says and in how he says it that supports your answer? Did the author hide his perspective?

2. Should an author hide his own bias or point of view when writing on such a controversial topic, or should he establish it from the start? Support your answer.

3. Who should be responsible for "placing a value on a human life" for insurance purposes? The federal government (if so, what branch or by what means?)? The private sector (if so, which group: Insurance companies? Attorneys? Physicians?)? The individual (if so, who? How?)?

4. What is meant by "informed consent"? Give an illustration.

5. Discuss the causes of negligent medical practice cited by the author (the incompetence of the physician, the obsolescence of the technique or method of treatment, and the inherent risk of new, highly technical and interpretive forms of medicine) plus any other causes you can add. How can society safeguard itself from these situations?

Exercise

Create a hypothetical medical malpractice suit. Write a description of the events in this case first from the physician's point of view, then from the attorney's point of view. Finally, write it as if you were the patient. Describe how the perspective you are using influences what you write and how you write it.

ROBIN ABRAHAMSON MASSON

Washington v. Davis: *The Death Knell for Civil Rights Plaintiffs*

At the close of the October 1975 term, the Burger Court put a formidable obstacle in the path of minorities seeking to challenge racial discrimination by government officials. In *Washington v. Davis,* 426 U.S. 229(1976), the Court announced that in order to sustain a claim that they were denied equal protection, plaintiffs will now have to prove the existence of discriminatory intent. The racially disparate impact of a law or practice that is neutral on its face will no longer shift the burden of proof to the defendants. Rather than standing as the touchstone of invidious discrimination, it is but one of the many factors to be considered in determining the existence of discriminatory intent.

One year later,[1] the effect of *Davis* remains to be seen, but it signals certain defeat for those unable to probe the minds of government officials in an effort to prove their intent and motivation.

---

[1]The material from which this article was taken was written in 1977.

In *Davis v. Washington*, black applicants to the District of Columbia Police Department who had been denied admission because of their failure to pass Test 21 challenged the department's admission procedures as racially discriminatory and violative of the due process clause of the Fifth Amendment. The essence of their claim was that because a higher percentage of blacks than whites failed the test, the test operated to exclude a disproportionate number of blacks from the force. Therefore, plaintiffs argued, the government was obliged to demonstrate that the test was job-related and not a discriminatory device.

The District Court ruled that the plaintiffs' showings (1) that the proportion of black officers was not equal to the proportion of blacks in the community, (2) that a higher percentage of blacks fail the test than whites, and (3) that the test was not validated to establish reliability in measuring job performance, shifted the burden of proof to the defendants. However, it also determined that on the undisputed facts, the defendants had carried their burden and the test was exonerated. In granting the defendants summary judgment, the District Court relied on several factors: (1) since August 1969, 44 percent of all new recruits were black, equaling the proportion of blacks in the fifty-mile radius from which the department recruited; (2) the department had systematically and affirmatively sought to enroll black officers who had passed the test but who had failed to report for duty; (3) the test was a useful indicator of performance in the training school program; (4) the test was not designed to and did not operate to discriminate against otherwise qualified blacks.

Plaintiffs appealed the decision to the Court of Appeals, presenting as the sole issue for review whether the use of Test 21 invidiously discriminated against blacks and hence denied them due process of law in violation of the Fifth Amendment. That court reversed the lower court and granted summary judgment for the plaintiffs.

However, yet another turnabout took place when the case was appealed to the Supreme Court. In *Washington v. Davis*, the Court said that evidence of the racially disparate effect of an official law or act is not sufficient to sustain an equal protection claim. In order to shift the burden of proof to the government, plaintiffs must show that the practice complained of is a purposeful device to discriminate. However, the decision gives future litigants little guidance about what kind of proof will be deemed sufficient to make out a prima facie case. When one looks at the many cases cited by the Court and the language quoted from them, its standards are even less clear:

A purpose to discriminate must be present which may be proven by systematic exclusion of eligible jurymen of the prescribed race or by an unequal application of the law to such an extent as to show intentional discrimination. *Akins v. Texas,* 325 U.S. 398, 403–404 (1945).

A statute, otherwise neutral on its face, must not be applied so as invidiously to discriminate (sic) on the basis of race. *Yick Wo v. Hopkins,* 118 U.S. 356 (1886).

A prima facie case of discriminatory purpose may be proved as well by the absence of Negroes on a particular jury (*Hill v. Texas,* 316 U.S. 400, 404 [1942]), or with racially non-neutral selection procedures.

The important question remains unanswered by the Court: What is necessary to make out a prima facie case? As Justice Stevens observed in his concurring opinion:

The line between discriminatory purpose and discriminatory impact is not nearly as bright . . . as the reader of the Court's opinion might assume. Frequently, the most probative evidence of intent will be objective evidence of *what actually happened* rather than evidence describing the subjective state of mind of the actor. For normally the *actor is presumed to have intended the natural consequences* of his deeds. *This is particularly true in the case of governmental action* which is frequently the product of compromise, of collective decision making, and of mixed motivation. It is unrealistic . . . to require the victim of alleged discrimination to uncover the actual subjective intent of the decision-maker. . . .

Although it is as yet unclear what effects *Davis* will have on future civil rights cases, it is safe to say that the decision bodes ill for victims of official discrimination. The Fourth Circuit, in *Richardson v. McFadden,* 45 U.S.L.W. 2130 (September 14, 1976), the only court thus far to construe *Davis,* held that South Carolina's use of the bar exam and the establishment of a cutoff passing score are sufficiently related to the state's objective of ensuring minimal professional competence and thus do not violate equal protection rights of black applicants who satisfy all requirements for admission to the bar, but fail the bar exam. The court interpreted *Davis* to say that where discriminatory purpose is not shown, it is inappropriate to adopt the more rigorous Title VII standard for the purpose of applying the Fifth and Fourteenth amendments.

In short, the future looks bleak for the prospective civil rights plaintiff. Not only must he hurdle the rational basis test, but now he must offer affirmative proof of discriminatory intent in order to survive a motion for summary judgment. The *Davis* decision has placed a strong barrier in the way of those hoping to rectify past effects of discrimination and prevent its recurrence. There will be few, if any, litigants who will be able to come forward with the kind of evidence *Davis* requires.

Comprehension Questions

Assimilation

1. *Washington v. Davis* went through how many different courts?
   a. one
   b. two
   c. three
   d. four

2. According to the author, the effect of this case:
   a. is bound to be overturned at a higher court
   b. will have a positive effect on discrimination suits
   c. remains to be seen
   d. none of the above

3. The Court of Appeals:
   a. upheld the lower court
   b. upheld the Supreme Court
   c. reversed the lower court
   d. reversed the Supreme Court

4. Test 21 refers to:
   a. voter registration
   b. job application test
   c. registration for the draft
   d. sobriety test

5. The Supreme Court decision gives future litigants:
   a. no hope
   b. detailed guidance
   c. little instruction
   d. great encouragement

6. *Richardson v. McFadden* was a case in:
   a. Circuit Court
   b. City Court

c. Supreme Court
d. County Court

Interpretation

7. The author's attitude in this article indicates she:
    a. does not take the outcome of *Washington v. Davis* seriously
    b. believes the Supreme Court decision will some day be vindicated
    c. clearly disagrees with the Supreme Court decision
    d. is optimistic that litigants will be able to work within the guidelines set down in this case

8. The writer of this article is well versed in:
    a. Circuit Court cases in Washington, D.C.
    b. legal cases of the Warren Burger Court
    c. legal terminology
    d. the many forms of racial discrimination

9. The tone of this article is:
    a. skeptical
    b. tolerant
    c. wry
    d. neutral

Main Idea

10. The main idea of the article is:
    a. In making intent rather than result the means to prove racial discrimination, the courts have put an impossible burden of proof on the plaintiff.
    b. Because it is patently unfair to civil rights litigants, *Washington v. Davis* will one day be overturned or replaced by a more just standard.
    c. The court system must be reevaluated and changed to bring it up to date in the area of racial discrimination.
    d. The weakness of the *Washington v. Davis* case is that it does not assist future civil rights plaintiffs in their fight against discrimination.

Analysis Questions

1. This article was written in 1977. What has happened since then? Was the author correct in her prognosis of a bleak future for prospective civil rights plaintiffs?

2. Does the precedent established by this case still hold? What reasons can you give?

3. How does the author's tone affect her thesis?

4. Comment on the title of this article.

5. What is meant by the phrase *motion for summary judgment?*

Exercise

Can you think of an incident that upset you although it had no direct impact on you personally? Write about that incident and your reaction to it. Include any action you took, if you were able to do so. What was the final outcome?

The Spirit of Law

The profession of law, I believe, abounds with frustration and with exhilaration, with hypocrisy and with idealism, with the most cynical selfishness and with devoted selflessness.

I find that our so-called legal science is nine-tenths sham—a sham that is usually unconscious, but sham nonetheless. I am also persuaded, and firmly persuaded, that the law is by far the greatest of all the professions.

Our legal system has, of course, sprung from the common law and the equity of England. The decided case was on the throne; it ruled, if Parliament did not put it off. But in real life, of course, the decided case cannot rule because it cannot ever recur. No new case can, therefore, be decided by the law of the old case, as theory would have it, but only by analogy to it. The correct questions should be: How close is the analogy? to this case? to that case? How significant are the differences that are so sure to exist? What interests would be served, what interests disserved, by using any particular analogy in deciding?

Here is where the sham began to grow; and it grew; and it flourished mightily. A fundamental quality of human thought, from the most primitive to the most sophisticated, is the tendency to construct abstractions. Sometimes this is a boon; sometimes it spawns arrant nonsense. The physical scientist could test and check his abstractions by experiment.

The legal scientist could not; hence his abstractions became sanctified—turned into sacred legal principles. Every question conceivable, it was thought and taught, could be answered by deduction from the legal principles. Judges never made law; they simply discovered it. It was a perfect, a foolproof system. And this was not so very long ago (as such things go). The Lord Chancellor in *Iolanthe,* only eighty years ago, would have found little dissent among the real chancellors and judges of England when he sang:

> The Law is the true embodiment
> Of everything that's excellent.
> It has no kind of fault or flaw.
> And I, my Lords, embody the Law.

Such nonsense has naturally made our profession vulnerable. It invited other ridicule, more damaging, such as that of Professor Fred Rodell of Yale, who in "Woe unto You, Lawyers," contended that the law is nothing but a successful conspiracy to bamboozle and to milk the laity, and that any judge or lawyer, to justify any decision, need only search a bit for some resounding legal principle (devoid of specific meaning) and then open it like an umbrella to cover himself. And the late Judge Jerome Frank, a less caustic and sweeping critic, called sharp attention to the crudities of our fact-finding machinery and the absurdities of our trial courts in their straitjackets fashioned by customs that are meaningless today.

Flashes of wisdom, giving new insights, can turn too easily into clichés. We grow used to them and think we agree, but do not always digest or absorb them as parts of ourselves. So it is, I think, with my next witness and my best one, Judge Oliver Wendell Holmes's tremendous aphorism: "The life of the law has not been logic; it has been experience." The house of cards of legal logic that Rodell mocks and Frank decries ought to have collapsed when Holmes wrote those words almost 100 years ago. His young genius already saw then what many of us are coming only now really to comprehend.

If, for the argument, you will agree momentarily with me that the law is far from being the systematic, harmonious body of principles that many great judges and lawyers see it to be, is it on that account inferior to other professions? Consider the physical sciences. They are cleaner, so to speak, more free from cant and hypocrisy. In them, you will say, intellect really does reign. Errors are found out and then corrected, not enshrined. Rodell could not make fun effectively of the physical sciences.

Those professions have triumphed, assuredly. They have progressed. They have revolutionized themselves while the law has plodded but a few steps forward. But wait: all that the intellect does is not necessarily good. The rigid logics of the physical sciences, it is true, have worked wonders in the mastery of man's environment in many ways. In their progress they have created the hydrogen bomb and the intercontinental missile; they have developed an incredibly lethal nerve gas; they have nursed and nourished a botulinus toxin so deadly that, like strontium 90, a spoonful would have the power to exterminate every person living on the earth. These are triumphs, surely, but they are gifts to man that men could well do without. In this perspective the blundering illogic of the law suddenly seems more bearable.

I suggest to you that the reason for the law's enormous appeal, in contrast to that of other occupations which may be more strictly intellectual, is that the law has a glorious subject: the peaceful settlement of human disputes. Human disputes were brought down out of the trees by our faraway prehuman ancestors. Just as today, survival was uncertain; there were perils enough without their fighting always among themselves. Truces, we may suppose, were arranged at times, possibly by gestures that antedated language. Peaceful settlements must at times have followed; and at some times these must even have been observed. So, in the dawn, the law was born. Nourished by custom, by token and taboo, by the urge to conform, by punishment, it grew and developed slowly—slowly, so slowly that we can hardly conceive of such immense stagnation. Hundreds of generations, tens of thousands of years, passed without any perceptible change; then some little change was tried, and for some odd reason or another, it was not suppressed.

The emerging law was imperfect and illogical, because human men were imperfect and illogical. They are so, still; behold the powerful figures, for examples, in Washington, Moscow, Paris, London, Havana. The weaknesses of the law are the weaknesses of people. The glories of the law are the glories of people. The law *is* people.

When we despair of the law because it is wanting in logic, we indulge a tendency, quite natural in man, to exalt and idolize man's one unique talent. We forget how feeble an instrument mind in fact is, incompetent to digest or even faintly to conceive of even any one of the four infinities that always embrace us: the infinitely big, the infinitely little, the infinitely complex, and that infinite brevity of the moment we call the present, in which all existence so fleetingly occurs. Indignation over the slightness of the influence of reason should yield to surprise that sometimes it can do so much—this when deep instinctual and emotional urges happen to almost balance.

Beyond logic and beyond reason, I happen to think, there is something more that we can glimpse, and know, at moments. This I will call, for want of a better word, *spirit*. It is an emanation from the life force itself. It has caused all the religious experiences of all the higher religions of all history, and all aesthetics, and all rejoicing of the soul. It transcends logic and often mocks it. It may be the drive for life and love and beauty. This drive for life, illogical, inconsistent, opportunistic at times, is the stuff of law. This drive holds some hope—though no assurance—of changing the ways of settling human disputes to ways without wars. This, as we have seen, is the law's very own subject.

Thus I conclude with one more quotation from a speech by Holmes:

> I think it not improbable that man, like the grub that prepares a chamber for the winged thing it never has seen but is to be—that man may have cosmic destinies that he does not understand. And so beyond the vision of battling races and an impoverished earth I catch a dreaming glimpse of peace.

Comprehension Questions

Assimilation

1. The roots of our legal system, according to this article, are:
   a. English
   b. Irish
   c. Latin
   d. Greek

2. In real life, the "decided case":
   a. cannot rule
   b. provides basis for useful analogy
   c. will never be exactly repeated
   d. all the above

3. *Iolanthe* is:
   a. a musical play
   b. a famous lord chancellor in Elizabethan England

    c.   an unknown judge who influenced the author

    d.   a professor from Yale who criticized the legal system

4.   Acerbic critics of the legal system are best exemplified by:
    a.   Rodell and Holmes
    b.   Holmes and Frank
    c.   Frank and Rodell
    d.   all the above

5.   Judge Holmes describes law as being based on:
    a.   experience
    b.   logic
    c.   intellect
    d.   legal science

6.   The author believes that the law's enormous appeal is its:
    a.   logical basis
    b.   nuances of language
    c.   colorful history
    d.   glorious subject

7.   The spirit of law:
    a.   is grounded in logic
    b.   transcends logic
    c.   redefines logic
    d.   is unknowable

Interpretation

8.   The author is:
    a.   biased in favor of law
    b.   biased against law
    c.   has no discernible bias
    d.   does not care about law

9.   The tone of the article is:
    a.   didactic
    b.   inspirational
    c.   dry
    d.   pessimistic

Main Idea

10. The main idea of the article is:
    a. Today's profession of law is based on English common law and history.
    b. Logic and reason are the cornerstones upon which our legal system is founded.
    c. The profession of law must transcend both reason and logic in its pursuit of peaceful settlement of human dispute.
    d. The physical sciences have produced weapons that can destroy mankind; legal science holds the key to preventing the destruction from taking place in our lifetime.

Analysis Questions

1. Willcox argues that law is based on experience rather than on logic. What evidence confirms his position? Denies it? After considering the evidence, do you agree or disagree with the author?

2. In order to work in a democratic society, the law must engender the respect and compliance of the people. Comment, with reference to Willcox's essay, on this statement.

3. Willcox states that in the name of progress, the physical sciences have produced the capacity for physical destruction of the world. "Progress" in legal science has also, on occasion, led to destructive injustices. What wrongs can you think of that have been produced in the legal system throughout its history? How have they been corrected?

4. What does Willcox mean by the "spirit" of law?

5. Willcox states that the purpose of law is the "peaceful settlement of human disputes." Trace the progress law has made to accomplish this purpose.

6. How has Willcox's bias toward his subject influenced his tone toward it in this essay? Is the result persuasive?

Exercise

Create different titles for this essay. Describe the impact of a title on a reader as the first input he has from the author. What exactly should a title accomplish?

COMPARATIVE ANALYSIS QUESTIONS:
SOCIAL SCIENCES

1. Both Masson and Willcox write on the broad subject of law, yet their articles are more different than alike. For each comparison below, identify which article corresponds to the appropriate term:

Optimistic	Citations of cases	Historical
Pessimistic	Literary allusions	Philosophical

Broad topic	Concrete	Timeliness
Narrow topic	Abstract	Timelessness

2. Rosen and Hendrix each identifies an important tool in business. What are the tools? How is each important? What other skills or areas of knowledge can be effective tools for business?

3. Does Bronfenbrenner's thesis contradict Norton's? Does it contradict the Bems'? Can one agree with both Bronfenbrenner and Norton at the same time? With Bronfenbrenner and the Bems?

4. Norton's field is history; the Bems' field is psychology. How did the respective discipline of each author influence the approach to the topic? (Consider the organization of ideas and the methods used by the authors to make their points.)

5. Grinols and Kahn write about a topic in their field of economics: regulation. Their approaches are different, however, one being a historical definition and the other a topical statement of the status quo. Which is easier to read? Why? Which will still be timely ten years from now? What do you consider to be the purpose each author had in writing his article?

6. Krebs is a professional in the area of international relations; Mattes is not. Does this difference affect their messages and their approaches to or treatments of them? How? How does the topic each writes about matter in terms of credibility? What if each wrote an article about the other's subject? What credibility would each have?

7. Kramnick's discussion of the British system of education points up several differences between it and the American system as discussed by Burris. Identify and discuss some of these differences.

8. How does Bronfenbrenner's triad approach relate to the hospice concept as discussed by Collins?

9. Explain how the Bems and Norton emphasize the importance of the recognition of women's role in society. How do their approaches differ? How are they the same? Which is more effective?

10. How does Boileau's issue of career planning fit into Burris's theme of education for mature students?

11. A theme in the article by Hendrix is the planning needed to successfully market a product: in this case, antiques. Boileau's article can be seen in similar terms: in this case, a person is planning to "market" herself to an employer. Point out the similarities and variations in this analogy. Consider motivation, ultimate goal, the types of planning involved, and so on.

12. For which of the articles below does bias, or point of view, figure heavily? Slightly? Is bias ever irrelevant?

Palmer	Ehrenberg	Collins
Norton	Krebs	Grinols
Masson	Willcox	Boileau

13. Willcox indicates that law's ongoing development is never-ending and that it is constantly getting to more accurately reflect what the people it governs believe to be fair, or just. How does the development of the medical malpractice issue fit into this thesis? Do you think that Palmer would agree or disagree with Willcox's thesis?

14. The main theme of Ehrenberg's article concerned cost/benefit analysis. Define this term as he used it. Then, examine how this term is applicable to the article by Kahn, by Grinols, by Palmer, by Bronfenbrenner, by Hendrix, and by Norton.

15. The social sciences comprise fields of study that are many and diverse. How would you explain the term *social science*? What other fields might have been included in this collection?

PART IV

Humanities

Thinking About Music

Sounds of music pervade modern America. Shoppers, commuters, travelers, workers, joggers, and diners are constantly assaulted by music chosen for its ability to soothe, motivate, or excite. A great industry has grown just to provide these sounds.

And sound it is, for most listeners simply do not understand what they are hearing. Apart from the investment of rather simple symbolism in whatever they hear, millions of listeners just do not comprehend music on its own terms. The average listener may associate a particular piece with a particular event in his/her own experience or, more typically, may relate a genre of music to a style of life—rock and roll to teenagers and adolescent rebellion, jazz to decadent hedonism, classical music to intellectualism, folk music to political causes of the left, hymns to organized religion, country and western music to blue-collar America, and so forth. Sometimes it is enough just to hear a characteristic combination of instruments or a tune to stir up these associations. Musical compositions with words help make these connections too. Purveyors of Muzak and advertising depend on these extremely strong yet simple relationships to carry messages to the consuming public. The advertising industry has taken cues from psychologists to effectively match music to a desired message. From our positions as consumers, then, we need to think about what music is and how it may influence our lives. We may become better informed consumers just by realizing (or guessing) the degree to which music is used to influence our thoughts about a product, a job, an event, or an environment. I think once we begin to realize the power of music in a commercial context, we can begin to appreciate some of the power and value of music in other, noncommercial, contexts. Indeed, having considered music as an environmental factor in our lives, we might be prepared to consider how colors, patterns, architectural features, and other artistic formations affect our thoughts and actions.

Music or, more properly, pieces of music, whether preconceived and performed according to certain specifications (the score in most Western music) or evolving on the spot (improvisation), have their own systems of logic (or antilogic) analogous to literary-linguistic, mathematic-physical, and legal-philosophic thought. Like expressions of other art forms, musical thought may be traditional—that is, related to a continuum of predecessors by application of principles of organization and expression. Or music may be atraditional and defiant or neglectful of traditions. It is both the creation from nothing by one or more individuals *and* an evolutionary-revolutionary event tempered by the cultural milieu from which it arises, even if it challenges that milieu.

Music's internal order (or lack of order) is perceived and can be described without resorting to jargon terms and specialized techniques available only to initiates (musicians). Musicians talk about techniques, structures, methods of construction, performance practices, and theories using specialized words and meanings. This jargon makes the description and teaching of music easier, but may also obscure music from people who do not have control or understanding of the terms and yet still wish to explore or explicate musical ideas for themselves. Thoughtful listening to music, as opposed to just hearing music as Muzak, provides its own rewards, just as careful attention to a painting is more rewarding than merely spending time in front of one.

A musical composition is composed of ideas. Ideas relate to one another in a variety of ways. Some are short, others are long; they have duration. Some are complicated with lots of parts, others are simple without many discernible sub-ideas. They have patterns sometimes but not at other times. Some parts are quiet; some are deafening. Some ideas are played by all simultaneously; others by a variable array of instruments and voices that are part of a larger group. Ideas may change their lengths, patterns, companions, and reciters in the course of a piece of music. Some pieces employ contrasts, both simultaneously and at different times; that is, loud and soft, high and low, slow and fast, differing instruments and voices, and/or a variety of rhythmic groupings may be employed at one time or sequentially. There are also repetitions of ideas; some exact, some not, some with variations, some with additions, some foreshortened, lowered, truncated, or hidden. A lot of music consists of a predominating idea and other ideas that are subordinate. Duration, complication, patterns, variation, loudness, speed, serial or simultaneous combinations are concepts that might as easily be applied to other artistic forms or to other systems of logic (illogic). Notice that nowhere above is used a jargon term such as sonata, anacrusis, or key signature. Just perceiving a piece of music in general terms will help the listener flex his/her analytical skills and, not incidentally, make music more interesting, less a sonic filler. Thoughtful listening does not take an enormous amount of time. It can be accomplished in bits while listening to a piece by selecting an element of the piece and focusing your attention on that element through the entire piece. The next time you hear the same work, focus on another element. This practice will sharpen your listening and provide a repertory of musical understanding useful in interpreting other pieces of music.

There are musical compositions that seem not to be organized in any logical way. Much music written during the last couple of decades seems to flaunt irrational, inexplicable, and un- or antitraditional elements. This flaunting suggests that traditional procedures, ingredients, and principles can be used as foils against which to listen to music. As more music not part of the Western European traditions becomes known and assimilated, more listeners will compare the new and exotic with the more commonplace. Much oriental music is organized on cyclical bases, like very complex clocks with wheels within wheels. Perceiving these cycles or even parts of the cycles (beginning and end, for instance) is a major accomplishment for Western ears, but one that opens up new mental and cultural vistas. Informed listening also provides a person with a richer, more flexible intellect.

This essay began with a short statement on the nature of Muzak and similar sounds provided for involuntary listening. Muzak is a cultural product, or perhaps by-product, since for most it is merely background to prosaic undertakings. Returning to another view of music as an expression of culture brings this essay full circle. Music that exists to serve a function or to accompany, herald, or set apart an event is more common than music written purely for its own sake. In a more rural, less industrial America, folk songs were written, played, and passed on to commemorate great moments, love, death, battles, journeys, fantastic occurrences, and so forth. We now write music for weddings, funerals, ceremonial occasions in an individual's or a group's existence. On these occasions, music is usually a nonessential extra without which the event could become utilitarian, pedestrian, strained, or too common.

For the most part, music is written so that it is accessible to its listeners. Most of what we hear, especially Muzak, is tuneful: we can hum, whistle, or sing the principal element of musical interest—the tune—and usually understand and repeat the text (partly because there are lots of repetitions). Alas, music of this sort is written or arranged, performed, and sold for reasons of profit. While many people enjoy this accessible music—rock, folk, punk, musical comedy, and other types—the reason for writing this kind of music is crass. On the other hand, so-called serious music, that written without much hope of profit making, is generally composed in ways that attempt to break new ground, use new techniques, exploit new sources of sound (from brake drums to computers to natural sounds). Much of this kind of music was and is written to express some sort of esthetic concept, philosophical notion, or poetic ideal; texts are often chosen and set to music in order to heighten the listener's chances of perceiving the intent of the piece. It is important to listen to this music thoughtfully and with as few preconceptions as possible, for this music is as much of our age, our wildly eclectic and permissive age, as is all that commercial-popular music written for profit.

So, to paraphrase the poet, listen well or neglect the music of our sphere. It is certainly not necessary to select one kind of music in preference to another. The real shame in Muzak is that its very consistency allows us to build the unfortunate habit of not listening thoughtfully and thinking about music.

Comprehension Questions

Assimilation

1. Music is not understood by most hearers because:
   a. of the necessity of understanding jargon and specialized techniques
   b. only the musicians themselves can truly understand the music they produce

    c.   only the composers can truly understand what they create

    d.   they do not listen carefully or thoughtfully

2. Musical technical terms cited by the author include:
    a.   sonata and scenario
    b.   duration and sonata
    c.   anacrusis and duration
    d.   key signature and anacrusis

3. Muzak is described as all the following *except:*
    a.   background sound for prosaic undertakings
    b.   a cultural by-product
    c.   tuneful
    d.   crass

4. The author's chief objection to Muzak is in regard to its:
    a.   marketability
    b.   consistency
    c.   dominance by one culture
    d.   lack of structure

5. The author characterizes much oriental music as all the following *except:*
    a.   wildly eclectic
    b.   difficult for Western listeners to perceive
    c.   organized on cyclical bases
    d.   like very complex clocks with wheels within wheels

Interpretation

6. Readers of this article can correctly infer that Keller believes that:
    a.   people should prefer one kind of music over others
    b.   all Muzak and similar "popular" music should be eliminated
    c.   serious music writers today are the only true symbols of our modern eclectic age
    d.   neither musical talent nor expertise is absolutely necessary to gain insights into serious music

7. The author's tone is:
    a.   scientific yet cynical
    b.   wry yet serious
    c.   petulant and accusing
    d.   self-serving

8. The author's style is:
   a. slang
   b. colloquial
   c. informal
   d. formal

9. The author's organizational pattern is:
   a. cumulative narrative
   b. chronological
   c. expository
   d. enumerative

Main Idea

10. The main idea of this article is:
    a. Intelligent listening to music provides new insights and stimulates the imagination.
    b. The vast majority of Americans who listen to popular music should listen instead to the many other forms of music available for their enjoyment.
    c. The mindlessness of Muzak, and its ubiquity in today's culture, has a numbing effect on the hearer.
    d. Like painting, sculpture, and other fine arts, music can be enjoyed by anyone, whether or not he has technical knowledge about the piece.

Analysis Questions

1. Without being talented or trained, how can the average person get the most out of the music she hears? Be specific.

2. Keller states that we should be aware of "what music is and how it may influence our lives." Discuss how music can be "used" by advertisers, dentists, political parties, schools, governments, and other individuals or organizations.

3. Keller indicates that commercial music (rock, folk, punk, new wave) is written for profit, while serious contemporary music, written without hope of profit, is composed in attempts to break new ground. Comment on your perception of the accuracy of this viewpoint.

4. What role does music have in your life? How important is music to you as an individual? As part of a group?

5. Do you listen to music while you study? Comment.

6. What is the author's opinion of Muzak? Do you share it? Explain.

7. Is music a form of communication? Explain.

8. Simply because music is written for profit, is it "crass" or bad? Doesn't any author/composer/artist want to be well-received? Can this translate properly into fame? Into profit?

Exercises

1. Make a list of eight to ten of your favorite songs or pieces of music. For each one, tell why it is a favorite.

2. The author compares listening to music to looking at a painting. In chart form, show what characteristics and properties a musical composition and a painting have in common.

MARTIE W. YOUNG

A Picture Is Worth Ten Thousand Words

Some old proverbs, like certain wines, not only travel well but seem to grow in stature with the passage of time. One such proverb comes to us from China. Of uncertain authorship and age, but of undoubted great antiquity, the proverb says that a picture is worth ten thousand words. As in the case of gunpowder, which the Chinese invented many centuries ago for the harmless purpose of exploding firecrackers, this ancient country has supplied us with something that has taken on a different meaning in the modern world. Today few would argue that, given a choice, most people would indeed rather look at a picture than face a dense block of text. A glance at any recent statistic about the number of television sets in American homes (or in Japanese homes, or homes anywhere in the world almost) would confirm the dominance of the picture in our age.

This fact of modern life may have done much to enrich the coffers of television broadcasters, but it has also sent many of our most venerable newspapers into despair and bankruptcy. The sad condition of our daily printed word was forecast gloomily by a number of writers well over a century ago. In the mid-nineteenth century, for example, the Russian novelist Ivan Turgenev borrowed, perhaps unconsciously, from the ancient Chinese when he had a character in one of his stories say "a picture shows me at a glance what it takes dozens of pages in a book to expound." Turgenev may have been only expressing the frustration many writers feel: it has always been difficult to get people to read rather than look at pictures. But it may be more than mere coincidence that about the time Turgenev was composing his novels, a French painter, Louis Jacques Daguerre, had perfected a technique whereby pictures could be made by a mechanical-chemical process we were later to call photography. Suddenly and swiftly, the age of science had produced a miracle that was to transform dramatically the art of picture making and seemingly make prophetic an ancient Chinese proverb.

Before the invention of photography, picture making was considered the domain of the artist, a being of extraordinary talent, gifted with powers beyond those of normal individuals. From the time the first cave man began scratching images on the rock wall, the idea of representing objects of the real or spiritual world held special fascination for humans. Through trial and error, and with painful slowness, artists eventually perfected a way of depicting the world that was satisfying, even though at times it seemed that the making of pictures could be as tedious and difficult as the writing of ten thousand words.

Photography, on the other hand, made picture making relatively easy. In a few score years after Daguerre proclaimed his invention, it was a tool readily available to those not possessing the perceptive eye and manual dexterity that had distinguished the gifted artist for thousands of years previously. Here suddenly was the means whereby Everyman could become picture maker, as Everyman earlier had become warrior with the discovery that gunpowder could be used to hurl lead at distant enemies. And just as Henry Ford took the internal combustion engine and made it fit an automobile that was within the financial reach of many ordinary persons, thus altering the physical landscape of the world forever, George Eastman developed a lightweight camera and film that could be mass produced like the Model T. And thus was altered the world of the artist forever.

The best artists knew that the new technology had changed things radically, of course, and they reacted quickly to the camera's sudden intrusion into their previously sealed realm. Most welcomed the new developments at first, and a few even embraced photography as a serious medium of artistic expression. But as more and more photographs were produced in the century following Daguerre, the more it became evident that the new technology raised as many questions about, as it supplied answers to, the problem of picture making. The first soundings of disenchantment came in the late nineteenth century when the great French painter and caricaturist Honoré Daumier observed that photography described everything but explained nothing. It was a point many were to agree with, and it still seems relevant today. A photograph of an abandoned gas station on a deserted interstate highway may be graphic and riveting in its descriptive powers, but it informs us of nothing beyond what is immediately before us. Photographs, like all isolated images without context, can be as mysterious and as ambiguous in their meaning as a point of light moving across distant space. In other words, to describe was not enough. What photography did was to call into question the whole idea that accuracy of depiction was the end goal of picture making. What had been so arduously sought by thousands of artists over hundreds of years—a way of capturing the observed world accurately—was now seemingly in easy reach. Ironically, it left the artists bewildered.

What photography did accomplish was something else. Ultimately, photography relieved the artist of the necessity to simply describe and left him with the richer world of explanation. Now that the outward world could be captured by light refracted through a lens onto a coated piece of chemically treated paper, the need for the human hand to transfer the visible onto a flat surface by careful application of paint or some other material was lessened considerably, if not gone completely. The artist was free to redefine his role and become explainer, not describer. In the decades after Daumier's observation, there came in rapid succession a series of artistic movements, whose names we know but whose theories are often jumbled in our minds: Impressionism, Surrealism, Dadaism, Expressionism, to name a few. At their root, each of these movements was responding to the changes wrought by technology. Artists turned inward, looked at the workings of the mind, and concerned themselves with structure and form in art. They were no longer merely picture makers.

Once the element of representation was removed from art, it was only another step to nonrepresentation, or abstraction. Just where and when the first abstract art appeared is a matter of some dispute, but it is not an important issue here. What is clear is that by the end of World War II, in the late 1940s, a movement international in scope but largely centered in New York, dominated the artistic mind. Without realizing it, the abstract artists of the postwar years were readdressing the ancient Chinese proverb, but now words and pictures were fused. The abstract movement was distinguished from previous art movements that reacted to the age of science by the fact that it had at its core a strong literary component. Around such abstract painters as Jackson Pollock and Franz Kline was grouped a number of leading art critics and writers. They were the theoreticians of the abstract movement, the explainers, as it were, of the new picture makers. It was the critic Harold Rosenberg, for example, who coined such phrases as "action painting," and described the abstract expressionists as artists who used the canvas as an arena for action. What was important in the new movement was not the picture, but the process. The large gesture on the canvas, the explosive energy of splashed paint, the elimination of all traditional marks on the surface (meaning representation)—these became the goals of the new picture makers. And in the process they confused and dazed a public still captivated by the older technology of picture making, a public getting its first glimpse of the electronic image in the development of television. And the more recalcitrant the public, the more vehement explainers seemed to become.

By the early 1960s, the abstract artists were moving aside for new developments that came with bewildering speed: Pop Art, Op Art, Minimal Art—new terms were seemingly coined with the regularity of a school semester. One graduating class was followed by another one totally different, each headed by its leading spokesman. Indeed, the seasonal change of art movements after the abstract expressionist period seemed as related to fashions on Fifth Avenue as to anything else recognizable in society. And to give order to this dynamic changing art world came the printed word. Reams of copy were turned out to explain the new trends, the new school, the *new* period. So much writing about art appeared in recent years that it threatened to overwhelm the art itself. As the writer Tom Wolfe declared, in a controversial article a few years ago, the explanations about the art *became* the art—the "painted word" as he termed it. Or to put it another way, one could say that in modern art, ten thousand words is worth a picture.

Comprehension Questions

Assimilation

1. The title of this article comes from a Chinese proverb attributed to:
   a. Confucius
   b. Turgenev

c. Kang Ho
d. none of the above

2. The proverb in the title is compared to all the following *except:*
   a. gunpowder
   b. certain wines
   c. a line in a Russian story
   d. fashions on Fifth Avenue

3. Ivan Turgenev and Louis Jacques Daguerre were:
   a. compatriots
   b. contemporaries
   c. writers
   d. painters

4. A criticism of photography mentioned in the passage is that:
   a. it is only as good as the photographer
   b. it eliminates the aura of mystery from art
   c. it describes everything but explains nothing
   d. it is too graphic and riveting in its descriptive powers

5. The first reaction of most good artists to the introduction of photography was one of:
   a. skepticism
   b. jealousy
   c. enthusiasm
   d. apathy

6. The abstract movement differed from previous art movements owing to its:
   a. strong literary component
   b. immediate acceptance by the public
   c. rejection of photography
   d. emphasis on the picture itself

Interpretation

7. The basic structural pattern employed by the author is:
   a. chronological
   b. descriptive enumeration
   c. problem–solution
   d. spatial

8. The phrase "painted word" refers to:
   a. graphics and other artistic signs
   b. writing about artistic development
   c. photographs touched up with paint
   d. none of the above

9. The author has used all the following modes of development *except:*
   a. quotations and other examples
   b. references to events outside the world of art
   c. vividly detailed analysis of art forms
   d. terse, colorless exposition

Main Idea

10. The main idea of this article is:
    a. An ancient Chinese proverb seems to be tested by developments in modern art in the West.
    b. Photography and abstract art are extremely opposite examples of the forms art can take.
    c. Today's "modern art" is so vague it cannot be understood without written explanation.
    d. Artistic expression takes many forms, including painting, literature, music, and photography.

Analysis Questions

1. Do you consider photography to be a "serious medium of artistic expression"? Discuss.

2. How appropriate is Young's title to this essay? Does he make effective use of it? What title would you suggest?

3. Define *art*.

4. In his chronologic approach to his subject, Young ends with the early 1960s. What artistic developments have emerged since then?

5. How important is it that today's undergraduate college student take a history of art course? Should it be required?

Exercises

1. Make a comparison chart of painting and photography by heading two columns with the two terms and then listing appropriate attributes, advantages and disadvantages, examples, descriptions, and the like under each heading.

2. In the form of a hypothetical debate, write a page or so defending photography as an art form and then another page attacking the idea. Finally, consider: In the process of completing this exercise, how have your own opinions on the position been affected?

RICHARD H. PENNER

The Renovation of Classic Hotels

*A*pproaching the building through the wrought-iron gate on New York's Madison Avenue, one realizes that this hotel is like few others in the world. The stone facades of the landmark Villard Houses, designed by architect Stanford White in 1882, contrast with the ubiquitous steel-and-glass office towers of midtown, and the interiors, glimpsed through the arched windows, show none of the standardization of the newest hotels. Once inside, the visitor is not disappointed. The principal hotel space is the two-story lobby with an elegant two-tiered crystal chandelier and a grand marble staircase leading from the lower floors. The landing features one of the hotel's several tours de force, a stunning fireplace of red Verona marble set between two intricately carved fountains.

Several of the public rooms are equally elegant, replete with original materials and details. The Gold Room, the first owner's music room, is used for breakfast, tea, and evening cocktails, the last two accompanied by musicians playing from the gilded balcony. The ceiling is decorated with exquisite gold-leaf plaster ornamentation, the walls with carved wood panels, and the floor with intricately patterned inlaid marbles. Throughout the hotel, works of the best artists of the last century—Tiffany windows and glassware, La Farge paintings, and Saint-Gaudens sculptures—are set beside the superbly detailed gold-leaf, wood, mosaic, and marble work of the nameless craftsmen of their time.

The Helmsley Palace is remarkable not only because it represents the careful restoration of a landmark building, but also because it is the antithesis of the modern American hotel. During the 1970s, two major design trends developed: the atrium hotel pioneered by Atlanta architect John Portman and the mixed-use project. In the former, introduced by Hyatt Hotels and now extensively copied, a major lobby space, often ten to twenty stories high, is located in the middle of the building, with the guest rooms grouped around it on the upper floors. The guest corridors, actually balconies encircling the lobby, afford the visitor continual views of the activities below in the lobby and restaurants. The mixed-use development, even larger in scale, combines in one megastructure commercial, office, hotel, entertainment, and other functions, to create a dense block of activities. Both these types of developments are in many ways symbolic of the past decade, when bigger was better and when projects competed with each other on the basis of little more than their spectacular size.

Although many of the hotels designed and built in the past twenty years have become classic themselves, their imitators have often lacked grace and distinctive style. In response to the inhuman scale and banality of many of the newer hotels, architects and developers sought other appropriate concepts—ones that would not only be profitable investments but would also provide the community with the best in architectural design. One particularly successful approach is the renovation or restoration of older hotels, run-down or out-dated. There are several compelling reasons why that technique has found favor, from the reduced construction cost and myriad tax benefits to the maintenance of the community's architectural heritage.

During the last century, the existence of a local hotel was evidence of a town's emergence as a commercial center and, as such, was a source of great civic pride. Today, people's pride in their cities is based partly on this business, social, and cultural past, represented, in many respects, by their famous older hotels. Where, only a few years ago, great blocks of buildings would have been summarily torn down, the current interest in landmark preservation has applied pressure on developers to maintain and restore the existing buildings. Frequently, a renovated downtown hotel becomes the centerpiece for urban revitalization efforts. For example, in Philadelphia, the landmark Bellevue-Stratford closed in 1976 soon after the outbreak of

Legionnaires' disease at a hotel convention. For two years all ensuing proposals for the site included the wrecking ball; yet none received city approval. Finally, in 1978, a buyer came forward who intended to restore the hotel to its former grandeur. Thus the largest preservation project ever in that historic city's downtown was begun. But without public pressure, without an abiding interest in the cultural history that the hotel represented, without an appreciation of the architectural qualities that the building offered, the hotel would have been lost.

Usually there is a tension between the more economical and cost-effective design and the one that is more appealing esthetically. But in the renovation of older, classic hotels, the two divergent goals unite; the renovation not only offers the better investment opportunity but also clearly provides a chance to strengthen the architectural richness of a city.

The financial advantages, less obvious than the esthetic, make renovations extremely attractive to the hotel developer. In most cases, the renovation of an existing structure is less expensive than new construction. In addition to the obvious reason—that it uses fewer new building materials—the recycled building can be completed and occupied in less time and so produces earlier revenues and lowers financing costs. No less important, however, are the various tax incentives: laws allow developers an investment tax credit of up to 30 percent of the project costs and permit accelerated depreciation and, in some cases, forgiveness of real estate taxes for a specific period.

While the developer analyzes the economic factors of a project, the future hotel operator studies the market conditions and the demand for a hotel of a particular quality at a specific location. Older hotels frequently are located on the best sites—close to transportation, near office or retail centers, overlooking a historic park—which helps ensure high occupancy. Perhaps less easily quantified is the potential effect on the market of the high-quality spaces found in the older hotel. The high ceilings and oversized rooms, the ornate moldings and crystal chandeliers, the marble floors and paneled boardrooms all assure a competitive advantage over the newer hotels with less sumptuous interiors. When one considers the reduced cost and earlier occupancy, the tax advantages, the central location, the unique building, even the image of the developer as one who conserves the historic environment, there seem to be few reasons to raze a building if it has the qualities and location suitable for renovation.

But the picture is not entirely bright. Older hotels are inefficiently designed, with long corridors and poorly located service areas. They require extensive upgrading, not only to meet more stringent life-safety codes, but also to bring the mechanical, electrical, and plumbing systems up to current standards, to install new elevators and sophisticated fire-protection systems, and to increase the building's insulation and weather-tightness. To make major changes in the planning or layout of an existing building or improvements in its systems and equipment is both more difficult and more costly than installing these in a new structure. In addition to construction problems, some developers may worry that the older hotel does not fully enough suggest the high level of service and amenities they plan. They may also worry that the renovated project—in contrast to their other new hotels—undercuts their efforts to create a uniform marketing image nationwide.

What types of hotels are suitable for renovation? Many that have been successfully renovated are found in such secondary cities as Memphis or Providence. But wherever it is located, the older hotel needs, more than simply a strong site, a building with undeniable character, a hotel that has, in hotelier Alan Tremain's words, "a creative life and style of its own." What does a renovation entail? Much more than a simple cleaning and redecoration. Often the kitchen and restaurants must be relocated to get the dining areas close to the lobby and to the street, where they can, in a visible and easily accessible position, attract not only hotel guests but people from the community. Such changes require complete replanning of the public spaces, redesign of the ventilation and other mechanical systems, and, of course, totally new concepts for the restaurants and lounges themselves.

In addition, the older hotels are notorious for having small guest rooms—originally planned for the price-conscious businessman. Various techniques are common for enlarging these rooms; the most typical is removing the wall between two adjoining rooms and making one room approximately twice as big. For example, the Statler-Hilton in Boston was reduced from 1,200 to 750 rooms mostly by this approach of enlarging the old guest rooms. In addition to replanning, most hotel renovations emphasize major upgrading of the interior materials and furnishings. Often the finishes are stripped away to reveal the original surfaces: the marble floors that had been covered with linoleum or the stained-glass skylight that had been hidden by a suspended ceiling. Many designers take pains to study the original architecture and decoration, assuming that the initial design of these grand hotels reflected the best taste at the time they were built.

Some hotels require less extensive renovation or remodeling because the owners or operators never permitted them to become obsolete or rundown. New York's Plaza and Waldorf-Astoria hotels have been meticulously maintained since their construction sixty years ago and, in fact, each property currently includes in its budget approximately $5 million a year for the continual upgrading of the facilities.

More typical, however, of the renovation trend is a project like the Bellevue-Stratford. Owned and operated by a single family since it was constructed in 1904, the hotel had long since fallen from glory when it closed in 1976. No buyer would touch it; the building was a liability, for the value of the land exceeded the perceived value of the old structure, especially with the twin albatrosses of the outbreak of Legionnaires' disease and a tasteless mid-1950s redecoration. At that time the prominent decorative details—the elegant moldings, the lobby chandeliers, the immense clock, the brass hardware, the oriental carpets—had all been replaced with bland substitutes. The 1978 redesign, which cost $22 million by the time it was complete, was no less than a restoration of the formerly grand public rooms and a modernization of the guest rooms—the latter, though, entirely in keeping with the style of the original hotel.

Similarly, in 1974, developers purchased Los Angeles' Biltmore Hotel, the largest hotel west of Chicago when it was built half a century earlier, but poorly maintained and no longer competitive with the city's best hotels. While the elegant and gracious interiors were completely and painstakingly restored, the architects chose to play off against this background a selection of the most classic modern furnishings. The great lobby, featuring a fantastic carved and painted wood ceiling and a theatrical Spanish grand stair, was decorated with a simple parquet floor, small seating groupings, and simple plantings. Most of the guest bedroom areas, where the original architectural spaces are less grand, were simply decorated in a contemporary style. This juxtaposition of the old and new, this effective contrast of the gracious older spaces with the best in newer furnishings, draws attention equally to both the quality of the original building and the skill of the designers.

Perhaps the best known of the recent proliferation of restored hotels was, in fact, not originally a hotel at all. Instead, the Helmsley Palace, described earlier, was created out of private mansions, with the addition of a new high-rise tower containing the guest rooms. As it happens, the earliest proposals for the project did not include the restoration of the interiors—not protected by the Landmarks Preservation Commission—but only the exterior facades. This plan met with immediate strong and vocal resistance from numerous public interest groups concerned with preserving the historic and architecturally rich character of buildings in their entirety. After several years of hearings, design reviews, compromise, added economic incentives, and, not the least, intense public and media pressure, the developers evolved the revised plan that was eventually effected. The owner admits with some pride, "What started out as a commercial venture ended as a work of art."

These projects point out the variety of ways in which older properties, buildings that a decade ago would have been torn down for renewal projects, can be rehabilitated or restored. The advantages are obvious. How unfortunate that it has taken us so long to recognize the value of our historic architecture, the importance of renewing our inner cities, and the visual benefits that result.

Comprehension Questions

Assimilation

1. The Helmsley Palace is described as an example of:
   a. a typical modern American hotel
   b. the atrium hotel
   c. the mixed-use project
   d. the restoration of a landmark

2. The Bellevue-Stratford Hotel closed in 1976:
   a. following an outbreak of Legionnaires' disease
   b. due to public apathy in its restoration
   c. because its downtown location was no longer appropriate
   d. because the city's commercial interests failed to appreciate the cultural history the hotel represented

3. Advantages to restoration of old hotels include all the following *except:*
   a. the high-quality spaces found in older hotels
   b. location within the city
   c. tax incentives
   d. size of guest rooms can be maintained

4. Disadvantages to restoration of old hotels include all the following *except*:
   a. the kitchen and restaurants usually have to be relocated and completely replanned
   b. restoration is successful only in the largest cities
   c. mechanical, electrical, and plumbing systems are below standard
   d. service areas are often found in inappropriate areas

5. Examples of restored hotels cited by the author include all the following *except*:
   a. the Portman Hyatt Hotel
   b. Los Angeles' Biltmore Hotel
   c. the Statler-Hilton in Boston
   d. the Bellevue-Stratford Hotel

Interpretation

6. The author's structure is basically identified as:
   a. interrogative
   b. how-to
   c. cumulative narrative
   d. chronological

7. The author's belief in the value of restoration of hotels:
   a. is entirely subjective, thus attempts to prove it are irrelevant
   b. causes him to omit consideration of the problems and costs involved in restoration of old hotels
   c. is pointed out through illustrations and opinions rather than by statistics
   d. is a minority opinion, and thus not likely to prevail

8. Penner's bias toward his topic is most likely to be that of:
   a. a scholar
   b. a government specialist
   c. a sculptor
   d. a builder

9. The author's tone in this article is best described as:
   a. diffident
   b. neutral
   c. cynical
   d. enthusiastic

Main Idea

10. The main idea of this article is:
    a. The 1980s have reflected a return to traditional ideas in hotel architecture as well as in other art forms.
    b. It is both emotionally and economically rewarding to renovate, rather than replace, old, classic hotels.
    c. It is necessary to consider each hotel on its own merits when conducting a cost/benefit analysis relating to possible renovation.
    d. Without the strong and vocal support of the public, many old, classic hotels would have been razed rather than restored.

Analysis Questions

1. The author attempts to reconcile preservation of our heritage with making a lot of money. Does he convince you that both interests can successfully coexist? Which points are most persuasive? Least persuasive?

2. What are the advantages to restoring old hotels? Disadvantages?

3. Who should decide which hotels will be restored and which destroyed? Owners? Taxpayers? Federal government? Local government? Architects? Local community members? Discuss.

4. What makes a hotel "classic"? What does that term actually mean?

5. Is the restoration of older buildings (perhaps on your campus or in your home city) something that has interested you previously? If so, how has this essay affected your interest? If not, has this essay aroused your interest? Discuss.

Exercise

The Helmsley Palace was the product of a restoration process described briefly in the article. Penner quotes the owner of the Palace as saying, "What started out as a commercial venture ended as a work of art." Briefly describe what this comment means and relate it to the information about the Helmsley Palace in the article.

ROBERT D. MACDOUGALL AND
BONNIE G. MACDOUGALL

Buildings and Their Meanings

*A*rchitects consider esthetic questions to be the most important and challenging ones of their profession. To be sure, anyone who is in the business of designing buildings must be concerned with technological and functional issues as well. Yet any number of different design solutions have the joint properties of structural soundness and functional adequacy. Among these, some will be judged by informed people to be more correct, elegant, or beautiful solutions than others, and therefore to be better designs.

The new building materials of the past century—particularly glass, steel, and concrete—combined with technological innovations such as high-speed elevators, brought to the cityscape spare "modern" architectural forms that at first shocked the public as capricious and irrational departures from tradition. Designers themselves believe that esthetic decisions are never capricious. They believe that beauty in design is logically derived from a set of underlying principles that is universal and true. These underlying principles relate buildings to some still more general system or order—that is, to some larger scheme. The notion that there is a logical and universal basis for esthetic judgment in architecture is a conviction that has united designers through time and across cultures.

What then makes a beautiful building, and to what kind of more general scheme does it belong? Although designers in any given setting believe they have absolute answers to these questions, inspection of the evidence reveals that standards of beauty and theories about order in architecture are functions of cultural orientation. Indeed, there are as many perspectives on esthetics in architecture as there are cultures on earth.

The technological change experienced by our own society in the last century has created many new options in design and hence has stimulated a variety of opinions on the subject of the sources of beauty in architecture. In traditional India, on the other hand, there has generally been only one opinion. According to South Asian tradition, the gods who created and govern the world revealed the principles of universal order as they apply to buildings through Visvakarma, the god of architecture. The challenge for the traditional designer in India is to emulate the creative example of Visvakarma, who is credited in legend and myth with great architectural works both in the celestial realm and on earth. To this end, the designer must study and master specific design prescriptions that apply to order in houses, temples, palaces, and cities. The rules were written down in ancient times by wise men who were learned enough to comprehend divinely revealed knowledge or, in some cases, as legend has it, by Visvakarma himself.

The core of the traditional Indian theory rests on the assumption that the universe is governed by harmonies that affect order in all things: the movement of the planets, the coming and going of the seasons, the fortunes of men. A building is an intervention in this order and thus a potentially disorganizing influence on the entire system. Beauty in architecture is therefore defined by referring to those principles that the gods revealed to give the works of man a compatible place in the overall order. The greater the degree of compliance with these principles, the better the design.

The conviction that a building must become part of a harmonized whole helps to explain the Indian preoccupation with orienting it in both time and space. According to formulas that vary with the particular circumstances, dwellings, palaces, temples, and other structures must be ordered with respect to the cardinal points. They must be sited so as to avoid invisible cosmic forces that travel in lines. They must be built under compatible astrological conditions. Finally, particulars in the design of ornament and in the proportions and real sizes of interior spaces and apertures are generally derived from an absolute rule.

Ideas about beauty and order in Indian architecture therefore derive from a belief in an ordered universe. As in many other cultures, the theory of order that gives rise to the definition of beauty has a religious dimension in that it relates a seemingly ordinary event of daily life, such as building a house, to cosmic realms and divine origins. The architectural theory is therefore more than a collection of assertions about what is and what is not beautiful and orderly. It relates architectural design to a universal design and therefore provides sound reasons for making esthetic decisions in a particular way.

In the Indian tradition the esthetic particulars are formulated as prescriptions and collected in books that constitute part of a long, established written tradition. Yet the process that infuses an architectural design with more general significance is not dependent on an academic tradition and can be found in societies in which there is no written literature at all.

The Dogon, an African people indigenous to central Mali, have produced a domestic architecture that has been extensively photographed by architects because of its sculptural plasticity. Foreigners find this tradition beautiful and so, very likely, do the Dogon, but perhaps for different reasons. In the Dogon world, a properly designed homestead is one that is organized in an oval pattern. Again, the appropriateness of the solution is derived from a more general model of how the universe is ordered. The Dogon say that the entire universe grew out of a placenta or egg. This pattern now represents the universe on the largest scale. The homestead is also based on this ovoid pattern, and its component parts are further said to represent a copulating deity in his human form. Accordingly, certain parts of the house are said to represent his hands, belly, penis, and so on. A similar conceptual scheme applies to the organization of entire villages. The ideal organization of the dwelling, therefore, is built on a model, in this case frankly anthropomorphic, which unites the image of man with the organization of houses, settlements, and the cosmos as a whole.

These ideas from India and Africa about a total order in which architecture participates are also organizing themes in the Western tradition to which we are heir. In Greek and Roman times, and later during the Renaissance, the design principles were couched in the language of Pythagorean mathematics, which proposed that the fundamental harmonies that ought to be reflected in architectural proportions were united through number. Numerals in this system not only had the property of number, they were associated with qualitative oppositions such as good and evil and with geometrical concepts such as plane, point, and line. Universal rules of order revealed through this system were said to be reflected in the perfectly proportioned human figure that fit, according to a drawing first produced by the Roman architect Vitruvius, into the perfect geometry of a circle. In Renaissance times this mathematical vision of universal order became wedded to a Christian worldview. Contemplation of the perfect proportions of the human figure became a way of comprehending a divinely inspired order that, in turn, was to be translated into architectural form. The churches of the Italian Renaissance for example, were built on a centralized plan in the belief that the circle represented perfection, beauty, and the abstraction of the perfect man created by the all-knowing God.

And now for the "modern" architecture of our own time. The reader may be warily anticipating the revelation of a heretofore unpublicized link between the spare, unornamented idiom that has come to be called the International style and a set of mystical beliefs held by architects. Although the search for universals has not been abandoned, most contemporary architects operate in a secular realm and do not contemplate God. An exception is Paolo Soleri. He has linked a Buck Rogers vision of the city of the future (in one version he would construct crystalline towers containing millions of people) with a personal theology about which he has written independently and extensively. Soleri sees the imposition of a unifying physical order on the city as part of a process in which man evolves to a higher spiritual plane. The culmination of this process is an ultimate order that to Soleri represents God and perfection.

The fantastic dimension in Soleri's work sets him apart from the architectural mainstream of our time. Yet his view of man as an "order maker" and "divinity creator" echoes beliefs held by architects who have been far more influential. The architect Le Corbusier, perhaps the single-most important influence on theory in the twentieth century, saw beauty in architecture as derived from the principles of geometry. He was much impressed by the clear, purposeful design of the machines of the new industrial age, and he imagined that other areas of life and thought would eventually achieve a new precision through the application of geometric principles. Architecture and modern art were two areas he specifically mentioned. Le Corbusier also wrote that geometry was a system *created by ourselves*. Recall that the traditional European view was quite different and saw mathematical regularities as divinely directed. For Le Corbusier, geometry was, instead, our means for creating a material world that *represents* to us perfection and the divine. There are no explicit mythological themes set forth in his work, yet a familiar idiom remains:

Harmony, reigning over all things, regulating all links of our lives, is the spontaneous, indefatigable and tenacious quest of man animated by a single force: the sense of the divine and pursuing one aim: to make a paradise on earth.[1]

And so, modern architecture has now turned to insights from a secular mathematics for that wider understanding of order which has seemed so necessary to designers everywhere and which has enabled them to create architecture in this world that is judged to be so beautiful that it seems to have come from some other.

Comprehension Questions

Assimilation

1. According to the authors, an architect's biggest challenge concerns:
   a. technological problems
   b. cultural considerations
   c. esthetics
   d. functional issues

2. Modern architecture is characterized by:
   a. the importance of astrological conditions
   b. ovoid patterns
   c. emphasis on "the fantastic dimension"
   d. application of geometric principles

3. The South Asian god of architecture is:
   a. Visvakarma
   b. Paolo
   c. Dogon
   d. Hermes

4. The domestic architecture of central Mali is noted for its:
   a. emphasis on the harmonies of invisible cosmic forces
   b. sculptural plasticity
   c. circular motif
   d. lack of ornamentation

---

[1]Quoted from *The Modulor* (Cambridge, Mass.: Harvard University Press, 1954), p. 76.

5. Contemporary architects operate in a context that:
   a. is a return to traditional esthetics
   b. has its basis in mythology
   c. views mathematical conformity as inspired by God
   d. is secular

Interpretation

6. Of prime importance to architects throughout the world, according to the authors, is:
   a. increased understanding of order
   b. knowledge of the myths that permeate architecture
   c. the development of one acceptable standard of esthetics
   d. usage of mathematics in architectural design

7. The authors believe that the reason there are a great many esthetic perspectives in architecture is:
   a. the number of different cultures in the world
   b. widely divergent religious attitudes
   c. the development of new building materials that make new structural forms possible
   d. the constant development of new schools of thought over the years

8. The organization pattern of ideas in this article is best described as:
   a. chronological and enumerative
   b. descriptive and enumerative
   c. spatial and descriptive
   d. interrogative and spatial

9. The tone of the article is:
   a. expository
   b. exuberant
   c. strident
   d. cynical

Main Idea

10. The main idea of this article is:
    a. Buildings are dedicated to gods, but are built for the people who live in them.
    b. True beauty in architecture rests in the appreciation of the builder.

c. A single building style may be considered pleasing to one person or culture, yet displeasing to another.

d. Esthetic judgments in architectural design are functions of cultural orientation.

Analysis Questions

1. The authors describe the architectural themes of several cultures. What (if anything) do they have in common?

2. Do you have a preference for a specific type of architecture? Can you tell why? Would you live in it? Study in it? Work in it?

3. How does function influence form in designing buildings? What buildings on your campus are most conducive to learning owing to their style? Why?

4. If Indian and Dogon architectural designs are based on their respective understanding of order in the universe, and indeed illustrate that order, speculate on what the trend toward glass, steel, and concrete modernity illustrates in our modern culture.

5. Describe what the authors mean by "that wider understanding of order which has seemed so necessary to designers everywhere."

Exercises

1. Visit the library on your campus or a nearby public library. Consider the relationship of form and function. Write a description of the library including your opinion of how its form and function complement (or fail to complement) each other.

2. Do a freewriting exercise on the word "architecture."

What Is Greek Tragedy?

D efinitions of *tragedy* and *the tragic* are essentially unsatisfying, largely because the concept of what is tragic is simply too broad to be exactly defined. But we can define *Greek tragedy,* because it is something specific, a body of thirty-two plays, the noble remnant, left to us by the ravages of time and the destructiveness or indolence of men, of hundreds of plays that were produced at religious festivals in honor of the god Dionysus, in Athens, during the fifth century B.C. We can debate whether to bestow the term tragedy on the plays of Seneca, the sole Roman imitator of the Athenians whose work has survived; or on the Elizabethan imitators of Seneca; or on such plays of Shakespeare as *The Tempest* and *Romeo and Juliet;* on the sociological and psychological dramas of the modern theater of Ibsen, O'Neill, Tennessee Williams, and others. To the body of Greek plays the term tragedy cannot be denied.

This purely external definition—Greek tragedy is the group of Greek plays called tragedies—is what we must start from. Obviously, it does not take us very far. Neither does the word *tragedy* itself, though it does convey one essential, if rather amorphous, message. The word means, literally, "goat song," and that may be interpreted as "song sung by goats," that is, sung by a chorus dressed in costumes imitating the half-animal, half-human attendants of Dionysus called satyrs. That has been the dominant theory in modern speculations about the origin of the genre. But another interpretation has recently gained a strong following: the goat song is sung not by but *for* the goat, the prize for which competing choruses sang and danced. And behind the concept of prize and contest there lies that of sacrifice; the goat is the sacrificial offering, the *pharmakos,* that brings ritual purification and atonement to the community by its death. Both speculations are almost wholly theoretical; evidence from antiquity is meager indeed. But both point to a fundamental element of Greek tragedy: the sacred choral dance and choral song.

Two other items of ancient evidence yield the same emphasis: Aristotle, our earliest scholarly witness to the beginnings of tragedy, tells us in the *Poetics* that tragedy began as a rudimentary dramatization of the dithyramb, a public religious performance consisting of choral singing and dance in honor of Dionysus. Most striking witness of all is the original shape of the Greek theater, no longer visible in most of the ancient theater buildings that have survived, because these were modified during later antiquity from their earliest form: a round dancing place, the orchestra, with an altar sacred to Dionysus at the center. Not a stage, but a place for sacred choral dancing, lies at the heart of the theater of Greek tragedy.

All the plays we now possess, even the earliest of them, from the first half of the fifth century, have a relatively complex form far beyond the choral dance; and in some of the latest of the extant plays, produced toward the end of the century, the chorus has retreated to a subordinate or even a marginal place in the action, and our attention is focused on the actors and on the myth they are enacting. It is not quite always a myth. One surviving tragedy is based not on myth but on history; and that one is, curiously, the earliest we have. Aeschylus's *Persians,* produced in 470 B.C., dramatizes very current history indeed: the battle of Salamis in 480. More exactly, the drama is the reception in the Persian capital of the disaster suffered at Salamis by King Xerxes' fleet. The playwright himself fought in the battle. Even the action of the myths can be very close to contemporary life. In some of the plays written by Euripides during the Peloponnesian War, the brutality and moral chaos of the siege of Troy, as portrayed, for example, in *Hecuba* and *The Trojan Women,* reflect the same intensity of anguish and horror that we find in certain chapters of the account of the Peloponnesian War given by the historian Thucydides. The distinction between myth and history is not, in this respect, essential.

When we consider the general question of just what the action of Greek tragedy is and does, we may find a sharp division between the attitude of the professional scholar and that of the more casual reader.

To those whose acquaintance with Greek tragedy is slight, Greek tragedy often seems rather formulaic, devoted to one of a few well-worn topics: innocent and helpless human beings hounded and brought low by a mysterious and meaningless "fate"; or human *hubris* (usually mistranslated as "pride") suffering its inevitable and therefore rather monotonous fall; or the admirable hero reduced to ruin by a *hamartia,* which is all too often identified with that "one defect" to which Hamlet ascribes the ruin of a man whose "virtues else" are "pure as grace." But Greek concepts of fate are not ours; *hubris* means violence more than it does pride; *hamartia* is not, or not primarily, a moral flaw, but a disastrous mistake; and the Greek tragedies cannot be reduced to easy formulas, no matter how convenient for the extraction of moral truisms this simplification would be. These clichés are the detritus of centuries of efforts by critics to summarize the genre, and like most summaries they are misleading.

Of course, fate and *hubris* and something that can reasonably be called *hamartia* have their places in the tragedies, but they seldom explain any one specific play satisfactorily, and it is difficult to characterize a "typical" Greek tragedy. The scholar, conscious of individual differences, is likely to react in the spirit of Brian Vickers's comment[1] that "once you've seen (or read) one Greek tragedy, you have thirty-one to go." The greater our familiarity grows, the less confidence we have in summing matters up in broad generalizations.

Nevertheless, it is possible to describe some aspects of the plays that characterize their action and their presentation of the human predicament. The play that has most often been described, not without a measure of validity, as a drama of fate is Sophocles' *King Oedipus.* In the traditional myth, which Sophocles inherited from earlier tradition, Oedipus is doomed, from before his birth, to kill his father, Laius king of Thebes, and marry his mother. Yet this predestination is not, on the whole, what Sophocles' play is about. Instead, the playwright keeps the initial emphasis of the play concentrated on the efforts of Oedipus, as king of Thebes, to rid his city of the blight that is destroying it by discovering and banishing Laius's unknown murderer, whose presence is the cause of the blight. Oedipus, who once before saved Thebes from the ravages of the Sphinx, is determined, no matter what the cost, to save Thebes again. Gradually

---

[1] *Towards Greek Tragedy* (London: Longman Group, Ltd., 1973), p. 41.

the emphasis of the play turns from the search for the identity of Laius's murderer to the search for the parentage of Oedipus. But of course, the two discoveries are one, and though our attention becomes riveted more and more on Oedipus himself, we cannot forget that he does, in fact, by his ruin save Thebes, and by self-destruction, symbolized in the play by self-blinding, fulfill his heroic role.

The element of fate is present, of course, but the dramatic power depends largely on a series of ironic contrasts: between the magnificence of Oedipus the king and the pollution and guilt of Oedipus the man; between the keenness of Oedipus's pursuit of his search and the blindness of Oedipus to his own self; between the achievements of heroism and the disaster of human imperfectness; between the omniscience of deity and the ignorance of man. These are what create tragedy in this play, and we cannot even find solace in the thought that it was Oedipus's own fault, except for being human and imperfect and yet reaching for heroic fulfillment. Nor can we say that it was divine jealousy or disapproval. Sophocles has Apollo predict the fate of Oedipus but does not suggest that he imposed it. Sophocles is not, in this play at least, undertaking to answer the riddle of human suffering. It is in the action and the characterization that the greatness of the play lies, not in religious pronouncements or moral instructions. To reduce the play to a drama of fate is to lose the real drama and the real meaning.

Most of the principal characters of Greek tragedy, including Oedipus, are figures of pride. Ancient Greek moral judgment had little use for humility and found in the kingly self-esteem of an Oedipus the quality of *megalopsychia,* "greatness of soul," a quality to be admired, not condemned. *Hubris* is quite another matter; it is related to pride, but violence is in its nature. A tyrant is guilty of *hubris* not by reason of arrogance but when he commits acts of violence that transgress the natural laws of moral conduct. When Agamemnon, in Aeschylus's play of that name, makes his regal entrance as the conqueror of Troy, it is not his pride in what he has achieved that condemns him, but what we learn from his own lips and what the playwright shows us in the theater about the nature of the sack: the sacred shrines of Troy were razed, and, even worse desecration, Cassandra, the sacred virgin priestess of Apollo, comes before our eyes as a part of the spoils of Troy, as Agamemnon's concubine. *That* is *hubris.* But that is far from conveying the whole theme of the play or the trilogy of which it forms a part. In Sophocles' *Antigone,* to King Creon the action of the princess in defying his edict and burying the corpse of her traitor brother is *hubris;* but he is wrong, and before the play is over we know that his violation of human decency in leaving the body to rot is *hubris,* as well as folly.

Aristotle, in the *Poetics,* uses the term *hamartia* to describe the fatal error (or proneness to error; neither Aristotle's usage nor that of other Greek writers permits us to be exact about the nature of the fault expressed by the term in this passage) by which a heroic and high-minded character falls from prosperity into misfortune. Aristotle is a critic we do well to take seriously—he was, after all, closer to these plays than we can be—and since tragic action in which this kind of "reversal" *(peripeteia)* takes place is highly praised by him, it is not unreasonable for critics and readers to have looked for *hamartia* in the tragic heroes of the Greek playwrights. It is not hard to find imperfections, especially in the self-willed and impetuous heroes of Sophocles, and there is no reason to doubt the significance of these imperfections for our understanding of Sophoclean tragedy, whether or not this is really what Aristotle meant in his use of the term. But the usefulness of *hamartia* for the understanding of Greek tragedy has limitations. The concept is wholly irrelevant to Aeschylean drama, and in many of the tragedies of Euripides (whom Aristotle calls "the most tragic of the poets") the search for *hamartia* is quite misleading. When, in *Hippolytus,* the goddess Aphrodite destroys Phaedra by forcing upon her an uncontrollable sexual passion for her stepson, simply in order to take revenge on Hippolytus because he has spurned and rejected her divine influence, the notion of *hamartia* has no place. If we interpret the action literally, divine might enforces its prerogatives without regard for human suffering; if deity in the play is taken symbolically, the conflicting forces that operate within the unfortunate Phaedra are her earnest wish to preserve her conventional virtue as wife of Theseus and, overwhelming this wish, the irresistible and disastrous force of her sexual desire for Theseus's son.

More often than not, Euripides' tragic "heroes" are mainly victims. In *Hecuba,* the queen of Troy, who on a single day first sees her daughter Polyxena led away to be slaughtered by the Greeks as an offering to the shade of Achilles, then is presented with the corpse of her murdered son Polydorus, and finally exacts from his murderer a savage, bestial revenge, stands as a symbol of the anguish and degradation wrought by war. Even in her revenge she loses, pathetically, because she loses her very nature.

Tragic heroes are no longer "heroes": Euripides' Orestes is a cowardly neurotic; his Jason, though behind him lies the glorious legend of the voyage of the *Argo* and the Golden Fleece, becomes a contemptible opportunist who abandons Medea for a marriage connection with the royal house of Corinth. At the end of the play, when Medea has completed her revenge for Jason's infidelity, and children, princess, and king have all met brutal deaths through Medea's cunning and violence, we are left with the two unlovely, decidedly unheroic figures of Jason and Medea wrangling over the dead bodies of their children, before Medea flies off in a magic chariot to escape unscathed from the consequences of her murderous deeds. Jason is to die a fittingly inglorious death, struck on the head by a timber falling from the hull of the rotting *Argo*. There is nothing here that fits any standard mold of heroic tragedy, and yet the tragic action has clear and powerful meaning. There are, moreover, plays of Euripides much farther removed from any conventional pattern of tragedy: *Iphigenia Among the Taurians* is a romantic adventure; *Helen* is high comedy; *Orestes* is close to black comedy.

What we have from ancient Athens is not a monolith that we can measure and neatly assess, but a body of extremely varied poetic dramas, not all of equal power to attract the attention of readers and audiences down through the centuries, but constituting overall the most durable and perennially influential of our artistic heritages from antiquity. What is perhaps the most astonishing fact of all is that the best of the tragedies, including all that have survived, were produced within the span of seventy years in one city, Athens.

Comprehension Questions

Assimilation

1. The thirty-two surviving Greek tragedies were written in honor of:
   a. Athena
   b. Zeus
   c. Dionysus
   d. Seneca

2. The earliest Greek theater included all *except:*
   a. an altar
   b. a stage
   c. a place for choral dancing
   d. none of the above

3. Greek tragedies were based on:
   a. myth

b. history
c. both myth and history
d. neither myth nor history

4. The most correct meaning of the Greek word *hubris* is:
   a. fate
   b. violence
   c. pride
   d. moral flaw

5. The dramatic power of Sophocles' *King Oedipus* is derived mainly from:
   a. the element of fate
   b. the Oedipus complex
   c. the self-blinding of Oedipus
   d. a series of ironic contrasts

6. An attribute prized highly according to ancient Greek moral judgment was:
   a. pride
   b. humility
   c. a sense of humor
   d. wisdom

7. According to the author, one of the most surprising facts about the best of the Greek tragedies is that:
   a. they were written by three men: Sophocles, Aristotle, and Euripides
   b. they were all produced in one city: Athens
   c. they were all produced within a span of fifty years
   d. they were all of nearly equal importance and appeal

Interpretation

8. The title "What Is Greek Tragedy?" is:
   a. appropriate, because the author answers the question in several different ways
   b. inappropriate, because the author never really answers the question
   c. appropriate, because although the author never answers the question, he doesn't intend to: it is a rhetorical question
   d. inappropriate, because the author spends too much time discussing other topics

9. The author's tone is best described as one of:
   a. disgust concerning the action of the characters in the plays
   b. despair over the loss of other plays written during this period

    c.   admiration toward the main characters in the plays

    d.   enthusiasm concerning the durability and influence of the plays

Main Idea

10.   The main idea of this article is:

    a.   The fact that only thirty-two Greek tragedies survive is an irreparable loss to the heritage of mankind.

    b.   The most remarkable contribution of the ancient Greek tragedies is their impact on moral instruction.

    c.   The characters, themes, and plots of Greek tragedy have greatly influenced major writers from Seneca to Shakespeare to Tennessee Williams.

    d.   The thirty-two ancient Greek tragedies that have survived to our day are a remarkably varied group of plays, impossible to sum up in a few generalizations, yet sharing the characteristics of high seriousness of topic and poetic creativeness in execution.

Analysis Questions

1.   Is it helpful to be familiar with the plays Kirkwood mentions in order to understand his essay? Is it necessary?

2.   How does Kirkwood define Greek tragedy? What was *your* perception of Greek tragedy before reading this essay? How has that perception changed?

3.   What examples of *hubris* can you think of in literature other than Greek tragedies? In motion pictures?

4.   Kirkwood is obviously enthusiastic about his subject. Did you find his enthusiasm contagious?

5.   How relevant is the study of classics today? Does relevance matter? What is meant by *relevance?*

Exercise

Make a list of the Greek terms used in this article and their definitions. For each one briefly describe an illustration or example either from the article or from your own invention.

How Johnny Can Write: Thinking About a Composition Theory

*I*n recent years, encouraged by attention to a national writing crisis, teachers of writing have focused on the process of writing itself, defining the sets of skills by which a student completes an assigned writing task. This writing process, is, however, no neat series of discrete steps. To understand the complexity of the process, one need only consider the work that students of writing must accomplish in the course of fulfilling an essay assignment.

Students must shape and develop their ideas to the needs of their audience and to the forms of their particular mode of writing, while generating individual sentences according to linguistic conventions and grammatical norms. They must keep in mind these individual tasks even while the actual process of writing is constantly uncovering to them new dimensions of inquiry that may require them to modify and alter what has already been said or what is being planned.

At the same time, everything students have learned about writing itself and about themselves as writers advances or retards their work, encourages or discourages their task, even as the whole host of associations that the act of writing and the subject of their writing reifies broods over their work or smiles upon it. Writing is nothing less than an activity to which a student brings her entire psychological, sociological, and cognitive history.

In this project, the research into the nature of the writing process can be of considerable importance. Not only does revelation of the multilayered task of writing lay to rest some misconceptions about how good students write (such as that all good writers first organize material into outlines), but it gives us a more accurate basis for learning the actual process of writing. Researchers conclude that this process consists of recursive periods of thinking, writing, and revising, as the writer makes her way through a stage of incubation or "prewriting" to first-draft writing and revision. Recent analysis of process by Linda Flower[1] suggests that in good writers revision consists of transforming the first draft, or "writer-based prose," into writing that is intelligible to readers, or "reader-based prose."

But studies of writing process alone are not enough. They leave unexamined the intellectual content of writing, the structure of ideas a student brings to a writing task. The process is, after all, the molding and shaping of ideas, the refinement and elaboration of them; but the ideas themselves are known to the writer via the organizing principles by which she sees herself and her world.

Before there is a writing process, there is a cognitive process. The work of a writer's process of cognition is to understand the world so it may be written about. The work of writing is to modify that understanding continually as the writing of an essay progresses. If we attach to the conceptualizing of a writing process the conceptualizing of a process of cognition, we can question how these concepts overlap and mutually reinforce, or possibly subvert, each other.

It is not enough, however, to see writing and thinking as simply related. To understand the work of writing an essay we must see more clearly the nature of that relationship, and if possible the degree to which thinking and writing can be understood as separate and distinct from each other. To help understand this distinctiveness, such analysis as the Perry scheme

---

[1]Linda Flower. "Writer-Based Prose: A Cognitive Basis for Problems in Writing," *College English* 41 (Spring 1979), 19–37.

of intellectual and ethical development in college can be useful.[2] The Perry scheme describes the developing world view of students as they are exposed to college-level knowledge across four years of undergraduate life. Based on yearly interviews that charted the intellectual development of eighty-four Harvard undergraduates, Perry evolved a scheme that describes the structure of ideas by which students order and evaluate the content of their university education. The particular contribution of the scale to the teaching of writing is its positing a state of cognition at the outset of the writing process. This state of cognition affects the competence with which a student can complete the task.

An example from Perry's studies helps the argument that a model for teaching writing must, to some degree, accept the separateness of cognition and writing. Since it is the work of this essay to suggest that a particular model of thinking and writing is legitimate, it may be useful to see the distinctiveness of the two activities before we begin to argue for their interrelationship. On page 4 of his book noted above, Perry describes the experience of a student answering an essay question that had been written assuming a cognitive conception of the reality of ideas that this student had not yet grasped. The student was asked to write an essay comparing the concept of the tragic heroine as it is exemplified by Cordelia and Antigone. The student's response, typical of a failure of many students reading the question, compared the characters themselves, failing to see that he was to compare *concepts* of tragic heroines.

Explanations of this student's difficulty that do not take into account how a student structures ideas might suggest that the question had not been read properly, without asking if the question *could* have been read properly, or might ask if class notes had been taken down, without asking if they *could* have been taken down properly—given the limitations of the student's ability to understand. Nor does Perry equate this failure with level of intelligence, saying that successive academic performances by such students belie assuming the problem is caused by a failure in intelligence.

If we accept Perry's scheme as a description of cognitive awareness of the world of ideas, we must consider, as Perry does, whether the very idea

---

[2]William G. Perry, Jr. *Forms of Intellectual and Ethical Development in the College Years: A Scheme* (New York: Holt, Rinehart and Winston, 1970).

of legitimate alternative constructs to explain a single reality (the state of the tragic heroine) was one such a student could assimilate.

However dutifully the student studies, if the idea of legitimate competing concepts is an alien one, one that can be accommodated only slowly, and, as Perry suggests, at some cost to one's sense of self and one's prior network of ideas, then that idea will not be understood as it was presented. The new information, seen as anomalous, will be denied or altered.

On the other hand, we cannot divorce learning how to think from learning how to write. Cognition and writing stand in some relationship to each other, like the container and the thing contained. The container shapes the thing contained, and in this case the thing contained can also shape the container. Cognition is the container, the structure by which ideas are given shape and ordered. Yet these ideas, the thing contained, are expressed in language and can, through writing, erode and reshape the container. Thus cognition both precedes the writing process and is then influenced by it.

Comprehension Questions

Assimilation

1. The writing process:
   a. is simple, with the right approach
   b. is complex
   c. is impossible to grasp
   d. does not really exist at all

2. In an essay, students must:
   a. formulate their ideas to the needs of their audience
   b. shape their ideas to the forms of their mode of writing
   c. follow linguistics conventions and grammatical norms
   d. all the above

3. All good students write:
   a. from notes on three-by-five cards
   b. in pencil so changes can be made as they go along
   c. from material organized into outlines
   d. in successive drafts of writing and revision

4. Writer-based prose becomes reader-based prose:
   a. when someone actually reads the material

b. through thinking, writing, and revising
c. only in the final finished product
d. when the writer gets the material down on paper

5. The writing process:
   a. is preceded by a cognitive process
   b. eliminates the cognitive process
   c. precedes the cognitive process
   d. is eliminated by the cognitive process

Interpretation

6. Cognition refers to:
   a. skills
   b. the actual writing process itself
   c. understanding
   d. the final draft

7. According to the author, thinking and writing are:
   a. separate but equal
   b. separate but related
   c. mutually exclusive
   d. the same thing but in different forms

8. The tone of this article is:
   a. diffident
   b. instructional
   c. satiric
   d. negative

9. The text of the article is best described as:
   a. complex, scholarly
   b. easy to skim
   c. informal
   d. colloquial

Main Idea

10. The main idea of this article is best stated as follows:
    a. The writing process is defined by sets of skills by which a student completes an assigned essay.

b. Students must follow specific prescribed rules in writing their essays.

c. The skill of writing is based on an understanding of the interrelationship between thought and writing.

d. The limitations of the student's ability to understand a topic will impede his or her ability to write about it.

Analysis Questions

1. The author indicates that changes must be made to convert writer-based prose into reader-based prose. What do these two terms mean? How does the writer make these changes?

2. Brody uses a formal, theoretical approach. What different approach might have been used?

3. Define *cognition*. How does it apply or relate to the writing process?

4. How does the process of writing affect the content of what is actually being written?

5. Brody states that learning how to think cannot be separated from learning how to write. Comment. (What about learning how to read?)

Exercises

1. If you were asked to speak or write about something you have learned in a major course this year, what influence would your prospective audience have on your approach to this task? Prepare something for your professor; then rewrite it for your roommate.

2. "Writing and reading meet in the printed word, forming a bridge between someone with a message and someone else willing to receive it." Make a concept map of this statement.

3. Write a brief statement about something you have learned from your college experience this year as if for a diary (for your eyes only). Then rewrite it as if for another reader of your choice (for example, friend, grandmother, brother, faculty advisor, or pastor). How does the intended audience, or reader, affect what you write in terms of content? Style? Tone?

Beyond Rules to Writing

"*B*ut I was always taught that you should never start a sentence with 'because.' " "You want five paragraphs in this essay, right?" "Yes, I know that the experience is about me, but I changed it to 'she,' because I remembered that you should never use 'I' in papers."

Every year freshmen arrive in our introductory writing classes, not only graced with varying degrees of skill and enthusiasm, but also armed with a number of false assumptions about the craft of writing. We sometimes take private pleasure in releasing them from the spells under which they have been laboring. Our pride is held in check, however, by at least two phenomena. First, there is a look of suspicion on the faces of many students that translated would read, "Okay, if you're changing the rules again this year, what's the point of digesting this? It's all going to swing back in a couple of years anyway." Second, most of us have received letters from former students who assure us that their success in writing, if not their career or life in general, is based in part on their strict adherence to our warning never to use infinitives or parenthetical expressions, always to start an essay with a personal anecdote, whatever—some bit of advice that, try as we may, we cannot remember ever having proffered. Or, if we do recall having said something about the subject, the student's version is generally a distortion of a suggestion that was intended to encourage flexibility or curb excesses.

So it is not only junior high and high school teachers who nurture in student writers this allegiance to rules, many of which prove to be—at best—half truths. However unwittingly, we do too. Why does it happen? Surely we enter the classroom intending to show students the wealth of possibilities open to them. Why then do some of them leave holding up the amulet of what they believe to be inviolable truths against the vampire of error?

How do we feel about rules ourselves? Do we deplore only those that are wrong or misapplied? Or rather do we regret the fact that—on balance—too many students see too much of the whole writing process as rule-bound? I would argue that the latter is the major problem; it is, indeed, their urgent search for rules that leads some students to embrace anything that sounds like one and to construct others where none is needed or exists. What is wrong with that impulse toward regulation? At its worst, it prevents students from doing the real work of writing and revising, of playing with words, of developing their own internal standards for language that says what they want it to, the way they want it to. It suggests that the right way is out there somewhere, an occult science into which they will try—although, they fear, without much success—to gain entry. Paradoxically, students with the tightest, most rule-bound sense of writing are often those least likely to absorb the conventions that *are* important. Unfortunately, in many ways large and small, we encourage their quest for absolutes. We foster it in the ways we present those rules that we must teach, in the ways we respond to student papers, and in the methods by which we dissect, organize, and distribute our curriculum among the various courses in our writing programs. If we understand which tendencies in our students (and in our teaching methods) encourage the passion for rules, we may be able to minimize their effects.

We are not entirely to blame. There are, after all, the temperaments, the learning methods, and the mental habits of students themselves. Certainly the weaker writers among them, those who have not had the chance to gain confidence in their own judgments and choices, are frustrated by their history of failed attempts. That they would yearn for something as unequivocal as the Pythagorean theorem from which to launch their college writing careers is entirely understandable. Furthermore, very few of us are entirely anxiety-free as we enter unfamiliar waters. We are inclined to feel buoyed by a few secure rules or even by the illusion of rules.

Of course, I don't mean to say that the codes of writing, which our students try to follow, are all illusory. Indeed, by violating them, students occasionally make us conscious of conventions we had never fully articulated before. And when we teach writing, we do and we must trade in some "rules." For example, we require that students document the sources of their research materials, both quoted and paraphrased. Flexible as we may be about the license good student writers take with sentence structure, happy as we are to applaud the trenchant fragment, we insist that they recognize that most sentences need a subject and a verb and should stop at particular places for reasons we are eager to recite. We ask them to distinguish between the semicolon and the colon and to use the dash with discrimination rather than as a substitute for every other mark of punctuation. While we affably acknowledge that the ability to spell correctly has virtually nothing to do with either intelligence or skill in writing, we nevertheless insist that they look up the words that they don't know how to spell in order not to distract their reader from their message.

The list of axioms that students need to assimilate is, although longer than that just given, still blessedly short. Also, thanks to the growing maturity of our discipline and to our belief that students would understand and develop their own processes of writing, these regulations are no longer the lifeblood of college writing classes. Very few of us any longer believe that a detailed knowledge of the system of grammar leads inevitably to better writing. Such linguistic study seems more appropriate for students who are already strong writers and who want to pursue it for their own interests. No, with classes or with individual students, we raise these rules when failure to observe them has led to serious problems in our students' texts.

Yet I suspect that we could improve the way in which we raise them, so that these rules do not seem to be at the heart of writing, but rather necessary and generally reasonable tools for achieving far more interesting goals. From time to time we take our stand and declaim conventions in the hope that *this* will be the speech to end all speeches on the subject, to drive the point home at last. But, by reciting these regulations in voices more forceful than those we use to engage students in the more substantial matters of audience, tone, literal and figurative language, development, originality, and integrity, we skew their importance and reinforce the idea that to master the rules is to seize the brass ring. Perhaps the surest way to avoid that misapprehension is to state explicitly the lowly but necessary function of standard conventions. Students would then know that they will not alter opinion or the course of history by executing sentences that are merely correct; yet should they have the skill and good fortune to shape events by their writing, their sentences will have to be correct.

Furthermore, we should be careful not to present as rules those suggestions about writing that have no absolute value. For example, when we exhort students to make their main point clear near the beginning of their paper, we should not give them the impression that the thesis statement always appears at the end of the first paragraph or even, necessarily, in the first page. Nor, in encouraging them to consider thoroughly both—or all—sides of a controversial issue before asserting a position, should we imply that the use of the first person singular introduces an indefensibly subjective point of view.

If we unintentionally reinforce the yearning for rules in the classroom, when we can see and hear the effect we are having, how much more likely we are to do so in the shorthand with which we respond to students' papers. It occurred to me as I was writing "passive voice" for the fifth time on a paper that, for all the student knew, I might have been congratulating him for a distinctive and effective syntactical structure. "Use the active voice" is scarcely more helpful to someone whose understanding of the difference is shaky. Nor does either make clear the effect of those constructions on the sense of the sentence. So what I really should have said is, "Come in to see me so that we can talk about alternative ways to structure your writing." This, in fact, is what we often intend by the marks of identification and correction with which we read students' papers; we hope that the weight of the ink on the page will encourage students to seek us out to discuss their work. It is easy for students to misinterpret them as proof that they have once again got it wrong.

We can improve the way we comment on papers. We can ensure, for example, that at least as much, preferably more, of our commentary is devoted to the substance of the argument, the narrative, the proposal, the poem. We can ask, in the margins and at the end, such questions of the writer as we would ask if she were right there telling us the story or making the argument. We can then place in their rightful, subordinate context, questions about the technical elements of the writing. We can ask how the way the student has structured the sentences and the paragraphs influences the reader's understanding of her intentions. By engaging the student's interest in convention on those terms, we place the power and the responsibility for clarity in her hands. Also, when we have put the technical elements in their proper perspective, we are inclined to be more selective about those we choose to highlight, allowing students to digest the more important principles before moving on to the finer tuning.

Finally, we intensify the devotion to rules not only in what we say and write to students but also in the way we construct our curriculum. We categorize our classes as developmental, introductory, and advanced; as expository and creative; and as professional, technical, and journalistic. We further divide creative writing courses into those that specialize in poetry or prose and professional writing courses into sections for business and the sciences. These categories are sensible, even necessary; they allow students to take courses that follow a reasonable sequence of difficulty and specialization, and they allow us to teach majors of particular disciplines in the most precise possible way. Unfortunately, however, they also provide students whole new arenas in which to overvalue and to misapprehend rules. Students are likely to misconstrue or, equally regrettable, worship whichever conventions the genre highlights. Students in developmental classes are prone to see their goal as the perfect sentence, those in professional writing classes to become obsessed with format, and those in technical writing classes to believe that absolute devotion to the passive voice or voicelessness guarantees objectivity.

We should make conscious efforts to minimize these tendencies. We can, for example, start each new semester, each new course, by stressing to students that we find most compelling the qualities of good writing that transcend genre: clarity, specificity, richness of language, a sense of personality, and a degree of passion. We can say directly that no particular conventions of the genre will ever be more important than those qualities and that we hope students will improve in these critical ways. Furthermore, we can make explicit the pitfalls as well as the benefits of the particular conventions of the genre, contrasting good examples of the craft with poor ones. For instance, in technical writing we can share with students not only examples of dry and dull writing in the discipline, but also those in which writers relied on the active voice, made the subjects clear through figurative as well as literal language, and were engaged by, even joyful about, their subjects.

If we think that joy is too much to hope for from student writers—if it is a rare commodity even in our own writing—certainly pleasure is not. That is perhaps the greatest gift that a writing teacher can impart: pleasure at the power of creating with language, pleasure in knowing how alternative ways of expressing our ideas and our experiences affect our readers, and pleasure in sentences that transcend pedestrian accuracy. If we can move beyond rule-based instruction and encourage our students to think in larger terms, if we can empower them to struggle with their visions and revisions, then the rules based on conventions and codes will practically teach themselves.

Comprehension Questions

Assimilation

1. According to the author, college freshmen:
   a. enjoy their writing classes
   b. are proficient in writing skills
   c. never write to their writing instructors after they leave college
   d. are skeptical about what they are taught

2. The overemphasis on rules in writing is due to:
   a. teaching methods of high school teachers
   b. temperaments and learning habits of students
   c. teaching methods of college writing teachers
   d. all of the above

3. The author stresses the validity of rules in all the following aspects of writing *except:*
   a. correct spelling
   b. placement of topic sentence
   c. appropriate documentation
   d. punctuation

4. One suggestion Penner makes to teachers of writing is:
   a. to stress the qualities of writing that transcend genre
   b. to eliminate the categorization of courses as developmental, introductory, and advanced

CATHERINE S. PENNER

c. to eliminate rules about sentence structure
d. to eliminate the categorization of courses as expository and creative

5. The author states that an instructor's typical intention for making many corrections on a paper is:
a. to encourage the student to go see the instructor
b. to scare the student into working harder
c. to make the student realize that college writing has stricter standards than high school writing
d. to give the student all the information she needs, so she will not need to see the instructor outside of class

Interpretation

6. The author's introduction:
a. is an excerpt from a student's paper
b. consists of typical comments made by students in college writing classes
c. refers to several inviolable rules in writing
d. covers several rules concerning punctuation

7. The phrase "vampire of error" is an example of:
a. alliteration
b. simile
c. personification
d. allegory

8. The author believes that the worst aspect of too much emphasis on rules in writing is:
a. that students confuse the rules
b. not enough attention is paid to the writing process
c. the rules change too often to try to learn them
d. there are too many rules to try to learn them all

9. The thesis–proof structure of this article highlights its:
a. weak thesis
b. lack of proof
c. persuasive tone
d. formal style

Main Idea

10. The main idea of this article is:
    a. The instruction in writing that students receive in junior high and high school does not prepare them for the level of writing that is expected of them in college.
    b. College writing instructors themselves are to blame for much of the problem that students have with learning the rules of good grammar and punctuation in writing.
    c. Both in the classroom and in their responses to students' papers, writing teachers will have greater success in teaching the necessary rules and conventions if they subordinate them to the more important qualities of good writing.
    d. Although good writing skills alone do not guarantee a college graduate a job in the field of his choice, they will prove invaluable in finding and keeping a job in almost any field of endeavor.

Analysis Questions

1. What is meant by the phrase "to seize the brass ring"?

2. What is the impact of the author's introduction? Do you identify with any of the statements made in the introduction? Discuss.

3. This article was written by a college writing instructor and addressed to other college writing instructors. How would it have been written if addressed directly to the student?

4. What are the *necessary* rules that the author says must be followed? What others can you think of?

5. The author states, "We are inclined to feel buoyed by a few secure rules or even by the illusion of rules." Explain this statement as it is used in the essay. Can you think of your own examples, other than in the learning of writing, when this statement is valid?

6. How does the information in this article compare with what you have been taught in writing classes? Discuss.

Exercises

1. Rewrite the introduction to feature an example of a student's writing that illustrates the author's point.

2. Write some comments you have received on your papers. Identify them as to whether they pertain to inviolable rules, to flexible rules, or to the writing process itself.

3. Write a paragraph or two using the passive voice. Then rewrite it in the active voice. Describe the effect of the voice on what you wrote and its impact on a reader.

WILLIAM J. KENNEDY

Rhetorical Discovery in Yeats's
"Leda and the Swan"

*T*hough rhetorical criticism in the twentieth century has tried many comebacks, it still seems the oldest living has-been. Three distinct modes of approach to rhetorical criticism share the same prejudices and presuppositions. I refer to the widely divergent modes of positivistic antiquarian scholarship, structuralism, and post-structuralism. They all accord primacy to figures and tropes and to an idea of communication that operates in a one-way direction from author to audience and vice versa.[1] Nearly every theorist of rhetoric (and certainly the best of them from Plato and Aristotle to Chaim Perelman, Roman

---

[1]For a sterile antiquarian approach, see Brian Vickers, "Rhetorical and Anti-rhetorical Tropes," in *Comparative Criticism: A Yearbook,* vol. 3, ed. E. S. Shaffer (Cambridge: Cambridge University Press, 1981), pp. 105–32. For a structuralist approach, see Jacques Dubois, *Rhetorique générale* (Paris: Larousse, 1970). For a poststructuralist approach, see Jacques Derrida, *Of Grammatology,* tr. Gayatri Spivack (Baltimore: Johns Hopkins University Press, 1976).

Jakobson, and Walter Ong) has expressed difficulty with these ideas.[2] The models of structuralism, poststructuralism, and antiquarianism take little or no account of the important factors of voice and address. These factors, however, constitute frames for the entire rhetorical act.

As frames, voice and address allow one to focus on the terms of the referential function.[3] These terms include not only the object of the discourse (the thematic argument) but also its subjects (who is speaking to whom). On the simplest level such an act implicates two agents: the speaker and the audience. On more complex literary levels it may implicate several, such as a speaker or narrator distinct from the author, fictional characters in turn distinct from both, even a fictive audience distinct from the empirical reader.[4] The rhetorical functions that evoke a system of relations between these agents are voice and address. Since each agent has his or her own set of attitudes, experiences, and expectations, a certain distance necessarily separates them. Thus there might ensue a structure of complex dynamic relationships quite different from the structure of words that they modify and inflect. These relationships are grounded in rhetorical structures of voice and address. The crucial part of any rhetorical analysis of a literary text involves a qualitative judgment on these relationships.

The structure of voice and address in Yeats's "Leda and the Swan" offers a good example for analysis:

A sudden blow: the great wings beating still
Above the staggering girl, her thighs caressed

---

[2]See Plato, *Phaedrus,* tr. R. Hackforth, in *Collected Dialogues,* ed. Edith Hamilton and Huntington Cairns (New York: Pantheon, 1961); Aristotle, *The "Art" of Rhetoric,* tr. John Henry Freese, Loeb Classical Library (London: Heinemann, 1926); Chaim Perelman and L. Olbrechts-Tyteca, *The New Rhetoric,* tr. John Wilkinson and Purcell Weaver (Notre Dame: University of Notre Dame Press, 1969); Roman Jakobson, "Linguistics and Poetics," in *Style in Language,* ed. Thomas Sebeok (Boston: MIT Press, 1960); and Walter Ong, S.J., *Rhetoric, Romance, and Technology* (Ithaca: Cornell University Press, 1971).

[3]See Paul Ricoeur, *The Rule of Metaphor,* tr. Robert Czerny (Toronto: Toronto University Press, 1975), and Paolo Valesio, *Novantiqua* (Bloomington: Indiana University Press, 1980).

[4]See William J. Kennedy, *Rhetorical Norms in Renaissance Literature* (New Haven: Yale University Press, 1978).

By the dark webs, her nape caught in his bill,
He holds her helpless breast upon his breast.
How can those terrified vague fingers push
The feathered glory from her loosening thighs?
And how can body, laid in that white rush,
But feel the strange heart where it lies?

A shudder in the loins engenders there
The broken wall, the burning roof and tower,
And Agamemnon dead.
                              Being so caught up,
So mastered by the brute blood of the air,
Did she put on his knowledge with his power
Before the indifferent beak could let her drop?[5]

This poem requires the audience to recognize the myth of Leda; the rape by Zeus; and her subsequent conception and birth of Helen and Clytemnestra; the later role of her daughters in the Trojan War, and, following that, the victory of the Greeks, the rise of their culture, the exile of the Trojans, the founding of Rome, whence the Roman Empire, Christendom, and all the history of the Western World down to the present day. In line 9 the seed implanted during the rape engenders much more than "The broken wall, the burning roof and tower, / And Agamemnon dead." It engenders the blankness of space on line 11 between the antinomic words "dead" and "Being," which is capable of being filled up by all the events of Eurocentric history from that moment till now.

The poem makes another, more tenuous, demand upon its audience to enter rhetorically into the action. In the welter of participles in the first three lines the audience must withhold its expectations about the action until the delayed climax of the fourth line. "How" on line 5 and "And how" on line 7 involve the audience fully in the rhetorical situation of an implied address. The questions imply the presence of an audience once and

---

[5]Quotations from W. B. Yeats, *Collected Poems* (New York: Macmillan, 1956), reprinted with the permission of A. P. Watt Ltd. on behalf of Michael Yeats, Macmillan London, Limited, and Macmillan Publishing Company. Copyright 1928 by Macmillan Publishing Co., Inc., renewed 1956 by Georgie Yeats.

for all, pressing it to respond in at least a fictive manner. Its participation, however, is at best spurious. Not only is there a temporal distance between the audience and Leda, but there is an emotional one as well. The audience cannot really be expected to respond to these questions; and yet the questions are more than merely rhetorical ones. At the very moment that they invite the audience into the poem, they frustrate its power to respond as it seems it should. Leda is powerless to alter the course of the action as Zeus overwhelms her; the audience is powerless to articulate its response as the questions overwhelm it.

The last six lines of the poem change the rhetorical situation drastically. In the shudder of sexual climax between Zeus and his victim, power passes from one to the other. For Zeus the shudder may be psychological as well as physical. With his divine foreknowledge Zeus can glimpse the historical consequences of the moment. Among many they entail his own transmogrification first into the god of later Greek mythology, then into the god that later Roman myth would conflate with its own Jupiter, finally into the dead burden of the past that Christianity with its own God would surmount, only in turn to be surmounted by the post-Christian gods, whoever they may be. Each step into the future is a step toward extinction.

Zeus knows this condition, and he accepts it with resignation, maybe even with indifference, if we allow the adjective in the poem's final line to suggest more than sexual satiation. Zeus's knowledge of the future is, of course, linked with his power as a god to enforce fate and affect human destiny. Leda, by conceiving Helen and Clytemnestra, has left her mark on history. She thus puts on Zeus's power in a decisive way, but, as the final question addresses its audience, did she put on his knowledge of the future as well? Could she fathom the significance of the act? Once more the question brings the audience into the poem, and once more it frustrates the audience's power to respond. Not only does the speaker's interrogative voice rise unexpectedly in the middle of the sentence, but it comes with a displacement of tense to past ("did she put on") from present ("he holds," "how can," "engenders the"). This temporal distancing further obscures the audience's relationships to the questions and obfuscates its intellectual and emotional response.

The audience, never named or summoned in direct address, is only implied by the insistent questioning. Nor does the speaker play any less ambiguous role in the rhetorical situation. He is trying to articulate in his own voice what is inarticulable, certainly not merely the brute blood of a rape, but the question of consciousness and an awareness of one's place in history. Yeats's speaker wonders about the future, hoping that his words will confer at least an imagined being on what is absent and desired. As with all speakers who desire something, if this one can't fully comprehend what he lacks, at least he can seek words to aid his understanding.

My analysis of the poem has focused on its rhetorical situation, its principles of voice and address, the roles of its speaker and his relationship to the audience. It has evaded its diction and figures of speech, its theme and substance. Those concerns occupy conventional rhetorical analysis. My argument, however, has been that one can understand the poem in and through its strategies of voice and address. I doubt whether any of us is willing or able to abandon our interest in elocutionary devices or thematic content, but I also know that we might find other stable resources to strengthen our critical awareness. Some of those resources are available in such concepts of rhetorical criticism as I have stressed.

Comprehension Questions

Assimilation

1. The rhetorical modes of structuralism, poststructuralism, and antiquarianism:
   a. are coming back into vogue
   b. take no account of the factors of voice and address
   c. are overlapping viewpoints of rhetorical criticism
   d. negate figures of speech in communication between author and audience

2. The thematic argument refers to:
   a. positivism
   b. Chaim Perelman's theory of rhetoric
   c. the object of the discourse
   d. the subject of the discourse

3. The crucial part of any rhetorical analysis of a literary text involves:
   a. analysis of traditional figures and tropes
   b. the dynamic relationship between fictive audience and empirical reader
   c. qualitative judgment on relationships between voice and address
   d. none of the above

4. The Swan is also:
   a. Leda
   b. Zeus

    c. Clytemnestra

    d. Yeats

5. In the conclusion to the poem, power passes:
    a. from Zeus to Leda
    b. from Zeus to Jupiter
    c. from Zeus to the Swan
    d. from Zeus to Agamemnon

6. In the poem, the audience:
    a. is implied by the insistent questioning
    b. is summoned in direct address
    c. is personified by being named
    d. is ignored

Interpretation

7. Kennedy's analysis is focused on all the following *except:*
    a. diction and figures of speech
    b. rhetorical situation
    c. principles of voice and address
    d. role of speaker and his relationship to the audience

8. Kennedy's approach is best described as:
    a. jocular
    b. analytical
    c. simplistic
    d. cynical

9. You can infer from the article that the author:
    a. prefers thematic content as an approach to literary criticism
    b. emphasizes conventional rhetorical analysis
    c. believes in a variety of approaches to literary analysis
    d. emphasizes depth over breadth in critical awareness

Main Idea

10. The main idea of this article is:
    a. Meaningful literary criticism evolves from thorough analysis of theme, characterization, and the rhetorical strategies of voice and address.
    b. The models of structuralism, poststructuralism, and antiquarianism take little or no account of the important factors of voice and address.

    c. Rhetorical criticism is at best a narrow but legitimate approach to literary analysis, at worst, the "oldest living has-been."

    d. To analyze rhetorical structures of voice and address in a poem like Yeats's "Leda and the Swan" provides significant insight into the poem's meaning.

Analysis Questions

1. Do you find Yeats's brief poem easy or difficult to understand? Why?

2. Kennedy states that he is analyzing Yeats's poem through consideration of voice and address. What is meant by those two terms?

3. How does Kennedy's analysis of this poem assist your understanding of it?

4. How important is your knowledge of Greek mythology in appreciating "Leda and the Swan"?

5. Do you find the information given in the footnotes helpful? Relevant? Worthless? Comment.

Exercises

1. Identify the rhyme scheme of "Leda and the Swan." Find or create a poem with the same rhyme scheme.

2. Rewrite the poem as prose—that is, narrative. Or rewrite it as a news article.

The Golden Handcuffs

Some had dismissed his work per-
functorily. One reviewer had grudgingly admitted that the writing was
relatively good and there were moments when the book came alive; but,
he had reiterated, they were just moments. A few others had indicated that
the book possessed an almost Kafkaesque quality to it, but it was "almost"
and he wasn't Kafka. . . . So it was a dismal cocktail party and Ronden
was the first to admit it, although he kept up his facade and amiably
discussed his new novel with all well-wishers and future detractors. His
writing aside, one did have to admit that he possessed an immense reservoir
of stubbornness, and thus, by mere youthful persistence—if nothing else—
he qualified as an artist.

The old lady had aroused his suspicions almost from the start. He had
noticed her standing aloof from the party. What particularly caught his
attention was the way she observed him as he worked the crowd, her head
cocked to one side.

Her hair was silver and so sparse that he could make out the hint of pink
scalp. She was old; yet when she finally decided to edge toward him and
close the distance, Ronden was amazed to see this wizened old lady move
effortlessly—almost youthfully.

"I've read your book," she said, extending a wrinkled hand, which he accepted. It felt like dead flesh and he shuddered. "It's fairly good, you know," she continued.

"I think so," he laughed, trying to disarm her. But the old lady just puckered her lips and gave a noncommittal shrug.

"Needs work. Lacks polish."

"Hmmm," Ronden issued a noise he usually employed when he lacked words—which was rarely. She was senile, he told himself, and wanted to walk away. His spirits were low enough. The book, his first full-length novel, seemed doomed already on this day of its birth.

"Why do you rush so?" she asked, shaking her head from side to side; the loose skin on her face followed, out of sync.

"Rush?" he asked and couldn't help but notice that the green dress she wore looked like hand-loomed silk. Very expensive. Again he was gripped by the desire to flee, but this collection of aged tissues kept him anchored.

"Art takes time. You so lack patience," she said and played with her lips between her yellow teeth. Ugly, Ronden thought; they should all have been pulled out and replaced with a good denture.

"I don't have time. I didn't have time. God, I was lucky even to manage to get it all down," he said, and was amazed that he had admitted it. "I'm working six days a week delivering groceries, trying to support a wife and two children. How—" and then Ronden clipped short his outburst. His words had risen uncontrollably out of his chest like bitter, hot bile.

"Care for another drink?" he suddenly blurted out. "How about an hors d'oeuvre?"

"What's the most important thing in your life?" she asked in a low secretive voice that rumbled about his ears, ignoring his fumbling gesture of hospitality.

"Huh?"

The old lady repeated her question, the disks of her gray eyes widening.

"That's a strange question."

"Well, what is?"

"My wife and children, of course."

"Of course? Are you sure?"

"What do you mean, 'am I sure?' " Ronden snapped, and then, catching himself, glanced nervously about the room. He could feel the lines on his young face deepen just as the old woman, who had moved in closer, seemed to take on more life, her gestures quickened, her eyes more alert. "Well . . . I suppose my writing," he then grudgingly admitted.

"Good," she said in her husky monotone. "I'm just curious—one more question; then I won't trouble you further."

Ronden nodded his head in perplexed defeat, no longer asking himself why he was putting up with her prying.

"Is it the writing in itself as an art form that is the most important, or is it publishing?"

"When I answered your first questions I *did* mean writing. I could be happy just writing—the publication is something incidental, a little money to provide momentary reprieve from the treadmill. Now, if you'll excuse me. . . ."

The months passed and Ronden's book, which had shown scant promise, fulfilled his dismal predictions, disappearing off the bookshelves and being absorbed into obscurity. He continued to labor diligently at his writing, but found it necessary to take a second job pumping gas at night when his wife, who originally had been helping with support, became ill with a complicated pregnancy. It was as if nature herself had interceded to cast in front of Ronden yet one more obstacle.

Now, there was barely time left to write, at best fitful moments, but still he remained determined to continue writing; things couldn't get worse, only better. He was possessed and absorbed by his art and refused to relent. His life became an endless cycle of drudgery—of the grocery store, the gas station, and his writing. He felt bitterness gnawing at his soul, but fought to overcome it, refusing to succumb to despair. Writing, which previously had emerged with relative ease, became a painful chore. The harder he labored at it, the less came. His exhaustion grew. Ronden's originality as an artist was rapidly deserting him, and he knew it.

This grueling existence continued for thirteen months. It was then that a messenger arrived at his home with a note. It read: "I would like to meet with you regarding your writing," and was signed E. Holmes, together with an address and a suggested appointment time.

Ronden was elated. He didn't know who the man was, but was positive this was good news. He danced around his apartment with his two little girls, jubilantly telling his wife that this must surely be the big break he had been dreaming of. Then, when his initial enthusiasm subsided, he began to mull over the name. Holmes? Holmes? He had never heard of it as connected with any publishing house or magazine. Who could Holmes be? The address given was a well-to-do residential part of the city.

The following day he called in sick at work and appeared at the given address. Nervously he rang the doorbell, trying to gauge his ring somewhere between timidity and self-assurance. It was promptly answered by a servant, who showed him into an elegant apartment with thick carpets and luxurious upholstery. Its opulence suddenly seemed to drive home to him the shabbiness of his own cramped rooms. He sank down on the edge of a deep sofa, feeling the familiar pain of discontent pressing against his chest, but convinced that his salvation was finally at hand.

The door to the living room opened and in stepped the same old woman he had met at the cocktail party more than a year ago. Her white hair was set in the exact same bun, and she even wore that same green silk dress. Only her face hinted at any degree of change. It had aged even further in the intervening year. She extended that limp hand to Ronden, who stood and uncomfortably accepted it.

"Do you remember me?"

"Yes," Ronden answered, his voice revealing the level of his disappointment.

"I asked you a question a year ago. Do you remember it?"

"Yes, as a matter of fact I do, and very clearly. I don't know why—"

"You remember it because it's a vital question, and now it's an exceedingly pertinent one. Is writing still the most important thing?"

"Of course! I haven't stopped writing since that book."

"Yes, I know that," she said matter-of-factly.

"How do you know?" Ronden's voice suddenly picked up the edge it had developed at their first encounter.

Ignoring his question, she continued, "You now make barely two hundred dollars a week. Perhaps, in a short while, you'll get a raise—"

"But—"

"Let me finish," she insisted, as if she knew she was now in command. "Can you make ends meet with your salary?"

"Barely. I owe a little money here and there, but I'm sort of gaining on my debts now."

"I see," she said, nodding her head thoughtfully. "I have an offer for you. I will employ you for four hundred dollars a week," the woman said, her narrow lips issuing the words without any emotion.

"What do I have to do?" Ronden asked skeptically, suddenly sitting up erect.

"Write, that's all. Just keep writing."

"And what do you get out of it, besides the satisfaction of supporting the arts?"

"The manuscripts you produce during that period are to become my property."

"Oh, I see," Ronden answered. "You buy them cheaply and resell them at a profit."

"You're deceiving yourself. I have sufficient resources so that my actions aren't motivated by profit."

Ronden remained in a state of puzzled silence, trying to make sense of her unusual proposal. In essence, he reasoned, the old woman was offering to act as his patron. It was hard to comprehend in this day and age. In fact, it was nothing short of miraculous! He began to regret his skepticism, his near rudeness to her. A soft smile passed over his face, and he extended his hand to the woman. This time she did not accept it, but gave a stiff formal nod in return.

"Thank you very much. Are there any other conditions?"

"None, except that you keep writing. I won't support a loafer."

"Don't worry. I'll keep writing!" he said, unable to restrain his delight in her humorless presence.

Ronden hurried home to his wife. Bubbling with joy, he told her of their good fortune; how, with her offer of money, the old woman had jerked him free from the shackles of grocery store and gas station. Not only would they be able to repay all their debts, but he could finally, after all these years of squandered effort, devote all of his energies and time to writing.

Spurred on by unlimited optimism, he immediately launched into writing a new novel. It was one he had wanted to start for a long time, but for which he had lacked the necessary span of uninterrupted concentration. True to his word to the old lady, Ronden labored day and night, writing and rewriting, line by line. Slowly the novel began to take form, gaining a life of its own, prose pure, plot intricate. Into this work, he poured more of his heart and diligence than into any other piece, and with it came the polish the old lady had found lacking. And when it was finally completed, he felt an exhausted exhilaration experienced only by the artist who has tried his best and knows he has brushed hands with near perfection—that uplift which comes at best once or twice in a lifetime.

After the manuscript had been corrected and retyped, he gave the old lady—as agreed—all the copies. She thanked him and asked that he return the following day. The next morning she greeted him with one of her rare smiles, and he treasured it as a reward.

"Yes," she said. "It's indeed the best you've done, but I know you can do *still* better."

"I don't know. It's sapped me of every bit of blood."

"Well, take a short rest and begin again. You have more ideas, don't you?"

"Yes, of course. That's one thing I never seem to lack."

"Beginning next week you'll be getting five hundred dollars a week."

Ronden thanked her profusely, but then couldn't keep himself from asking, "But what are you going to do with the manuscript?"

"That's my concern, not yours. Remember our agreement? Is writing still the most important thing?"

"Yes," he replied without any hesitation, still feeling the glow of success. "But—"

"Good. Then be thankful I let you write."

Ronden took a week off and then returned to work. He continued to labor, but this time he began a series of short stories. Holding himself in strict discipline, he made sure each word, each sentence, conveyed the precise feeling and meaning he desired. In the collection of short stories he then wrote, Ronden had finally become master of his own technique. And now he guided his intuition instead of letting his typewriter follow it blindly.

When the stories were completed, corrected, and recorrected, he presented them to the old lady, who once again complimented him and then asked the same question, "What's the most important thing to you?"

"Writing of course, but—"

"But what?"

"You just keep putting the manuscripts away. Aren't they good enough to publish?"

"What I do with the manuscripts is *my* business. You just continue to write."

"But—"

"That is, unless you want to cancel our agreement. Then everything you produce is your own. But, in that case, you are once again returned to your grocery store and faced with the dilemma of support. Surely the cumulative amount of money you've already received is by far more than what you would have gotten had you been able to sell your novel and short stories?"

"Yes," he answered hesitantly.

"Well, then, there's no problem. Surely you don't think I'm taking advantage of you, do you?"

Taking a long, deep breath, Ronden shook his head and left. He returned to his typewriter, but as he continued to write he began to be plagued with doubts, suspicions that he had mortgaged himself to the devil. How could she just let his work be buried in a drawer? To his surprise, the weekly check he received from the old lady was suddenly increased to $600. Ronden felt himself straddling fences of need, guilt, and art. It was, as he explained to his wife, like wearing a pair of golden handcuffs. Nevertheless, he went on experimenting with new ideas and, determined to remain honest to his patron, presented her with all copies of his finished works.

One day a short, well-dressed man appeared at his house, introducing himself as Mr. Berne, a prominent international publisher. Ronden invited him in, and Berne explained that he had discovered Ronden's book, his first and only book to be published, and had been exceedingly impressed by it. He was curious if Ronden was still writing. Ronden promptly replied yes, and upon the man's request gave him the copy of his newest short story, which was intended for the old lady. Mr. Berne took the manuscript with him and returned one week later, brimming with enthusiasm.

"This is excellent work. In fact, I would call it exceptional. I'd love to publish it as part of a collection. Do you have any more?"

"I do. But I can't give them to you," Ronden said, and avoiding the publisher's startled glance, took back the story.

"Is someone else already publishing them?"

"No. No, but I'm not free to sell them," Ronden tried to explain to a puzzled Mr. Berne. "Look, can I talk to you in a few days? Maybe something can be done."

Berne agreed, and Ronden went directly to the old woman's apartment. She gave him a friendly welcome and invited him in.

"Have you finished something new?"

Her words provoked Ronden.

"What do you plan to do with my manuscripts?" Ronden insisted petulantly.

"My manuscripts, you mean," she said with a smile, refusing to catch the contagion of his anger. Her calmness served only to goad him. "Are you just going to bury them?" he began to shout.

"That's my business. What's the most important thing to you?" She asked her familiar question.

"For God's sake, stop that!" He clenched his fists at his side.

"Do you want to end our agreement?"

"Yes, yes! I want to end it if you refuse to tell me what you're going to do with them!" Ronden's body trembled.

"I refuse," she retorted in her measured, husky voice.

"Then I want to end it. Give them back!" Ronden shouted.

"That won't be possible. You forget," she explained patronizingly, "they are my property. But why do you want them back?"

"Because they're publishable. No," he caught himself, "they're better than that! You're holding the best work I've ever done. There's a piece of my life in every line, on every page." Ronden began to weep with frustration. "Don't you see? I'm like a painter. I need to have my pictures hung in a gallery for the world to see," he pleaded, "not stored away in a dark closet."

"Good-bye, Ronden," she said, turning to leave the room.

"Thief!" he called after her. "Selfish old—" He chased after the old lady, but the butler intercepted him and helped Ronden find the door.

Ronden returned home. He tried to write, but it soon became apparent that the woman had fiendishly robbed him of his art. He had given her his best. And all just for the money.

Berne appeared again, and Ronden told him that the manuscripts were not available, but that he was writing a new novel. Berne then left his card, asking Ronden to call him as soon as it was completed. Ronden never called.

He returned to work in a store, and every working day he cursed the hideous old woman in the green dress.

Almost a full year later, Berne returned again and asked if the novel was finished. Ronden fought back his tears. He explained to Mr. Berne that he was finished as a writer. Berne said he understood, and once again left his card in the event things took a turn for the better. "They sometimes do, you know."

A week later a package wrapped in brown paper arrived. Ronden opened it and, to his amazement, found in it all the original manuscripts he had given the old lady. There was a short note that read: "These are yours now. Ask yourself my question just once more."

Ronden tore up the letter and laughed at the stupid old woman. He was free now, free to have them published. He could feel new life infused into his blood. Without wasting a moment, he jumped into his car and drove to the city, to the address on Berne's card. When he arrived, he learned that there was no Mr. Berne and no such publishing company.

Comprehension Questions

Assimilation

1. Ronden is:
   a. a famous novelist who wants to write short stories
   b. a poet
   c. a talented but unknown writer
   d. a father of twin girls

2. Adjectives used to describe the old woman include all the following *except:*
   a. stupid
   b. hideous
   c. clever
   d. selfish

3. "The golden handcuffs" refers to:
   a. the name of his first novel
   b. part of a simile used to describe his relationship with the old woman
   c. the name of the jewelry store where he bought earrings for his wife
   d. the name of the store where he worked after he broke the agreement with the old woman

4. Near the end of the story:
   a. Ronden is grateful to the old woman
   b. Ronden considers the old woman laughable
   c. Ronden is finally content not to publish his work
   d. writing becomes the most important thing in Ronden's life

5. The story indicates that the old woman's name was:
   a. Holmes
   b. Berne
   c. Ronden
   d. Lieberman

Interpretation

6. The reader can infer that Ronden had to take a job at a gas station because:
    a. he had lost the job at the grocery store
    b. his wages at the grocery store were reduced
    c. his wife had to quit her job
    d. it was part of his agreement with the old woman

7. Ronden was *most* deeply motivated by which of the following:
    a. money
    b. recognition
    c. his family
    d. the subject of his text

8. In this story, the passage of time:
    a. goes faster and faster
    b. stays the same rate
    c. varies from scene to scene
    d. slows down as the story progresses

9. The organizational pattern of this text is:
    a. expositional
    b. analytic
    c. narrative
    d. formal

Main Idea

10. The main idea of this story is:
    a. People will do anything for money.
    b. People often do not mean what they say or say what they mean.
    c. When opportunity arrives, do not ask foolish questions.
    d. A stitch in time saves nine.

Analysis Questions

1. "The Golden Handcuffs" is an example of fiction; the other selections in this book are nonfiction. What differences do you find between these two genres? Consider style, structure, tone, technique, approach of the author, and main idea.

2. Dialogue is a technique used extensively in the story. Is it effective? How else could the author convey the same information? Would this method be as effective?

3. The story is written in the third person, or by "all-knowing author." What does this terminology mean? How would the story change if it was written in the first person by Ronden's character? By Berne's character? By the old woman? What is the significance of perspective in a story?

4. Is Mr. Berne real? A figment of Ronden's imagination? Someone hired by the old woman? What are the results of his visits to Ronden?

5. The author refers to "an exhausted exhilaration experienced only by the artist who has tried his best and knows he has brushed hands with near perfection. . . ." Comment.

6. What is Ronden's true answer to the old woman's question? What is your answer to that question?

7. What role does suspense play in this story?

8. Why is the title appropriate? What other title choices could be considered appropriate?

Exercises

1. Is there some explanation for the ending (other than fantasy)? Make up another ending for the story. Or continue the story for another page or so, to a new ending. (Try this exercise more than once!)

2. Suppose that you are a student in a class in which you must turn in a full-length essay on various topics each week, that the essays were never returned, and that you never knew the grades they earned. What effect would this situation have on the effort you put into the essay? Your enjoyment of writing the essays? Your opinion of the class? Compose a letter to your instructor reflecting your response to the situation.

Scuba: A Pleasure in Search of a Purpose

*A*mericans will go to great lengths to disguise their pastimes as purposeful activities. Whether a remnant of the Puritan tradition or an echo of pioneer days, this trait makes it hard for them to allow themselves to do something just because it's fun. As a result, the reasons people give for doing something—good solid reasons—are often just rationalizations. But those rationalizations force them to organize the fun activity into a structure that often doesn't make much sense.

Scuba diving offers a particularly good example. People are attracted to scuba diving for the same reason they wish they could fly: Freedom from gravity signifies freedom from obstacles. Moving effortlessly underwater, scuba divers enter a new world, disengaged from day-to-day pre-occupations.

But no sooner do divers gain access to that liberty—by becoming comfortable with their equipment and their environment—than they divest themselves of it. Americans are accustomed to spending their time usefully and expect to have something to show for the investment of time in an activity. Newly qualified divers display this compulsion by setting themselves tasks in their underwater world. They start out by mapping their territory, much as the pioneers must have done in their new land. They take plastic reference books down with them in order to identify every variety of parrotfish or distinguish every type of coral. They challenge themselves to play with the moray eels, and they tame the natural fear the barracuda inspire.

The problem is that these activities are quickly exhausted in the intensive diving that goes with a multidive vacation package. In consequence, novice divers return home having invested hundreds of dollars in equipment, thousands in travel—and describe themselves as "dived out." The act of diving, with the sensation it confers of mastery of at least one world, still holds its appeal. But there is nothing left to *do*.

At this stage one of two things occurs. The expensive equipment takes up permanent residence in the attic, eventually to appear in the classified ads when the diver finally acknowledges that he or she is an ex-diver. Or the diver discovers a purpose that will justify a pastime that is neither a sport nor a hobby but an activity, like walking, that people feel a need to structure. However, while people can say they walk to get somewhere or to keep in shape, neither of these goals applies to scuba diving. How then do task-oriented Americans legitimize diving?

The justifications divers have found have only one thing in common: they have nothing whatever to do with the yearning for liberty that constitutes the original appeal of scuba diving. They range from the serious (environmental research) to the ridiculous (scuba poker). But they all impose a structure and a purpose on an activity whose essential structure is freedom and whose essential purpose is experiencing and reveling in that freedom.

Underwater photography is the justification divers choose most frequently, if the advertisements in diving magazines are any indication. This is a natural extension of the one characteristic that sets scuba diving beyond most people's reach: the almost prohibitive cost of the equipment. Like a child learning to walk, beginning divers are sustained by the conviction that the new activity holds limitless possibilities. In this belief, they plunk down their money—lots of it—and acquire a full set of diving gear along with their diving certification.

Committed to the activity by the amount of their investment if by nothing else, when its horizons narrow, divers naturally try to expand them again by increasing their investment with the purchase of photographic equipment. To reinforce this mechanism, dive shops at popular diving destinations have installed photography professionals who give lessons, rent or sell equipment, process the day's shots, and critique the photographer's technique.

You don't have to be a professional to see that many and perhaps most of these divers have taken up photography only to give shape to their diving experience. A close look at their snapshots reveals that they have not even mastered basic diving skills. Dee Scarr, formerly photo pro at a leading dive resort and now an independent diver guide, says that people tell her they suddenly have problems staying level when they start to take pictures. Without realizing it, they have been using their hands to help maintain their buoyancy, and underwater photography takes two hands. The divers tell Dee they need a third hand, but she tells them they really need to master their buoyancy control—something they should have learned in their first diving classes.

Just ask these people—who readily admit they never expect to get more than two good pictures to a roll—why they expose all those costly rolls of underwater film. Their answers are limp: "Because our friends back in Dallas (Chicago, Cleveland, and so on) don't dive and we want to show them what we see." Two weeks of nonstop photography for this? One imagines roomfuls of Dallasites fleeing the five-hundredth shot of a French angelfish.

Meanwhile, if you listen to the self-styled photography addicts talk, it is clear that the act of diving is still what appeals to them. What fires their enthusiasm is how far they descended, how much air they expended, and what it was like down below—not what exposure they found most successful or how they just missed getting the perfect shot.

There is even more of a contrast between the ostensible and the actual purposes of the folks who dive the shipwrecks off the Atlantic Coast. These divers plan for months to take a boat out of Morehead City, North Carolina, and scour wrecks in the Gulf Stream for brass fittings that they will haul to the surface in bulging "lift" bags. They say they will spend the winter months returning that brass to its polished beauty. (Images of bored Dallas suburbanites give way to images of inland homes overbedecked with brass ship fittings.) At least that is what they say if you ask them why they do it, but if you listen to them talk, all you hear about is "double eighties" and "hang bottles" (diving with two tanks to be able to go deeper, and breathing from a tank hung halfway to the surface as a way of staying underwater longer).

Food foraging is another activity divers have taken up to give meaning to their pleasure. Countries with coral reefs have banned spear fishing to avoid depleting a resource that attracts tourists. But divers looking for an excuse to go diving still take up the chase—now for lobsters off the New Jersey coast, another time for oysters on the floor of the Chesapeake Bay. Granted, those lobsters or oysters cost less than they would at the fishmarket—but only as long as the cost of the boat trip and the air fills is not taken into account. But does anyone doubt they are just an excuse to go diving?

The utility of taking up marine biology is less questionable. This is the approach the real workaholics favor, particularly those whose normal pursuits are intellectual. Organizations such as Earthwatch swell their research coffers with the tax-deductible payments of over-achieving divers, longing to spend their vacations diving but loath to give in to frivolity. By joining a marine research project, paying their own expenses, and putting in a hard day's work, they justify their attraction to underwater life with the claim of making a contribution to science.

When I spotted two dive boats reserved for "Underwater Sports" one day, I thought the era of the "dive jock" had finally begun. I envisioned underwater relay races, where divers passed eels instead of batons, and worried about obstacle courses that might damage the coral. There was no need to fear: the underwater sports turned out to be a group of overweight auto dealers from New Jersey on their annual holiday.

Aside from jousting on a sunken telephone pole at a well-known dive site in the Bahamas, underwater sports—a seemingly logical justification for diving—have not attracted many divers. Perhaps that is because so few divers are actually athletes. One of the attractions of scuba diving is that neither age nor obesity hinders full participation in the activity. Still, games may have a future: one dive shop in the Washington, D.C., area enlivens diving in a nearby quarry with monthly rounds of scuba poker, and caps the season with an underwater Thanksgiving turkey hunt. Then too, divers on pogo sticks have already been featured in a dive magazine.

Is there no end to the lengths Americans will go to legitimize an essentially purposeless but pleasurable activity? It is probably too soon to say, at least as far as scuba diving goes. Given the expense of scuba, few people can afford to take it up before middle age. This means that the baby boom generation is just reaching the years in which sizable numbers of people acquire the income to afford such expensive pursuits. As this most-numerous-ever group of Americans pours out of the rock concerts and off the ski slopes into the deep, it will transform the underwater realm as it has transformed every other territory it has invaded. Maybe this unusual cohort—the one that declared it was all right to stop and enjoy a flower just because it was pretty and smelled good—will grant scuba divers the freedom to enjoy diving for no other purpose than to have a good time.

Comprehension Questions

Assimilation

1. Scuba diving is likened to flying in that:
   a. both are expensive hobbies
   b. both are dangerous activities
   c. both are concerned with freedom from gravity
   d. both require extensive training and equipment

2. Justification used by divers, according to the author, include all the following *except:*
   a. environmental research
   b. staying in shape
   c. food foraging
   d. diving shipwrecks

3. According to the author, underwater sports:
   a. have proved popular because divers tend to be natural athletes
   b. are harmful to delicate coral formations
   c. are dangerous and should be avoided
   d. have not attracted many divers

Interpretation

4. One can infer that the author believes that divers' justifications for diving are all the following *except:*
   a. silly
   b. varied
   c. oriented toward physical fitness
   d. necessary

5. American scuba divers are described as being:
   a. lazy
   b. task-oriented
   c. athletic
   d. carefree

6. Riche's bias comes from:
   a. her own enjoyable experience scuba diving

b. her lack of interest in scuba diving
c. the fact that she has never actually gone scuba diving
d. information not given

7. The tone of this article is:
   a. humorous
   b. dry
   c. acerbic
   d. advisory

8. The primary purpose of this article is to:
   a. educate readers about a hobby
   b. entertain readers while making a point about American attitudes
   c. warn readers of dangers of scuba diving
   d. chastise scuba divers for their contradictory attitudes

9. The organization of ideas used by the author is basically:
   a. spatial
   b. thesis–proof
   c. compare and contrast
   d. descriptive enumeration

Main Idea

10. The main idea of this article is:
    a. Scuba diving is a hobby that is worth the considerable expense and training and has many practical purposes besides fun.
    b. A close look at scuba diving shows how Americans carry the work ethic into their leisure pursuits.
    c. Because age and stamina are not factors, scuba diving is a hobby open to almost everyone who can afford it.
    d. Most Americans who take up scuba diving give up the hobby because they can find no useful purpose for it.

Analysis Questions

1. Does Riche's description and treatment of scuba diving stimulate your interest in this sport? Explain.

2. Consider a hobby or sport that you enjoy. Is simple enjoyment the only reason you participate or are there other reasons? Does your experience confirm or refute Riche's view? Comment.

3. Do you think that scuba divers would enjoy this article more or less than nondivers would? Why?

4. What are some of the reasons adults take up sports? Can these reasons be classified as good reasons or bad reasons?

5. How do adults' reasons for taking up a sport or hobby compare with children's reasons? Contrast the sports you enjoyed as a child with those you enjoy now.

6. In the last paragraph of her essay the author relates some demographic-based information. Identify this information and describe how it ties in with the subject of the article.

Exercise

Make a list of any sports you enjoy or have enjoyed in the past, both as a participant and as a spectator. For each one, tell why you enjoy(ed) it. Identify those for which your enjoyment came from the actual activity itself and those for which the enjoyment came for other reasons.

Climbing High Places

*R*ecently thousands of people in Chicago and New York have been surprised by the sight of daring figures moving quickly and smoothly up the outsides of their cities' tallest skyscrapers. Far removed from the concrete walls of the cities, thousands of climbers enjoy the sport of moving up and around on rocks, mountains, and even the ice formations of wintry waterfalls.

Have you ever wondered how these apparent madmen (and women) protect themselves from the obvious danger of falling? Is the sport really as dangerous as it appears, or are there ways of pursuing it that make it no riskier than walking across the street?

As improbable as it sounds, one can engage in many facets of climbing for years without significant accident or injury. In fact, a case can be made that the most dangerous aspect of the sport is driving to and from the climbing site.

What makes these claims plausible is a combination of creative thinking and modern technology. Ingenious safety systems, always rooted in the principle of greatest simplicity, use modern ropes that have breaking strengths as high as 8,000 pounds. Even electronics is involved: mountaineers traversing avalanche-prone areas carry battery-powered beepers to signal would-be rescuers.

The basic principle in all safety systems is called *belaying*. The word belay is a nautical term meaning to secure a rope to a post or other fixed object. In mountaineering the term refers to a climber's securing him/herself to a fixed object using the rope. The fixed object is usually another person, called the *belayer*.

It is easy to envision a belayer at the top, standing or sitting (which is actually far more stable), holding a rope that drops down to a climber below. We further refine the system by *anchoring* the belayer to a tree, a large rock, or a Mack truck. Anything will do as long as it won't get pulled over in the event of a major fall. Finally, we teach the belayer an efficient system of taking in slack rope as the climber moves up and an effective braking technique that relies on friction rather than muscle. With a little practice a ninety-pound weakling can catch a two-ton Tommy.

You can see that someone following a rope belayed in such a manner can attempt any kind of climb with very little risk. Since climbing ropes stretch or bounce with a fall, the worst that can happen to a climber in this method of top-rope climbing is turning into an involuntary human yo-yo for a yard or two as the belayer stops the fall. Aside from bumping or scratching against the rock, there is no real danger in this form of climbing, provided the belayer is well-trained and stays alert.

Okay. You're convinced this follower of the rope can safely climb and bounce around the rock until the cows come home. Invariably someone asks, "But how did you get the rope (and the belayer) to the top in the first place?" Often the answer is simple. There may be a path going around the steep rock face that leads to the summit. The rope is carried up and dropped from the top. This explanation prompted one student to ask, "Then why climb the rock rather than take the path to the top?" This perfectly logical question left a roomful of rock climbers speechless. We will return to this subject later in the article.

Sometimes the solution is not so simple. No path beckons. To reach the top means to climb the rock; there is no other way. Now the sport becomes dangerous.

There is a saying among climbers, "We need a fool to go first." This is humor masking the serious truth. There comes a time in mountaineering or climbing when one man or woman must go out ahead of the belayer.

The risk multiplies, then multiplies again, and some climbers venturing into this realm of *lead climbing* never make it home.

The lead climber can protect himself, but far less effectively than a follower can. A rope around his waist that would drop him fifty yards below where it's held by a belayer will do no good at all if he falls, unless . . .

If he can find a place on the way up where he can secure an anchoring system, then pass his rope through that anchor in a way that allows him to continue climbing as the rope slides through the anchor, the leader has established a *protection point*. Thus, if he falls when he has climbed five feet above the protection point, he will drop five feet to his protection and five feet below it (owing to the original five feet of slack).

"That's no big deal," you might say, but before you grab a sturdy clothesline and head for the hills, consider these complications.

The situation described above is a best-case scenario. Ideally, protection points are found and secured every ten feet or so. However, rocks are not always so accommodating. A good protection point requires an appropriately sized crack or fissure to hold the anchor the rope will pass through. The anchoring device is usually an odd-shaped piece of metal called a *chock*. It must fit exactly, both to stop a downward fall and to be retrieved by an upward pull as the last climber goes beyond it. (The more commonly recognized *piton* is no longer in use as an anchor; it required permanent placement, a feature that proved both expensive and environmentally unacceptable.)

Suppose you can't find a good-sized crack, and you're climbing higher and higher? Remember, you must multiply the distance to your last protection point by two to determine the full extent of your fall. A *runout* (the term used to indicate the rope length between lead climber and last protection point) of twenty feet is not uncommon. Thus, a forty foot fall would result.

Since a forty foot fall by a full-sized adult generates a tremendous amount of force, all of which is transmitted to the nearest anchoring system, one can rarely be certain that a protection point will hold. Will the chock pull through that flimsy crack which was the only choice available and lengthen the forty foot fall to sixty feet—to an anchor that will stand firm?

Next the force hits the belayer at the bottom, who is serving as the ultimate anchor. The lead climber's prayer is a frantic petition that the belayer has learned his trade well and is not asleep at his post.

Finally, has the belayer anchored himself to the aforementioned tree, rock, or Mack truck? If not, the poor devil may find himself airborne in a hurry.

You can see how dramatically the odds shift when one leaves the secure world of following a rope up a climb and enters the realm of lead climbing. Every step and every maneuver in the leader's routine must be well-planned and carefully executed. Yet though the danger is greater, so are the rewards. Few human endeavors develop the ability to concentrate and the capacity to perform under stress as does leading a rock climb. The exhilaration upon successful completion of a lead is hard to beat.

Now, just when you thought you had learned all about the most dangerous aspect of a most dangerous sport, along comes ice climbing. This is an activity even rock climbers look upon with emotions ranging from healthy respect to sheer terror. As one expressed it, "Climbing ice is only one step removed from walking on water."

While the basic principles of protection are the same, there is an obvious difference in the elements that make up the system. Furthermore, it is by definition downright freezing when the sport takes place. This simple fact sends many a rock climber scurrying for a warm fire and a hot drink to reminisce about real or imagined exploits on good, solid rock.

For it is the instability of ice even more than the extreme cold (which, after all, one can dress for properly) that provides the quintessential danger of ice climbing. A leader on ice is not looking for a rock fissure formed thousands of years ago, but is drilling an ice screw into a slab of ice that changes hourly as temperatures and atmospheric conditions vary. The ice leader fears a fall much more than the leader on rock, as the protection placed in such a surface is far more likely to pull out.

Even the follower in this sport is facing greater odds than his or her counterpart on rock. Moving up on rock requires only dexterous use of the hands and feet that God graciously provided; movement on ice requires all four limbs to be armed with sharp and ominous looking instruments—crampons, ice axes, ice hammers, and the like. Picture the hardy winter enthusiast, flailing furiously with spiked objects: necessary for progress, yes, but quite dangerous when in close proximity to the safety ropes. A simple trip or fall can become a serious accident with so many sharp projections in the neighborhood.

These sober words are not meant to paint a bleak and frightening picture of the sport. Yes, it is riskier than rock climbing, but many a veteran ice climber lives and breathes, ready to inspire you to test the thrill and majesty of the sport. It is an awe-inspiring experience to stand at the foot of what was a thundering waterfall, now capped in icy silence. To stand at the top some time later, knowing you have exhausted your mind, body, and spirit to reach it, is an unforgettable experience. It produces euphoria and immense satisfaction in some; humility and reverence in others.

This is the answer to the student's question. Why not take the path to the top? Ice, rock, mountain, or skyscraper, one must go the hard way to achieve the peak experience. We live in an age when we can view not only all parts of the world but ever-expanding corners of the universe as well from the comfort of our living rooms. There are some, however, who forsake comfort and security to see with their own eyes and experience the danger along with the beauty. Though they use all their God-given intelligence and ability to lessen the risks, they have discovered that the deepest beauty and the deepest truths cannot be divorced from danger.

Comprehension Questions

Assimilation

1. Belaying is a system:
   a. protecting the climber
   b. using beepers
   c. dependent on muscle power
   d. known for thousands of years

2. The most dangerous possibility for a climber top-roping is:
   a. a friction burn
   b. getting bumps and scratches
   c. becoming a human yo-yo
   d. having an inattentive belayer

3. Chocks are:
   a. pitons
   b. a type of rope for lead climbers
   c. metallic pieces of gear
   d. tetrahedral in shape and two dimensional

4. In the author's opinion people climb:
   a. to prove they can do it
   b. to achieve a satisfying peak experience
   c. because they're daredevils
   d. because "it's there"

5. The primary danger in ice climbing is:
   a. cold temperature
   b. the impermanence of ice
   c. ice screws
   d. a cold, rigid safety rope

Interpretation

6. The author implies that since the dangers of ice climbing are greater than the dangers of rock climbing:
   a. it is a bleak and frightening sport
   b. one should scurry for a warm fire and a hot drink
   c. the satisfaction derived is therefore greater
   d. one must learn to rock climb first

7. Because climbing involves mind, body, and spirit, it is:
   a. exhilarating
   b. amusing
   c. frightening
   d. depressing

8. Which of the following was *not* suggested as a necessary part of rock climbing:
   a. climbing rope
   b. emotional endurance
   c. anchors
   d. exceptional strength

9. A side benefit to rock climbing that the author mentions is:
   a. physical fitness
   b. increased ability to focus
   c. greater dexterity
   d. meeting others with similar hobbies

Main Idea

10. The main idea of this essay is:
   a. Rock and ice climbing are two of the fastest growing sports in America, for a variety of good reasons.
   b. It is absolutely vital that rock climbers be aware of the dangers of their sport and the safety devices that are available on the market.
   c. In the sport of climbing, as in life, a sense of high achievement cannot be attained without risk.
   d. Rock climbing is dangerous and technical, but is worth the effort.

Analysis Questions

1. Does the humorous, colloquial style of this essay suit its topic? How does it add to (or detract from) the message?

2. Does the author's tone stimulate your interest in his subject?

3. What role should physical education play in the undergraduate program of today's colleges and universities? Why?

4. "The deepest beauty and the deepest truths cannot be divorced from danger." Comment.

5. Why do you think the author chose this title for his article? Does it have significance beyond its obvious meaning?

Exercises

1. Have you taken part in sports? If so, did your involvement affect you significantly in some way other than physically (mentally, emotionally, spiritually)? Write about one experience.

2. Go through the article and underline all places where the author's attitude toward his subject is evident.

COMPARATIVE ANALYSIS QUESTIONS: HUMANITIES

1. Compare the tone in the articles by Keller and Young. How does tone influence argument?

2. Moriah and Riche each write about a sport. In each case, how much attention is given by the author to the sport itself? In each case, the author's real message has to do with life, rather than a particular sport. What are those main points? How is the sport an effective vehicle for the author to make his or her point?

3. The MacDougalls and Richard Penner write about architecture. Each article is written for students without expertise in the subject of architecture. How does this influence the approach each author takes to convey the main idea of the respective articles?

4. Is it necessary to be an artist to appreciate Young's article? To be a musician to appreciate Keller's? Why or why not?

5. The ability to write can be considered an art. Is Brody's article like Keller's or Young's in any way? Explain. Can any of these articles be considered practical? Support your conclusion. How does Lieberman's story fit into this analysis?

6. Kirkwood discusses a type of drama and Kennedy discusses an aspect of poetry. What specific drama or poem does each use to help illustrate his point? Are these illustrations helpful?

7. All of the authors in this section can be said to have as purposes in writing their respective articles both description and persuasion. Refer back to the articles, if necessary, and identify what is being described. Then consider: Of what is each author trying to convince you? Which is the most effective? Why? Which is least effective? Why?

8. How does your interest in a subject influence your attentiveness to it and thus your understanding of it? Consider your interest in, and your understanding of, Kirkwood's or Richard Penner's article. The MacDougalls' or Kennedy's. Riche's or Moriah's.

9. Does Riche's article arouse your interest in scuba diving? Moriah's, in technical rock climbing? Do the authors intend to arouse your interest in the sports they discuss?

10. Catherine Penner's article is clearly directed to other teachers of writing. Consider the effect of audience on the writer. On the reader. Who might be Kirkwood's audience? Brody's audience? Reference your responses with information in the articles.

11. Have you ever written a short story? How does writing a short story differ from writing an essay? What stages in the writing process are alike?

12. Brody and Catherine Penner both wrote about the writing process. How do their points fit together? Do you find any contradictions?

13. When you read Young's article, did you identify with the photographer or with the painter? When you read Keller's article, did you empathize with the musician or with the listener? How did this affect your reception of the message?

14. Riche and Moriah wrote about leisure activities and our attitudes toward these activities. Explain how these issues fit into the subject of "humanities."

15. Consider the various topics covered in this section. Some are traditional; yet some may have surprised you—even stretched your mind in a new direction. What other topics would you have expected to find in this section? Pick a topic you like and write a brief essay about it. Consider your audience to be students without expertise in the subject. How does this limit you? Without visual aids, sound effects, or personal contact, what aspects of your subject are eliminated?

PART V

More Questions, a Rhetorical Guide, and a List

Supplementary Analysis Questions
Across the Curriculum

1. Several articles from various academic fields were concerned with the value of human life (Leman—chemical engineering, Kress—genetics, Palmer—law, and Collins—psychology). Examine the different approaches from the standpoint of the field of the author and of the topic of the article.

2. Several of the articles could be examined in the light of the theme of maximization, or realizing fullest potential (Groppel, Boileau, Leman, Ehrenberg, C. Penner, Ballantyne, Lieberman, R. Penner, and Riche). Show how each of these authors used this theme as a major or minor theme in his or her article.

3. Consider the topics by Kirkwood, Kennedy, Leman, and Frey. Does their relevance or importance depend on the reader's interest? Should it? If you have no intrinsic interest in a particular topic, how can you maximize the benefit from reading about it? Should a student try to avoid any topic that does not appeal to him? Can a student get *something* from a topic she finds boring or irrelevant to her main interests? Explain your responses.

4. There is a religious theme in Achtemeier's article and in the Mac-Dougalls' article. Explain the significance of this theme in their articles. Is there a religious theme in any of the other articles? Should a college student be concerned with religion and with religious themes in writing? Why or why not?

5. Peace is a theme in several of the articles. Consider Willcox, Mattes, Hoffmann, Bethe, and others. What should you be learning—and doing—about peace at this time in your life?

6. Examine the attitudes toward hospital patients expressed in the articles by Palmer, Craytor, and Collins. Have you or someone in your family ever spent time in a hospital? How did this experience affect your response to the above articles?

7. Compare the methods of persuasion by Bethe and Mattes. Kahn and Grinols. Ludington and Willcox. Keller and C. Penner.

8. Some articles refer to *he, his,* and *him;* others to *he/she, his/hers,* and *him/her;* and others to *she, her,* and *hers.* Which terms do you feel are most appropriate? Why? Does the subject of an article make a difference? Does your gender influence your responses to these questions? (How do you know?) What influence does your cultural background have on your opinions?

9. Consider the influence of culture in the articles by Krebs, Mac-Dougall and MacDougall, Kramnick, Riche, and Young. What is your own cultural perspective, and how does it enhance (or hinder) your understanding of these articles—or of any of the articles?

10. How does an author's style affect the impact of his message? How does her tone matter? Her organization of ideas? His bias? Consider these questions with any of the articles read. Draw some comparisons and contrasts between any two articles which differ in any of the areas mentioned above.

Rhetorical Guide

Organizational Patterns/Structure

For clear examples of the following common organizational patterns, refer to the articles listed below. It is important to note that, for added clarity and interest, many authors use a combination of patterns to express their ideas. In the list below, only one dominant pattern is listed.

Analytical:	Kennedy, Keller, Kirkwood
Chronological:	Burris, Norton, Young
Cumulative narrative:	R. Penner, Williams, Bem and Bem
Descriptive:	Leman, Clarke, Wells
Descriptive enumeration:	Ehrenberg
Expositional:	Groppel, Grinols, Palmer
Instructional (how-to):	Brody
Narrative:	Lieberman, MacNeill and Penfield
Problem–solution:	Kahn, Boileau, Collins
Question and answer:	Ludington

Spatial: MacDougall and MacDougall

Thesis–proof: Bethe, Bronfenbrenner, Kramnick

Style

As used in this text, style refers to the way an author writes, particularly concerning the degree of formality. Although style can vary within a single article, some examples of basic writing styles may be easily identified in the articles below as shown:

Colloquial, conversational: Bronfenbrenner, Kahn, Riche

Informal or semiformal: Rosen, Williams, Keller

Formal, scholarly: Brody, Kennedy

Bias

The author's bias is explained best as his point of view toward the subject of his text. Sometimes the subject is fairly neutral so that bias has no major effect on the author's writing or the reader's understanding of the material. The articles by Wells and Frey are straightforward, descriptive statements of geologic history of a specific area and of integrated circuitry, respectively, and thus are statements of fact rather than persuasive polemics. Bias plays a larger role in most of the articles in this text, however, as indicated below. Note that the list is limited to just one example of bias for each author. Note, also, that this is only a partial listing of articles reflecting strong influence of author bias.

Author	For	Against
Achtemeier	Belief in God	
Bethe	Nuclear disarmament	
Bem and Bem	Equal responsibilities and rights for men and women	
Boileau	Career planning	

Author	For	Against
Bronfenbrenner		Deficit model in child rearing
Collins	Active role of patient in terminal illness	
Craytor		Stereotyping of patients
Hoffmann	International communication among scientists	
Keller		Muzak
Mattes		Nuclear weapons
Rosen		Computer jargon
Willcox		Rigid legalism

Tone

The author's tone reveals her attitude toward her subject. It is greatly influenced by her bias and thus is a good indicator of that bias. Examples of tone in the articles in the text can be seen in the following partial listing:

Concerned:	Ballantyne, Craytor, Rosen
Cynical/skeptical:	Bem and Bem, Kramnick, Norton
Impersonal/neutral:	Frey, Hendrix, Leman, Wells
Optimistic/laudatory:	Groppel, Kirkwood, Willcox
Pessimistic:	Ludington, Masson

Authors Paired by Field

When two contributors from the same field write two independent articles, a comparative examination of their work can be of interest.

Often the topics are completely different (Ballantyne and Frey; the Bems and Collins) and appear to be as different as two articles prepared from completely separate fields. Sometimes the subject is much the same, yet the approaches to it differ greatly (self-regulation in the marketplace, Kahn and Grinols; attitude and knowledge in pursuing sport, Groppel and Moriah): This gives good evidence of the influence of the approach to a topic on the other elements of the author's packaging. And finally, sometimes the topics have enough relevance to each other to promote real discussion and understanding: Appreciation of each article is enhanced by the perspective contributed by the other (Masson and Willcox; the MacDougalls and R. Penner; Rosen and Hendrix; Brody and C. Penner). The articles referred to above are paired according to the authors' respective academic fields, as indicated below:

Architecture:	The MacDougalls and R. Penner
Business:	Hendrix and Rosen
Economics:	Grinols and Kahn
Electrical engineering:	Ballantyne and Frey
Law:	Masson and Willcox
Psychology:	The Bems and Collins
Physical education:	Groppel and Moriah
Writing:	Brody and C. Penner

Main Idea: Thesis

The following list gives, for each author, his/her professional field and the title and main idea of his/her article.

Author	Field	Title and Thesis Statement
Achtemeier	Meteorology	"The 'Apostles' Experiment': A Proof of the Existence of the Supernatural?" Any worldview that does not allow for the supernatural cannot give an adequate interpretation of the universe.
Ballantyne	Electrical engineering	"Why We Are Inferior to the Japanese" The United States is falling substantially behind Japan in its emphasis on

Author	Field	Title and Thesis Statement
		technology, and this lag has serious present and future economic consequences.
Bem and Bem	Psychology	"Egalitarian Relationships: The Sex-Role Revolution Begins at Home" America has actually experienced only half a sex-role revolution in the past 15 years; the role of women has changed, but not yet the role of men.
Bethe	Physics	"We Are Not Inferior to the Russians" The security of the United States and the world can be achieved through arms reduction, not through arms buildup.
Boileau	Career development	" 'So, What Are You Planning to Be?' " Career planning is as necessary for college-bound or already-degreed individuals as it is for those who plan no college training.
Brody	Writing	"How Johnny Can Write: Thinking about Composition Theory" The skill of writing is based on an understanding of the interrelationship between thought and writing.
Bronfenbrenner	Human development and family studies	"Alternatives to a Deficit Model for American Families and Children" The current formal diagnosis–prescription approach to families should be replaced by irrational total commitment to the child, worked out within the family, with support from outside, informal systems including the neighborhood, child-care center, school, and work place.
Burris	Education	"The Goal of Undergraduate Education: Can Colleges Serve Adult Students?" The enrollment of mature students in colleges and universities has revived an old controversy over what should be the role of undergraduate education.

Author	Field	Title and Thesis Statement
Clarke	Oceanography	"Year-to-Year Climate Fluctuations: The El Niño/Southern Oscillation Phenomenon" Scientists have identified and are beginning to understand the El Niño/Southern Oscillation phenomenon, the single most prominent signal in year-to-year climate variability.
Collins	Psychology	"Elective Death and the Hospice Concept" Terminally ill patients have a right to elect the kind of medical treatment they will receive, even if they choose palliative rather than curative care.
Craytor	Nursing	"Nurses' Perceptions of Cancer Patients and Cancer Care" Although nurses' perceptions of cancer patients and cancer care are both stereotyped and resistant to change, they can and must be altered.
Ehrenberg	Industrial and labor relations	"Evaluation Research and National Social Policy: An Academic Practitioner's Perspective" Benefits of evaluation research studies should be maximized through greater utilization when planning national social policy.
Frey	Electrical engineering	"Integrated Circuits: The Expanding Technology of Shrinking Structures" Enhancement of technology of integrated circuitry results in decreased cost and increased function.
Grinols	Economics	"Incentives and Self-Regulation" Today, as in Adam Smith's time, the selfish interests of firms and consumers are coordinated through the marketplace to achieve the common good.
Groppel	Sports medicine	"The Biomechanics of Sport" Human performance in sport can be improved through the application of scientific principles.

Author	Field	Title and Thesis Statement
Hendrix	Business	"Profiting from the Past: The Antique Marketplace" An appreciation of the relationship between demographics and the antique business can lead to more profitable marketing of antiques.
Hoffmann	Chemistry	"Two Unfortunate Trends" Contrary to current trends, we must put more resources into scientific education and research and increase our contact with Russian scientists.
Kahn	Economics	"Using the Market in Regulation" Government agencies should be looking for ways to reduce the cost and intrusiveness of regulations by using market forces to achieve their goals.
Keller	Music	"Thinking About Music" Intelligent listening to the music that accompanies many of our daily waking moments provides new insights and stimulates the imagination.
Kennedy	Comparative literature	"Rhetorical Discovery in Yeats's 'Leda and the Swan' " To analyze rhetorical structures of voice and address in a poem like Yeats's "Leda and the Swan" provides significant insight into the poem's meaning.
Kirkwood	Classics	"What is Greek Tragedy?" The thirty-two Greek tragedies that have survived to our day are a remarkably varied group of plays, impossible to sum up in a few generalizations, yet sharing the characteristics of high seriousness of topic and poetic creativeness in execution.
Kramnick	Government	"Britain: Summer of '82" On the surface all looked well in Britain in the summer of 1982, but beneath the self-congratulations and the good feeling lurked serious and staggering national problems.

Author	Field	Title and Thesis Statement
Krebs	International relations	"The Foundation of Diplomacy" Diplomacy is an exacting profession that demands expertise in cross-cultural communication, discipline obtainable only from first-hand overseas experience, and a reputation for accuracy and credibility.
Kress	Animal genetics	" 'Genetics Caused That?' " Since Mendel's discovery of genetics through studying garden peas over 100 years ago, scientists have made many discoveries about the genetic character-istics of living organisms.
Leman	Chemical engineering	"Profit by Design" The essence of design is the maximiza-tion of benefit and the minimization of detriment, rather than simply the ac-complishment of task.
Lieberman	Fiction	"The Golden Handcuffs" People don't always mean what they say or say what they mean.
Ludington	Agricultural engineering	"Man and His Environment" Man has a history of polluting his environment through his own igno-rance and carelessness; yet it is man himself who will ultimately suffer most.
MacDougall and MacDougall	Architecture	"Buildings and Their Meanings" Esthetic judgments in architectural de-sign are functions of cultural orientation.
MacNeill and Penfield	Biology	"The Scientific Method in Biology" The science of biology is based on a combination of inductive and deduc-tive reasoning and always involves ob-servations of some kind.
Masson	Law	"*Washington v. Davis:* The Death Knell for Civil Rights Plaintiffs" In making intent rather than result the means to prove racial discrimina-tion, the courts have put an impossible burden of proof on the plaintiff.

Author	Field	Title and Thesis Statement
Mattes	Citizen activism	"Exorcising the Nuclear Demon" If we don't change our way of thinking, civilization is likely to be destroyed in a nuclear holocaust.
Moriah	Physical education	"Climbing High Places" In the sport of climbing, as in life, a sense of high achievement cannot be attained without risk.
Norton	History	"Change and Continuity in the Lives of American Women" American women's lives have changed dramatically since 1800—or have they?
Palmer	Law	"Understanding the Medical Malpractice Crisis" Policymakers will find meaningful solutions to the malpractice problem by considering the larger social trends affecting modern medicine, rather than by simply trying to modify the doctrine of informed consent.
C. Penner	Writing	"Beyond Rules to Writing" Both in the classroom and in their responses to students' papers, writing teachers will have greater success in teaching the necessary rules and conventions if they subordinate them to the more important qualities of good writing.
R. Penner	Hotel architecture	"The Renovation of Classic Hotels" It is both emotionally and economically rewarding to renovate, rather than replace, old, classic hotels.
Riche	Freelance journalism	"Scuba: A Pleasure in Search of a Purpose" A close look at scuba diving shows how Americans carry the work ethic into their leisure pursuits.
Rosen	Business	"Righting Writing, in Business" Concerned by the deterioration of business writing in an era of rapidly expanding communication technology, the business community is acting.

Author	Field	Title and Thesis Statement
Sagan	Astronomy and space science	"Can We Know the Universe? Reflections on a Grain of Salt" Man's knowledge of the universe comes through its natural laws and his understanding of them; his fascination, from its mystery.
Wells	Geology	"Geomorphology of the Finger Lakes Region" Rivers of snow and ice, and the debris they carried, shaped the present look of the Finger Lakes region of New York State.
Willcox	Law	"The Spirit of Law" The profession of law must transcend both reason and logic in its pursuit of peaceful settlement of human dispute.
Williams	History of science	"How Are Scientific Discoveries Made?" Scientific discoveries and theories do not, as is usually thought, come simply from the observation of nature, but arise from the creative human mind and are then tested against nature by experiment.
Young	History of art	"A Picture Is Worth Ten Thousand Words" An ancient Chinese proverb seems to be tested by developments in modern art in the West.

Contributors

Achtemeier, Gary L. Ph.D., Florida State University; Professional Scientist, University of Illinois/Illinois State Water Survey

Ballantyne, J. M. Ph.D., Massachusetts Institute of Technology; Director and Professor of Electrical Engineering, Cornell University

Bem, Daryl J. Ph.D., University of Michigan; Professor of Psychology, Cornell University

Bem, Sandra L. Ph.D., University of Michigan; Professor of Psychology/Women's Studies, Cornell University

Bethe, Hans A. Ph.D., University of Munich; Professor Emeritus of Physics/Nuclear Studies, Cornell University; Chair: John Wendell Anderson Professor of Physics Emeritus; Nobel Prize, 1967

Boileau, Sandra. M.S., University of Illinois; Director, Special Programs and Community Services, Parkland College

Brody, Miriam. M.A., Boston University; Assistant Professor in the Writing and Reading Program, Ithaca College

Bronfenbrenner, Urie. Ph.D., University of Michigan; Professor of Human Development and Family Studies/Psychology, Cornell University; Chair: Jacob Gould Schurman Professor of Human Development and Family Studies

Burris, Helen Brown. Ph.D., Iowa State University; Assistant Professor of Human Service Studies, Cornell University

Clarke, Allan J. Ph.D., Cambridge University; Associate Professor of Oceanography, Florida State University

Collins, William. Ph.D., University of Michigan; Director of Learning Skills Center, Adjunct Assistant Professor of Psychology, Cornell University

Craytor, Josephine K. R.N., M.S., University of Rochester; Professor Emeritus School of Nursing, University of Rochester

Ehrenberg, Ronald G. Ph.D., Northwestern University; Professor and Director of Research, School of Industrial and Labor Relations, and Professor of Economics, Cornell University

Frey, Jeffrey. Ph.D., University of California at Berkeley; Professor of Electrical Engineering, Associate Director National Research and Resource Facility for Submicron Structures, Cornell University

Grinols, Earl L. Ph.D., Massachusetts Institute of Technology; Associate Professor of Economics, University of Illinois

Groppel, Jack L. Ph.D., Florida State University; Associate Professor of Physical Education and of Bioengineering, University of Illinois

Hendrix, Nancy. Ph.D., Vanderbilt University; Assistant to Chancellor, Vanderbilt University; previously taught at Tennessee State University

Hoffmann, Roald. Ph.D., Harvard University; Chairman and Professor of Chemistry, Cornell University; Chair: John A. Newman Professor of Physical Science/Chemistry; Nobel Prize, 1981

Kahn, Alfred E. Ph.D., Yale University; Professor of Economics, Cornell University; Chair: Robert Julius Thorne Professor of Economics

Keller, Michael A. M.A., SUNY Buffalo; Head of Music Library, University of California, Berkeley; 1983: University of California, Berkeley, Medal for Distinguished Service to the Carillon Program

Kennedy, William J. Ph.D., Yale University; Professor of Comparative Literature, Cornell University

Kirkwood, Gordon. Ph.D., Johns Hopkins University; Professor of Classics, Cornell University; Chair: Frederic J. Whiton Professor of Classics

Kramnick, Isaac. Ph.D., Harvard University; Chairman and Professor of Government, Cornell University; Chair: Richard J. Schwartz Professor of Government

Krebs, Max V. B.A. Princeton University. U.S. Foreign Service Officer 1947–1976, primarily in Latin America, final post: Ambassador to Guyana 1974–1976; Visiting Fellow, Woodrow Wilson National Fellowship Foundation; currently lectures in International Relations, Sand Hills Community College, Pinehurst, N.C.

Kress, Don. Ph.D., University of Wisconsin at Madison; Professor of Animal Genetics, Montana State University

Leman, Gregory. Ph.D., University of Illinois; Visiting Assistant Professor of Chemical Engineering, University of Illinois

Lieberman, Robert. M.A., Cornell University; Lecturer in Physics, Cornell University; three published novels: *Baby, Goobersville Breakdown, Paradise Rezoned*

Ludington, David. Ph.D., Purdue University; Professor of Agricultural Engineering, Cornell University

MacDougall, Bonnie G. Ph.D., Cornell University; Director of South Asia Program, Assistant Professor of Architecture, Cornell University

MacDougall, Robert D. Ph.D., Cornell University; Dean of Summer Session and Extramural, Assistant Professor of Architecture, Cornell University

MacNeill, Allen D. M.A., Cornell University; Lecturer in Biology, Cornell University

Masson, Robin Abrahamson. J.D., National Law Center, George Washington University; Lecturer and Staff Attorney Legal Aid Clinic, Law School, Cornell University

Mattes, Kitty Campbell. M.A., Cornell University; writer/editor; author: *In Your Hands: A Citizen's Guide to the Arms Race*

Moriah, David. B.A., Cornell University; Director of Outdoor Education, Cornell University

Norton, Mary Beth. Ph.D., Harvard University; Professor of History, Cornell University

Palmer, Larry I. LL.B., Yale University; Professor of Law, Cornell Law School, Cornell University

Penfield, Lorrie. M.A., Cornell University; M.D., State University of New York at Syracuse.

Penner, Catherine S. Ph.D., Syracuse University; Assistant Professor in the Writing Program, Ithaca College

Penner, Richard H. M.S., Cornell University; Associate Professor of Properties Management, Hotel Administration, Cornell University

Riche, Martha Farnsworth. Ph.D., Georgetown University; Editor: *The Numbers News;* Associate Editor: *American Demographics*

Rosen, Charlotte. Ph.D., Cornell University; Lecturer-Coordinator of Management Communications, Graduate School of Management, Cornell University

Sagan, Carl. Ph.D., University of Chicago; Director, Laboratory for Planetary Studies, and Professor of Astronomy, Cornell University; Chair: David Duncan Professor of Astronomy and Space Sciences

Wells, Grady. Freelance writer, Ithaca, N.Y.; Editor: *Pre-professional Publications*

Willcox, Bertram F. J.D., Harvard Law School; Professor Emeritus, Law School, Cornell University; Chair: W. G. McRoberts Research Professor in the Administration of the Law, Emeritus

Williams, L. Pearce. Ph.D., Cornell University; Professor of History of Science/History, Cornell University; Chair: John Stambaugh Professor of the History of Science

Young, Martie W. Ph.D., Harvard University; Professor of History of Art, Curator of Asian Art, Howard F. Johnson Museum, Cornell University